Decolonizing Consciousness

The book intertwines several strands of scholarship in Indian Philosophy, contemporary psychology and the lived Indian psychological practices inclusive of *Yoga, advaita, tantra* and *bhakti* to engage in an exploration of consciousness, cognitive science and philosophy.

The book examines the characteristics of consciousness by situating it in the historical and cultural contexts of Euro-American as well as Asian, particularly Indian philosophical tradition specifically, the Bhakti tradition and creative living. The volume decolonizes the understanding of the ecology of consciousness while accounting for the diverse strands, which have given us a unique understanding of the mind, psychology, cognition and philosophy of the mind.

This book will be of interest to students, teachers and scholars of psychology, consciousness studies, cognitive science, philosophy, social psychology, Yoga studies and Yoga psychology. It will also be useful for Yoga professionals, social workers, therapists and anyone who is interested to learn about consciousness.

Shilpa Ashok Pandit is an Associate Professor, School of Arts and Science, Ahmedabad University, Navrangpura, Ahmedabad, India.

Decolonizing Consciousness

Reclaiming the Indian Psychology of Well-being

Shilpa Ashok Pandit

Routledge
Taylor & Francis Group
LONDON AND NEW YORK

First published 2023
by Routledge
4 Park Square, Milton Park, Abingdon, Oxon OX14 4RN

and by Routledge
605 Third Avenue, New York, NY 10158

Routledge is an imprint of the Taylor & Francis Group, an informa business

British Library Cataloguing-in-Publication Data
A catalogue record for this book is available from the British Library

ISBN: 978-1-032-16090-0 (hbk)
ISBN: 978-1-032-37279-2 (pbk)
ISBN: 978-1-003-33620-4 (ebk)

DOI: 10.4324/9781003336204

Typeset in Sabon
by KnowledgeWorks Global Ltd.

Contents

Acknowledgements

This book is a long time of about 25 years in making. As a student of both the traditional Indian knowledge traditions and the contemporary psychological sciences, I was and am frequently overwhelmed and intimidated by the yawning gaps in theory and practices. Thus, the first offering of gratitude is to the universal Guru-tattva that animates the worlds and provides direction to the lost and wandering fools such as me. This Guru manifests in form or as a song or a smell or a memory long past. I offer my gratitude to the Guru as all the human and the non-human world and who came to my life experience as pain and its relief, pleasure and its retreat. The Guru thus allowed me to accept the possibility of what could be an unalloyed witness as well.

I acknowledge the help of teachers and colleagues in psychology, philosophy, Sanskrit, Music, Yoga and Biology, where conversations radiated beams of light and bits of insight to see the warp and weft, the interweave of knowledge.

I acknowledge the assistance provided by the editorial staff of Taylor and Francis. I also thank the generous anonymous reviewers of the book. I thank my research assistant – Ms Vaghela whose help in the review of literature was valuable.

I offer this effort to my children and students, who are old and ancient, even though their body-mind identities are young. They will also encounter questions and try and find answers – within, in relationships as well as in abstraction.

1 Decolonizing psychology

The ecology of consciousness in Indian psychology

The decolonizing movement in social sciences

This book is a modest attempt to offer a decolonized recasting of the academic discipline of psychology to a consciousness-based Indian Psychology. In attempting so, it assumes familiarity with several background debates on psychology as taught, practised and theorized in the developing world, including India. Some of the key debates and movements globally are presented as prefatory remarks.

The debate and movement to decolonize is alive in almost all humanities and social sciences across the world. The decolonial scholarship has, till now, primarily focussed on race and is a discussion point in South America and Europe, but it recognizes the devastating impact of colonization across the world: in Africa, South America, North America and Australia. Several landmark works have triggered these debates, such as the decolonizing of the research methods itself, by a Māori social scientist, Professor Linda Tuhiwai Smith (Smith, 2021), which plainly documents that social science research methods were by themselves methodologies of systematic loot and appropriation of both symbolic and material indigenous resources. One of the outcomes of colonization has been the effacement of the indigenous knowledge and wisdom traditions or the dilution and fragmentation of the knowledge systems into the Euro-American analytical and disciplinary categories. Societies have faced a clean rupture and break in the flow of their indigenous traditions, which has been recognized by scholars of decoloniality. This has been documented by psychologists on Indian psychological thought in India as well. Several issues that have further effaced the Indian knowledge traditions, post-independence, are conformity with the implanted existing university structures, the desperation to secure tenured academic positions, institutional stagnation, etc. Not only Indian psychologists but respected psychologists such as Moghaddam as well have discussed intensively why 'third world psychologies' are mimicking psychologies through a process of double reification and proposed that the solution lies in 'Omni culturalism' (see, Moghaddam, 1987, 2009; Moghaddam & Lee, 2006). This book holds the view that the route to

DOI: 10.4324/9781003336204-1

'Omni culturalism' first passes through decoloniality and the necessary reclaiming of the indigenous knowledge systems. Omni culturalism is an ideal state for a global psychology, where no adversaries or binaries exist, but its pathway is through intensive reflection and reclaiming of the indigeneity rather than papering it over. In India, this quest has frequently been 'dumbified' into going straight 'back to the glorious past' or that there are no differences, we are all one! Decolonization, as a process, will go through several churns and the initial versions of the articulation of decoloniality might struggle to find that exact note, given that there is a transition ongoing after a rupture. The argument in India that decolonization would be a 'right leaning' project is amusing; an evidence of the maturity and historical understanding of the critique! In this first volume, the assumption that the book follows is that the long and plural histories of India and its Indic consciousness will allow for multiple Indigenous psychologies – a glorious past with a healthy and mature recognition of the inglorious elements. This would be the healing as a continuous process.

WEIRD, cross-cultural and cultural psychologies: World-views and culture

Psychologists across the world have also increasingly acknowledged that psychology and knowledge construction, as we know it, is the psychology of WEIRD – Western, Educated, Industrialized, Rich and Developed countries (Henrich et al., 2010a, 2010b; Jones, 2010; Nielsen et al., 2017). When Moghaddam talked of a crisis in social psychology way back in 1987, he was identifying the hope for a new psychology that would truly reflect the multiple ways of being and becoming across the world. In the immediate aftermath of the second world war, the colonies that became newly independent inherited the category of 'modern' from their colonizers and started the academic disciplines of psychology with modern institutions such as the universities established by the colonial masters. It is not that the education systems did not exist earlier, in these colonies; they were deemed irrelevant and anti-modern. Around that time, the field of cross-cultural psychology started developing and was seen as a great advance, where psychologists recognized culture! Cross-cultural psychologists mostly embarked on comparative projects, where they essentially used their tools to compare different cultural cohorts on the concepts and constructs *as defined by them*! The key learnings from cross-cultural psychology were the idea of conceptual equivalence, the much-delayed understanding of etic/emic and the imposed etic (Moghaddam, 1987). The third and critical turn in studying culture came when cultural and indigenous psychologies were acknowledged as part of psychological knowledge canon, albeit in a marginal sense. In recent years, cultural indigenous psychology and cross-cultural psychology have increasingly gained acceptance in light of globalization (Berry et al., 1997; Kitayama & Cohen, 2010; Shweder & Sullivan, 1993; Valsiner, 2014).

If we were to locate this book in the mainstream psychology traditions, it clearly finds itself under the cultural psychology domain and not the cross-cultural psychology domain. Whereas cross-cultural psychologists, mostly from the Euro-American lens impose a universal as defined by them (imposed etic); Indian psychology is an insider emic psychology. As mentioned, the route to a truly global Omni cultural psychology will necessarily go through the reclaiming of an indigenous cultural psychology because the meta-theoretical assumptions of the indigenous cultural psychologies are starkly different from the mainstream Euro-American psychology meta-theory. An Integrative global psychology, especially for a colonized country such as India, can only be articulated through an emergent etic rather than an imposed one. Indic civilization has an unbroken history of possibly several psychologies; some common concerns continue to reverberate just like the background note of a tānpurā in the Indian civilizational context. The ontological categories, the epistemologies and the rhetoric, methodologies and the axiology of the Indic civilizational consciousness are largely *consonant*, without papering over the theoretical differences between schools of thought in the Indian Knowledge Traditions (IKT, hereafter). Even so, this book limits itself to the Āstikā systems within the broad Indic knowledge systems, which include the Bauddha and the Jaina traditions.

Two words have recently been coined – Indian Knowledge Systems (IKS) and IKT. The use of the term IKT is preferred in this book because traditions include all folk, multisensory, un-scriptured ways of being, becoming and practice, whereas the term IKS alludes only to the formal systems of knowing and being. Therefore, in this book, the term IKT is taken as the first important term. Some key and unique features of Indian consciousness-based psychology are identified below.

That the Indian society is hierarchical has been alluded to by several social science researchers. Another well-recorded discussion among social sciences and psychology has been the seeming contradictions in the Indian social context and the mindset. What seems like contradictions to non-Indians, the Indian mind addresses them in unique and contradictory ways. The Indian mindset has been discussed, most recently by JBP Sinha (Sinha et al., 2010). He has argued that the Indian mindset is very context sensitive. Just as Sinha discusses situations in the social context, this book holds the position that because the Indian mindset is hierarchical, not just based on social hierarchies, but task and ethical hierarchies as well, the Indian mind uses these *hierarchies as registers* to interpret the same words, concepts or frameworks according to the register and act differently. Indian psychology also uses levels of consciousness as a hierarchy. Some well-known examples of that would be – the seven higher and nether worlds in the Hindu Purāṅa-s, the levels of consciousness in the kundalini tantra system and the idea of three bodies in Yoga (sthula, sooksma and kārana). The key point to note, which is not seen anywhere in research literature, is that these levels of consciousness and the placement of concepts in an architectural frame yield both positive and negative definitions of the same concept. For example, emotions, when tied to the body, yield a negative definition, while when tied to spirituality, yield a positive definition. In flat conceptualizations of mainstream Euro-American psychology, this looks like a contradiction. Similarly, suicide is accepted as positive 'giving up of the body', when tied to completing one's duties; when running away from one's duties, suicide is not justifiable. Several more examples can be taken.

The second integrative feature of Indian psychology is that Indian applied psychology practice consciously maps the internal representation and external reality through *specific correspondences*. This conscious correspondence is called 'nyāsa' or placing. Nyāsa is seen in temples, in the human body, in the physical cities such as Varanasi or Ujjain and in the chakra system in the human body. This has been noted by scholars of religious studies, especially of the Tantra traditions (Dass & Das, 1979; Dyczkowski, 1988; Karasinski-Sroka, 2021; Samdarshi, 2019). While Samdarshi, in his 2019 paper, identifies these internal representations and external reality correspondence in architecture, the Hindu temples of India have always been seen with an internal representation correspondence with the external temple. Layered on the top, additionally, is the systems of yantra, which is again a correspondence with an internal and external reality just like the practice of Nyāsa, which is a conscious association of psychic elements with part of the body or the mantra. Just as Indian Psychology bridges the mind-body dualism through the practice of Yoga, the practice of tantra, bridges the internal and external duality or rupture, through its practices such as nyāsa. Sadly, most psychologists in India are unable to engage with Indian thought; these correspondences have not been studied enough. Very recently, some scholars have tried to assess the working memory of Buddhist monks, who by tradition, engage in the worship/practice of visualization of the Buddhas and their families called deity meditation (Kozhevnikov et al., 2009). Visualization is a very widely used practice in various traditions of Indian psychology, and this paper by Kozhevnikov is a mere initial confirmation of the effects of Indian psychology practices. The profoundly unappreciated part is the *consciously created correspondences* between external reality and internal representation. More research on this can be seen in Timalsina's work, who, though a scholar of religion, has identified these cognitive science connections with Hindu and Buddhist tantra, especially, in reference to embodiment, suffering and healing (Hayes & Timalsina, 2017; Timalsina, 2011, 2012).

The third integrating feature of the applied Indian psychology is empathy and mirroring, which is utilized to address the self-other separation. This has been fairly well studied in psychology of meditation, again albeit in a reductive sense. An influential paper by Metzinger, on 'minimal phenomenal experience' finds that meditators frequently feel a great sense of compassion (Metzinger, 2020a, 2020b), which Metzinger links to certain functions of the brain. In psychology and cultural anthropology literature,

Rasa theory has been well studied. Rasa is the outcome of this mirroring and the dissolution of self-other duality, which must begin with losing oneself! Rasa theory literature is quite vast to be cited here, but some studies can be further referred to (Pandit, 2011; Pandit & Misra, 2013; Sen & Pandit, 2013; Timalsina, 2007).

In summary, the diverse and rich theories in the Indian psychology context have primarily been to address the experience of duality, rupture and separation. Within the IKT, there are 14 vidyas and several ṣāstra-s. Vidya is understood as a pathway to learning and knowledge, whereas ṣastra implies a masterly application that cuts the constraints off. Ṣastra has been wrongly translated as 'scriptures' and most Indians also mindlessly use this translation. The Vidya that is the focus of this book is the 'Adhyatma-vidya' or the pathway to know the self. Adhyatma in the Indic ontological-epistemological tradition is centred on self-illumined reflexivity and examination of consciousness, across all binaries and dichotomies, which are otherwise seen in contemporary world-views on philosophy of science and psychology.

In this book, a basic architecture of Indian psychology is attempted to be reclaimed. This book references the arguments of philosophers in the contemporary context, especially in debates about consciousness, intelligence, artificial consciousness, etc. Across the chapters, the book uses several primary sources such as the Patanjali's Yoga Sutras and its commentaries, Advaita Vedānta texts – Brahmasutrabhasya and its commentary by Adi Shankara, Sribhasya, which is a commentary by great master Sri Rāmānujacārya. It also references the Upaniṣad and the interpretations of selected Upaniṣads, primarily the Māndukyopaniśad. For knowledge traditions, focussing on emotions and affective processes, the book has referred to primary texts of Abhinavabharati and the Bhakti text – Bhakti-Rasamrta Sindhu, apart from published papers by Indian Psychologists. For the chapter on mind-no-mind, apart from Patanjali's Yoga Sutra, the primary texts of Jīvanmukti Viveka by Sri Vidyaranya Muni have been used. Across the chapters, several points arise from the author's practice. Therefore, all mistakes are due to the author's inertia and sloth in practice and interpretation.

Towards the objective of reclaiming consciousness-based Indian psychology, this book has followed several path breaking attempts – especially, by contemporary teachers such as Prof Paranjpe and Prof Rao, who have earlier written the book, titled, 'Psychology in the Indian Tradition' published by Springer. Additionally, books such as 'The Handbook of Indian Psychology' and several other papers have been read and referred to. The aim of this book was to build on the earlier work and show new perspectives, according to one's training and practice. Several radical and profound insights, such as the deeper interpretation of the Māndukya Upaniṣad and the clear examination of concepts such as 'Adhyasa' or 'Rasa' is not possible in the book, which will be attempted separately. Even the applied psychology of Āyurveda, arising from the metaphysics of Sāmkhya, is not addressed in sufficient detail in this book. These are key mindful gaps and, hopefully, will be addressed by others in near future.

Some element of transitions from one familiar lexicon to another is required. The book starts with the chapter on consciousness, which sets the tone of an Indian psychology. This is followed by the chapter on body and embodied consciousness, as most psychologists have missed addressing and engaging with the sophisticated conceptualization of the body in the IKT. The chapter is imperfect and needs more details or perhaps another book but for the purpose of laying the basic architecture of Indian Psychology, this suffices.

Mainstream psychologists trisect the scope of psychology, into cognition, affect and behaviour. Assuming broad and deep familiarity of the contemporary psychology, on cognition, affect and behaviour, the next two chapters lay out the initial frameworks of affect and cognition from Indian psychology. The fifth chapter discusses social psychology from an Adhyatmic point of view and suggests Bhakti as an Indian social psychology. No psychologist in India till now has examined the notion that Bhakti movement represents an Adhyatmik social psychology and, therefore, a true Indian modernity, much before the problematic European modernity and the current ideas of multiculturalism! In general, Buddhism is presented as an alternative to the problems of caste in the hierarchical Hindu social systems. While the great Buddha was, indeed, the first of the Indian modernists, preaching in Pali, the project of modernity to address the issues of caste in Indian society is better addressed by Bhakti movement for two reasons: one it democratized knowing and being in a shared social sense, removing the barrier between monks/nuns as well as the laity and second, Bhakti is more embodied and infused with day-to-day lived experiences – with day-to-day rituals, music, dance and satsang. After the chapter on Bhakti and social selves, the sixth chapter lays the framework for a radical theory in Indian psychology of the 'no mind'. Transcending the 'mind' can there be freedom while living? What is the value of freedom otherwise? Continuing in this refrain the next chapter addresses what has been called as 'everyday' or small 'c' creativity. In contrast to the jazz and glamour of big 'C' creativity, in mainstream psychology, it is the everyday creativity, which keeps the 'self' loose and nebulous, in its moment-by-moment engagement with the ecology within and without. Everyday creativity not only brings joy to the self and others but completes the ecology of consciousness. Everyday creativity and its framework are thus conceptually stronger and grounded in an Indic ontology and episteme than the positive psychology framework. Everyday creativity also links the diverse and plural folk traditions of India, which were called 'little' by the colonizers. Finally, the conclusion chapter will identify the fallacies of academic reason if a universal rationality is assumed.

There is no claim whatsoever of any ethnic or religious superiority/inferiority. As the Pondicherry Manifesto of Indian psychology states, the term 'Indian' is used to honour that geography and a relentless search for the unbounded truth; this relentless search was carried by the best of its people – most radical in thought, compassionate in affect and ethical in behaviour – the Guru-s! In the last 150 years of the exchange between east and west, seekers of truth, beauty and love are found across the world. The key political point, without generating adversarial binaries between east and west, is the legitimate recognition and acknowledgement of the brutal loss to the Indic civilization and its ontological, epistemological and axiological frameworks due to colonization.

The most important purpose for Indian psychology is the key challenge that materialism or physicalism throws at humanity. At the core of the physicalist argument is the nature of self and whether humanity can be shaped and controlled by humans themselves or by others and/or non-human forces. Indian psychology presents an alternate world-view beyond the impurified ideas of 'God', non-human machines and an emergent consciousness from complex systems; a naturalistic philosophy, without the baggage of divinity and spirituality from the Abrahamic religions, such that all is recognized as divine and spiritual in a non-Abrahamic sense. The continued applications of Indian psychology towards well-being emphatically state that the human and indeed the whole universe is ever free; the only welcome bondages that the self-accepts are the bonds of ahimsa (love) and dharma (coherence). This is possibly the reason why Indian cultural psychologies and indeed Asian psychologies present a strong counter to the physicalist argument. For this reason alone, psychologists, not only from India but across the world, need to be galvanized for instituting and practising an Indian consciousness-based psychology.

References

Berry, J. W., Poortinga, Y. H., Pandey, J., Segall, M. H., & Kâğıtçıbaşı, Ç. (1997). *Handbook of cross-cultural psychology: Theory and method* (Vol. 1). John Berry.

Dass, B., & Das, B. (1979). Yogini cult in Orissa. *Proceedings of the Indian History Congress*, *40*, 91–98.

Dyczkowski, M. S. G. (1988). *The Canon of the Saivagama and the Kubjika: Tantras of the Western Kaula tradition*. SUNY Press.

Hayes, G. A., & Timalsina, S. (2017). *Introduction to 'Cognitive science and the study of Yoga and Tantra'*. Multidisciplinary Digital Publishing Institute.

Henrich, J., Heine, S. J., & Norenzayan, A. (2010a). Beyond WEIRD: Towards a broad-based behavioral science. *Behavioral and Brain Sciences*, *33*(2–3), 111.

Henrich, J., Heine, S. J., & Norenzayan, A. (2010b). Most people are not WEIRD. *Nature*, *466*(7302), 29.

Jones, D. (2010). *A WEIRD view of human nature skews psychologists' studies*. American Association for the Advancement of Science.

Karasinski-Sroka, M. (2021). When the poison is the cure – healing and embodiment in contemporary Śrīvidyā Tantra of the Lalitāmbikā Temple. *Religions*, *12*(8), 607.

Kitayama, S., & Cohen, D. (2010). *Handbook of cultural psychology*. Guilford Press.

Kozhevnikov, M., Louchakova, O., Josipovic, Z., & Motes, M. A. (2009). The enhancement of visuospatial processing efficiency through Buddhist deity meditation. *Psychological Science*, *20*(5), 645–653.

Metzinger, T. (2020a). Minimal phenomenal experience: Meditation, tonic alertness, and the phenomenology of 'pure' consciousness. *Philosophy and the Mind Sciences*, *1*(I), 1–44.

Metzinger, T. (2020b). Minimal phenomenal experience. *Philosophy and the Mind Sciences*, *1*(I), 1–44.

Moghaddam, F. M. (1987). Psychology in the three worlds: As reflected by the crisis in social psychology and the move toward indigenous third-world psychology. *American Psychologist*, *42*(10), 912.

Moghaddam, F. M. (2009). Commentary: Omniculturalism: Policy solutions to fundamentalism in the era of fractured globalization. *Culture & Psychology*, *15*(3), 337–347.

Moghaddam, F. M., & Lee, N. (2006). Double reification: The process of universalizing psychology in the three worlds. In A. C. Brock (Ed.), *Internationalizing the history of psychology* (pp. 163–182). New York University Press. http://www.jstor.org/stable/j.ctt9qg8nj.13

Nielsen, M., Haun, D., Kärtner, J., & Legare, C. H. (2017). The persistent sampling bias in developmental psychology: A call to action. *Journal of Experimental Child Psychology*, *162*, 31–38.

Pandit, S. A. (2011). The concept of 'Rasa' in Indian psychology: A preliminary qualitative study. *Journal of Psychosocial Research*, *6*(1), 139.

Pandit, S., & Misra, G. (2013). Emotions in Indian psychology. In *Psychology and psychoanalysis* (Centre for Studies in Civilizations, pp. 663–691). Indian Council of Social Science Research ICSSR.

Samdarshi, P. (2019). Spatial and architectural constructs of Tantric Buddhist Mandalas: A cognitive approach. In *Eloquent spaces* (pp. 69–87). Routledge India.

Sen, R. S., & Pandit, S. (2013). Exploring Vātsalyam: The emotion of love for the child. *Psychology and Developing Societies*, *25*(1), 165–193. https://doi.org/10.1177/0971333613477303

Shweder, R. A., & Sullivan, M. A. (1993). Cultural psychology: Who needs it? *Annual Review of Psychology*, *44*(1), 497–523.

Sinha, J. B. P., Singh, S., Gupta, P., Srivastava, K. B. L., Sinha, R. B. N., Srivastava, S., Ghosh, A., Siddiqui, R. N., Tripathi, N., Gupta, M., Srivastava, S., Mulla, Z., Vijayalakshmi, C., & Pandey, A. (2010). An exploration of the Indian mindset. *Psychological Studies*, *55*(1), 3–17. https://doi.org/10.1007/s12646-010-0001-x

Smith, L. T. (2021). *Decolonizing methodologies: Research and indigenous peoples*. Zed Books Ltd.

Timalsina, S. (2007). Metaphor, Rasa, and Dhvani: Suggested meaning in tantric esotericism. *Method & Theory in the Study of Religion*, *19*(1–2), 134–162.

Timalsina, S. (2011). Encountering the other: Tantra in the cross-cultural context. *The Journal of Hindu Studies*, *4*(3), 274–289.

Timalsina, S. (2012). Body, self, and healing in Tantric ritual paradigm. *The Journal of Hindu Studies*, *5*(1), 30–52.

Valsiner, J. (2014). *An invitation to cultural psychology*. Sage.

2 Consciousness

Sat-Cid-Ānanda

An incident triggered the thought process of this book. While taking a class on introducing consciousness for a group of students doing their master's program in psychology at an Indian university, a student raised her hand and asked the following question – 'what has consciousness got to do with psychology?' This question was stunning and revealed the fundamental ruptures in the mainstream psychology which we have been teaching and indeed practising in India – the assumptions of behaviourism, the disconnect with Indian wisdom traditions and implanted academic psychology in India and the labelling of psychological knowledge in Indian texts and material – as irrelevant and unnecessary. Indeed – What has consciousness got to do with psychology?! In this book, we will try to introduce and, thereafter, critically compare concepts, frameworks and models of consciousness and review whether consciousness has got anything to do with psychology, esp. Indian psychology. In the process, we will discuss contemporary ideas about consciousness as well as the sophisticated frameworks and perspectives from Indian knowledge traditions (IKT).

It would be interesting to consider that not only is consciousness a 'hot' topic in psychology, but 'non-dual awareness' is red hot topic in consciousness! (Josipovic, 2014, 2010, 2019; Josipovic & Miskovic, 2020). What has 'non-dual awareness' got to do with psychology? Does non-dual awareness have applied psychology implications? Does it reflect in neural correlates? These are exciting questions to consider. In the current context, since 2000s, psychology has been experiencing a 'consciousness boom' (Dreyfus, 2011) and this consciousness boom itself has been a result of several cross-currents of thought in the Europe and American history of ideas, including a long exchange of dialogues between the East and the West increasing in frequency from the early 20th century. Suffice to note: Several changes have occurred in academic psychology as a result of this long exchange, esp. in reference to health, well-being and the neuroscience of consciousness (Walsh, 2015; Walsh & Shapiro, 2006). In fact, positive psychology, which has been extensively taught in India, for more than ten years now, explicitly acknowledges its roots in several non-European world-views including the Indic consciousness-centred world-views. While calling

DOI: 10.4324/9781003336204-2

for the 'culturally pluralistic' rather than 'culturally deficient' theories of psyche, standard textbooks of positive psychology acknowledge the diverse Asian and Indian world-views arising from the Hindu, Buddhist and Jaina thought, just as they discuss Zen, Daoism, Christian and Athenian views. Psychologists in India took this question of positive psychology and its disciplinary roots through a vibrant special issue discussion on whether Indian Psychology is, in fact, the original positive psychology arriving from India or not (see Christopher, 2014; Rao, 2014; Salagame, 2014). Prof Rao, a teacher for a generation of psychologists in India, forcefully argued that the positive psychology movement that is so popular in the West has a very poor theoretical basis. He further wrote that a strong theoretical basis to positive psychology can be provided by the applied Indian psychological thought. Rao also acknowledged the strengths of the positive psychology movement.

Note that the central, organizing principle of positive psychology is well-being which has always been the central concept of being and living in IKT; well-being is definitional to consciousness in the 'non-dual' school of Vedānta! It appears then that consciousness is the elephant in the room that is frequently unacknowledged, even while intellectually cogent discussions are made about psychology and consciousness in India. Consciousness, understood in IKT, is transcendental as well as embodied in the world as the world. It is phenomenally 'recognized' by each one of us, moment by moment in our life – while being awake, in dream, in sleep and in advanced meditative states (Timalsina, 2008, 2011 and 2012). The phenomenal awareness of consciousness has not been investigated by the traditional Euro-American psychology for several historical reasons, and to reclaim Indian psychology is to honour the centrality of consciousness in human and non-human/animal psychology. Indeed, the questions of consciousness are ferociously debated in reference to machine cognition, with the help of new conceptual vocabulary such as 'sapience' and give novel interpretations to agency and consciousness, intelligence, sapience and sentience.

Why have the psychology students in India not explored consciousness? We will try to examine this question throughout as we also try to put forth what the Indian applied psychological texts say – from Yoga to Vedānta to Tantra. How have different systems – such as the Indian and the European-American systems, viewed consciousness historically and in present times? How have they seen the implications of their perspectives and approach to consciousness reflect in the psychology that they constituted as 'knowledge'? These are some of the questions that will be discussed along the way. We will return to this question and close this loop at the end of the chapter.

Booming inter-disciplinarity in mind sciences

The flavour of the current times is interdisciplinarity. Even as interdisciplinarity, multi-disciplinarity and trans-disciplinarity have been academic buzzwords for the last three decades or so, several intractable questions before humanity, such as climate change, global warming, economic and social inequalities, as well as the impact of technologies in our changing societies and cultures have made interdisciplinarity *imperative for solving these problems*. What do we mean by interdisciplinarity? It is generally understood that interdisciplinarity would mean that scholars from different disciplines would weigh in on a common topic from different perspectives. Independent perspectives remain independent and it is for the reader or the audience then to make sense of the different perspectives or not. Most times, the readers and the audiences still continue to see different perspectives in silos. There may or may not be a lateral or vertical *integration or transfer* of concepts, mental models and implications across disciplines. Often time, the metaphors of one discipline get transferred to the other, resulting in deep structure confusion. An example of this would be the metaphor of information processing for brain. Ironically, when computers themselves are re-fashioned as intelligent decision-making machines such as Siri or Alexa, the brain is viewed as a machine, and by implication, so is the self! This kind of inter-disciplinarity is similar to the story of the wise blindfolded men, describing an elephant that they can't see! We are not able to come to a combined or an integrated view. One of the pathways for interdisciplinarity could be where two professors/scholars/practitioners from two different perspectives do combined work together. An example of that is the combined work of Amos Tversky and Daniel Kahneman in the current times. Tversky was an economist and Kahneman is a social psychologist. They combined work and triggered a paradigm change in economics as well as in psychology.

In Indian history of thought, a radical foundational pathway of achieving inter-disciplinarity is integrality within the person. Polymaths such as Gurudev Rabindranath Tagore, Maulana Azad, Nikola Tesla or Edison, with deep interest and contributions in different contexts would be a case in point. The point to emphasize here is – we need true inter-disciplinarity to solve fundamental problems, which is necessarily a profound mindset, similar to a more trendy 'multi-cultural mindset'.

Precisely, this kind of interdisciplinary thinking is being attempted here and now in mind sciences. Cognitive neuroscientists, psychologists, philosophers, and monks have been discussing with each other since centuries, but more visibly in the last 50 years! Now, what are these 'mind' sciences? Isn't psychology about observable behaviour as any student of psychology in India would automatically profess?

As a result of a 100 years of dialogical process, the mind sciences are now changing and radically revising knowledge from single neurons to connections between neurons (called connectionism); from experimental psychology on single subjects to social and cultural cognition, and finally, implications for social policy. In this, cognitive neuroscience, behavioural sciences, lifespan development psychology, social psychology, law and policy come together at different levels of analysis as well as profound implications about how we want to move forward as a collective consciousness. Let me explain the levels of analysis – at the cellular and sub-cellular level, fascinating discoveries show the effect of behaviour on biochemistry, epigenetic triggers and phenotypal expression starting from fetal development, post-natally and indeed throughout lifespan development (McEwen et al., 2016; Meaney et al., 2013; Parent et al., 2012; Weaver et al., 2004). The development of brain and nervous system, which is studied as 'cognitive neuroscience' and lifespan development is linked with other systems such as endocrine system, immunity systems and genetics. *Behaviour is a 'key' that frequently triggers and moderates the locks/expression of these cellular and physiological systems.*

At the next 'body' level, we see the behaviour of the body as a coordinated system which is dually linked with the systems internally as well as the external environmental context; this is a dynamic adaptation with the micro-context and the macro-social context throughout the developmental lifespan of this person-the mind-body and several minds and bodies, in togetherness. Even at the level of the single 'body', it is emphasized that the dynamic adaptation to the context is intimately linked with bacteria, viruses and fungi systems, where the 'body' interacts with the micro-biome, viruses, etc., who further interact with endocrine systems, the nervous system and the mutation and expression of genes over a longer term. Finally, closely overlapping with the lifespan development, we see social psychology at the level of analysis of interpersonal relationships, community relationships and social structures and cultures. Note that social structures and cultures give the mental models, mindsets and epistemic assumptions to groups/communities and relationships as well as the individual as they navigate through life towards well-being or illness. Thus, right from the cellular to the trans-national social levels, there is an inter-linkage and this inter-linkage rests on consciousness –its perceptions, cognitions, affect and behaviour. Thus, consciousness appears as a system that accounts for subsystems of information generation, maintenance and exchange.

Importantly, this means that, if one systemic level is changed/modified, it would have an impact upwards and downwards. The key insight that one grasps in the IKT – which are consciousness centred and, therefore, applied psychological – is that these levels pivot from yogic/conscious behaviour, breath, emotion, cognition and/or social relations. It is fascinating that an applied psychology, with conscious action/behaviour is at the centre of this inter-system organization. If we look at knowledge this way, fundamentally, we need an interdisciplinary logic in these times, where fragmentation is mainstream and what we have is a WEIRD psychology (Heinrich et al., 2010a, 2010b; Jones, 2010). This seems to be happening in the European and American context in reference to cognition and 'mind sciences' and that is leading towards an appreciation of 'consciousness' as well as Indic ideas of consciousness. There is still a long way to go in terms of understanding the true import of this profound shift, but we have made a start.

Tragically, this welcome, albeit disruptive churn is not happening in the colonized Indian context where research, teaching and public discourse is still imported/mimicked and stagnant.

As the movement to 'decolonize' psychology and, indeed, the social sciences gains ground, several voices find space; welcome voices that critique not only external homogeneity but also internal homogeneity in discourse (Bhatia, 2017; Bhatia & Priya, 2019, 2021), we are hopefully moving towards are truly universal psychology, rather than the imposed Western European–North American psychology, with its debilitating theoretical biases as default universals. In this polyglot churn, this book is situated as a wholly indigenous and lived consciousness-based Indian psychology; not discounting, but rather welcoming the fact that there may be multiple psychologies in the Indic framework.

It is important to note here that, by decolonization, this book is not taking a transactional political position of East vs West or Hindu vs non-Hindu. Recognizing that the essence of Indian psychology has continued from the Vedas and the Vedānta, before the common era, there have been diverse plural traditions of living and these have indeed attracted seekers from across the world, the book also reiterates the position taken herein that the indigenous Indian psychology traditions were and have been brutally and indeed violently invisibilized by the colonization structures and practices (Asad, 1973; Cohn, 2020). This cannot be denied and needs to be emphasized as the 250 years of colonial rule and the politics of knowledge thereafter deeply disrupted the IKT and specifically possibilities of an Indian psychology centred on consciousness, which has been a lived reality of many, albeit not all people, communities since millennia. In the last 150 years, the West broadly has variously been inspired (through exchange), co-opted and/or distorted (through other practices) the traditional knowledge and wisdom from various colonized cultures. As mentioned, this has radically changed psychology from what it was 70 years ago to what we understand today. However, till the fundamental meta-theoretical assumptions of Euro-American philosophy of psychology and science are not revisited, the immense potential of Indian psychology, even if co-opted/inspired, will not fructify. The partial potential of applied psychology will also likely be commodified and hijacked by market-based discourses, reflecting a serious distortion of the aims of Indian knowledge systems.

Scholars have pointed out that early psychology, which grew out of philosophy in Germany and founded by Wilhelm Wundt did attempt to capture the lived experiences and the subjectivities of the people in a scientific manner calling it 'folk psychologie'. However, psychology shifted out of philosophy and was deeply influenced by the then extant philosophy of science. The positivistic, strict empiricist stance as a scientific method was privileged at the exclusion of all other methods of knowing because psychology aimed to solve concrete problems inspired by 'natural sciences'. In the early 19th century Europe, science and the scientific method was the hope for suffering humanity, and there was a widespread disillusionment with the church and theology. Philosophy in the European tradition was seen as analytical with little scope for application. In this context, science provided a solution to the masses in Europe; the scientific method and the philosophy of science consumed the philosophers themselves, such as John Mill, Francis Bacon, etc. In contrast and without papering over the serious philosophical differences among different schools of Darśana, the Indian context showed that Indian philosophy was always intimately connected with lived experiences, religion as well as social applications so as to be still able to solve human problems. Indeed, this linking and coherence were mindfully instituted by the scholars, practitioners and teachers themselves. We see this in Vedānta, Buddhism, Jaina thought, several schools of Hindu philosophy such as Yoga-Sāmkhya, Āyurveda, the Bhakti movement and the integrative Sufi-Islam and schools of tantra. Note that protest and resistance and reformation in religious traditions were and have been ongoing, without losing the scope for applications for well-being and the axiological assumption of liberating beings from misery and suffering.

Science and the philosophy of science since two hundred years prior has gone through transformations, particularly the 'paradigms shift' in physics from Newtonian mechanics to quantum and particle physics. Kuhn (Kuhn, 2012), a philosopher of science in the mid-20th century, located the idea of paradigm shift in the way, the hypotheses were framed, alluding to a confirmatory bias in science method. Further to Kuhn, Popper (Popper, 2005) further worked on the scientific method and specifically the framing of the hypotheses to address this confirmatory bias in the reasoning of the sciences. There have been several criticisms of the reasoning biases in the scientific method by the non-Euro-American contexts, including its focus on 'standardization', linearity, etc. This is primarily because the scientific method and the framing of hypotheses are fundamentally based on a split and a binary direction to how reality should be/is. Asian theorists, for example, have pointed out this flaw in the hypotheses framing and testing as it *fixes* the reality, that too in binary terms. Note that, Asian theorists have been influenced by Buddhism and Buddhism particularly advocated the middle path! Middle path meant that reality and, therefore, logic could not be binary reasoning, rather, could be *negotiated in terms of a dialectic process*. Thus, there are further logical possibilities with neither and both along with either/or. This is seen in Yogācāra texts, particularly sandhi-nirmochana sutra (often understood as 'breaking of the binaries'). It is remarkable that dialectics was seen as 'minor logic' in formal philosophy in European tradition! Of course, contemporary advances in psychology and, indeed, in artificial intelligence emphasize the fact that what is called as 'minor logic' by formal philosophical standards is the critical reasoning process of mature human beings, where contextual and dynamic adaptation to uncertainty are the hallmarks of human perception-affect-cognition-action nexus. It is ironic that mindlessly following this issue in formal philosophy of Europe, Indian scholars continue without questioning, even as there has been an attempt to decolonise research methods as such (Linda Tuhiwai-Smith, 2021).

Despite these criticisms, the mainstream scientific method and the philosophy of science underlying largely continues to follow the binary logic when setting and framing the hypotheses. The main point to note here is that in contrast to the mainstream of European philosophy, and not counting the anti-positivistic philosophers, Asian philosophies were always applied-analytical and psychological-lived in their orientation. This also means that Asian philosophies were always based on a continuous tradition of not only philosophers with the intellectual heft but also practices and lived experiences of an applied psychology (Paranjpe, 2019, 2012; Rao & Paranjpe, 2016; Shweder & Sullivan, 1993). Each of the Asian philosophies and perspectives was coherent to and from philosophy and living – with a set of ontological and epistemic framework. Since this was a lived and living philosophy, there is a broad agreement on the axiological values of emancipation and freedom from suffering. Paranjpe (Paranjpe, 2019; also see Cornelissen, 2008; Valsiner, 2014) has written extensively on these issues and identified this key value of freedom from suffering as the central organizing principle of all Indic psychologies. For example, there are different models discussed in Indian history on the relationship between political power, religion and spiritual power, where; most recently, Mahatma Gandhi, viewed political power arising out of spiritual power. At different points of time in the India, in history of ideas and action, different positions have been taken on whether political, religious and spiritual power can be combined in one institution or not. This is dialectically contrasted with the rupture of science, theology and philosophy in the European and American context. Thus, there are several differences between the history of ideas in the European and American context and the Asian and, specifically Indian context. Additionally, in the history of ideas in the European and American context, the relationship between power and truth is deeply problematic – with history of the genocide of the Jews, the abuse of powers by the church and its reflection in the philosophy of dialectical materialism of Marx. In the Indian context, one cannot homogenize to say that there was no conflict between political, religious and spiritual power or no questions of communities and caste or take a position that denies these questions. *However, it is clear that the way to organise these questions and resolve these conflicts has been particularly different than in the European and the American contexts, and these have been conflated wrongly by the contemporary thinkers.*

When the Western powers colonized much of the world, and indeed, the British colonized India, the intention was not just trade alone, just as early anthropologists did not seek knowledge alone! Historical research has shown that anthropology and ethnography were deeply political colonial enterprises and the intention of early researchers/anthropologists/historians was towards proselytization and the assertion of the supremacy of the Western civilization when the British, Portuguese and French and Dutch encountered the Indian context as the 'other' (Asad, 1973; Cohn, 2020; Dirks, 1989). This background brings us the central question about consciousness and psychology. Certainly, there was discrimination and marginalization in Indian society, but, equally, there were serious and deep efforts at philosophical, historical and social levels towards a greater coherence, a movement towards well-being.

Consciousness 'boom' in psychology

As mentioned in the earlier section, psychology split out of philosophy because it wanted to apply knowledge and/or move out of the speculative and analytical nature of European philosophy. In the early years, several psychologists such as William James continued to straddle philosophy as well as psychology, and therefore, there was a cross-fertilization of ideas from philosophy to psychology. As such, the mainstream of psychology always was influenced by a stream of philosophical thought called as positivism, realisms and/or empiricism. It is important to note here that, European philosophy had several other schools of thought as well including phenomenology, hermeneutics and interpretivism. However, these were and are not considered as mainstream. Till about 1950s, there was a distinction between the psychologies and the perspectives from Europe and the perspective from North America in psychology. Indeed, early theories and ideas in social as well as in lifespan development were quite different in foci. However, with the rising influence of North American psychology, at least in the global South, and indeed even in Eastern Europe, Asia, North America and Australia, North American psychology, which has been accused of methodological individualism became a default 'universal' psychology. It is in this context that we need to understand the approaches towards studying consciousness in psychology. Whereas early European thinkers such as Edward Titchener and Wilhelm Wundt were interested in the nature of mind and functionalists such as William James were interested in stream of consciousness, the issue of method and instrumentation, bogged them down seriously. With the influence of Watson, the radical behaviouristic line of thought came to be dominated; these exclusively focussed on reward and punishment or extractive models of learning. Clearly, learning among humans and non-humans is a much broader concept and not necessarily tied up to rewards and punishments; the dominance of the reward and punishment models and behaviourism, reduced learning to habit formation and observable behaviour theorized through stressed animal models, who were put into stress and then observed. Such an approach completely denied not only the existence of agency and self, a non-stressed approach to learning but also denied any research or academic interest in consciousness. Thus, we see that, from World War II onwards, whatever little interest that psychologists might have had in consciousness was completely relegated to invisibility because it could not be measured, or empirically or instrumentally observed. At this point of time, from the end of World War II to the 1970s and 80s, we see the split between European and increasingly American psychology and the rest of the world. However, radical behaviourism, with its main proponent Skinner reached its end of influence in the 80s. There were several co-mingling currents of thought that can be seen as responsible for this welcome relief. The first one was the advances in computer technologies. The advances in computer technologies had two world-view impacts; firstly, at the level of metaphor, now psychologists were able to study and move beyond the dead-end experimental psychology frameworks of memory, as ironically, it was computers that showed the way for re-understanding the human memory. When Atkinson and Shiffrin proposed a model of memory, they actually theorized something that was not clearly observable in terms of behaviour change; the workings of the computers led to working models of what mind might be. Note that Skinner and Watson denied the existence of mind since one could not 'observe' or locate the mind. Secondly, advances in computer technologies corresponded with the advances in the medical imaging technologies. Beyond electroencephalography (EEG), now scientists could study, even if by proxy and by correlation, the magnetic resonance imaging (MRI) and functional magnetic resonance imaging (fMRI) imagery that came alive in brain while neurons were 'firing'. Thirdly, earlier, brain structure and function were studied either post-mortem or in brains that had suffered insult, trauma, or disease. With the advances in medical imaging technologies, now the scientists could study live, non-traumatized brains. The advances in medical imaging technologies are also important because those satisfied the instrumental requirements of the behaviourist axiom about measurable and observable behaviour, at least by proxy and inference. The level of observability shifted down to neurons.

The broader advance in the thought was the 'crisis' in social psychology. By the 1970s, most social psychologists even from North America had recognized that Euro-American social psychology was in a crisis. The knowledge produced by the Euro-American default social psychology was dominated by data collected from white, Anglo-Saxon Protestant, college students, male! This could not be a universal psychology to be sure! Several scholars, such as Moghaddam have commented upon this crisis in social psychology (Moghaddam, 1987). Similarly, there was a crisis in mental health that led to a shift from clinic and hospital driven approach to a community driven approach to mental health. Alongside, the insularity of psychology was questioned by several psychologists within.

Finally, there has been an increasing exchange between the philosophers, meditation teachers, Yoga gurus, Buddhist teachers and practitioners from East Zen, Kung fu, tai chi, Hatha Yoga, and so on, with thinkers, psychologists, scientists and the general public. Many of the psychologists have been students of masters from the East. Similarly, due to the 60s hippy revolution, several people from Europe and North America travelled East and learnt wisdom traditions, imbibing the Eastern world-view in the process. Finally, it helped that, not only did we have the 'linguistic turn' in social sciences, but we also had an increasing focus on affect, culture and cognition and body as a site of phenomenological awareness.

Thus, we are able to 'see' from the 90s onwards, a slight but a sure shift that would inevitably lead towards the study of consciousness. Certainly, in the early years, the split between materialists, physicalists and integralists (Indian influenced scientists and philosophers) was and has been sharp, partly because of the body-mind dualism that European and American thought has been struggling with relentlessly as it derives its meta-theoretical assumptions from Greek logic and then Descartes. The physicalists understanding of consciousness is premised on the idea of body and the primacy of matter. Key physicalists and computationalists are Dennett, Churchland, Pinker and others. The integralist position is premised on the idea of the integrity of the mind-body-consciousness complex and the expression of consciousness as transcending while pervading the mind-body.

The Western philosophical ideas of consciousness and the meta-theoretical assumptions have created their own difficulties in terms of defining and understanding consciousness, intentionality, awareness and qualia and of their psychological conceptualization, including lived experience. This has implications for the applied psychologies of liberation and freedom from suffering and living while being free, as theorized in the ideal of Jīvanmukti or Bodhisattva. Let us see the conceptual vocabulary used to understand consciousness in the contemporary times

What is consciousness: Characteristics of consciousness

Defining consciousness is currently not possible for psychologists, given that it defies the available categorical terms. Consensus is difficult within contemporary European and American psychology, where there are several perspectives and philosophical positions (Cornelissen, 2008). This is comparable to the classical philosophical schools in India, where there are several differences about defining and understanding consciousness, but more significantly, in IKT, there is a broad agreement about the *centrality of consciousness as such.* The centrality of consciousness in the Indian perspectives is most profound as the unique identifier in the IKT and has been commented upon by scholars such as Rao and others. This is 'game changing' and redraws the landscape as all the meditative methods emerge out of this realization of the transformations or appearance of an embodied-enminded consciousness, which transcends both the body and mind and is *recognized* through meditation. The purely physicalist and computational perspectives have taken the position that consciousness is in the complexity of the neural function and structure of the brain; that there is no mind apart from the brain. The representationalist position acknowledges the importance of the brain but views the mind as layered on top of the neural activity, so to say.

Even within the assumptions of embodied consciousness, scientists have struggled to understand the changes in brain activity and consciousness due to alterations such as coma, anaesthesia, sleep, dreaming and wake cycles. Within the wake cycles, there are variations in consciousness in terms of awareness and focus/attention, such as reveries, day-dreaming and meditation. Thus, most psychologists and cognitive neuroscientists have focused on trying to understand *the characteristics* of consciousness. Some of those characteristics are below:

A **Subjectivity and phenomenal awareness** – Subjectivity and phenomenal awareness is 'big problem for contemporary perspectives! In the IKT, subjectivity is defined as a key characteristic of consciousness, even as consciousness transcends subjectivity. Self and subjectivity are centred on a sense and awareness of one's own self. Indeed, the question that IKT asks is – can one *recognise* an 'ownerless consciousness'? Can one be phenomenally aware but without the 'me and the mine-ness' of experience? These are some of the fundamental questions that comparative philosophers are asking, which IKT testifies as a lived. These questions are not only central for understanding Indian Psychology but also for understanding non-human machine cognition. From the IKT point of view – can humans, arrive at a pathway of experiencing the world without the 'me and the mine-ness' (mamakāra) of experience and, therefore, be free of suffering? From the point of view of non-human machine cognition, the question is opposite – can machines actually own up experiences and, therefore, be held accountable for their actions? On non-human animal consciousness, the question is – do animals have the 'me and the mine-ness' of experience? Do they recognize their agency? These are some of the fascinating questions in psychology, esp. cognitive and transpersonal psychology.

B **Qualia** – The quality of our experiences, the intensity and the variation in these qualitative aspects is a defining characteristic of consciousness. A simple example would be listening to music; the grasping/approaching and attending to music; the quality of our listening is differentiated by the experiences in our life, the acuity of our sense organs, their past training and the intensity of our attention – all affecting the quality of our experience. The quality of experience is also dependent on the context, the situation, the momentary affect and sustained moods that we experience. Music performers can (rarely) have a bad day when they cannot get the right pitch and tone, similar to students and novices, who certainly are trying to train their mind-bodies.

C **Unity and a unified field of awareness** – 'I' consciousness is distinguished from 'consciousness-as-such' in IKT. 'I' consciousness has been noted in the ancient Indian texts, where the self is understood as the

> unifying function of 'I' – me and mine-ness experience. The conventional self or 'I' consciousness identifies with the experiences is called the 'kartā (doer), jnātā (knower) and bhoktā (experiencer)' and thus is conceptualized as 'baddha-bound/linked/attached' to the experience, thereby, indicating to the possibility of living while being 'unbound' to the phenomenal world. In mainstream psychology, the question is framed in sensory-mind terms – the eyes see in rays of light, the ears hear in sounds, music and silence; the taste and the olfactory sense use molecule transformations and sense smell and flavour; touch is understood in terms of pressure and temperature – yet the brain coheres all the sensory inputs in a unified manner. How? Do we process the colour, the fragrance and the taste of the Kesar or an alphonso mango separately or is it only taste/smell/color; it is the same mango. Similarly, when we move in the markets, especially in the Indian markets; on the crowded streets of India we are deluged with intense colours, sounds, fragrances and tastes; all through, the experience is understood and processed seamlessly, cohereing in the subjectivity of the self and the unity of the market place, itself!

There are other characteristics of consciousness as well, but in this section, we have briefly tried to understand these key characteristics of consciousness. In contemporary psychology and the curriculum that we teach in India, we mostly focus on the waking states and briefly touch upon dreams and sleep states only in descriptive EEG terms! In the last two decades, there has been a differentiation of automatic wake states and deliberate wake states, which is sometimes attended to. There is a marginal mention of altered states of consciousness, typically in terms of drugs and substances abuse. This is appalling in comparison to the intensity of focus on consciousness and the subtlest, most profound discussions in the IKT, on consciousness as psyche-making, making India well-known across the world. Recent research in the European and American tradition has caught on and now started focusing on the availability of altered states of consciousness as legitimate frameworks across all cultures in the world and not just in India for enhancing a subjective well-being. Now, psychologists agree that subjective well-being through these altered states of consciousness is enhanced through trance states, lucid dreaming, hypnosis, religious chanting and the whirling dances of the derveshes!

The mainstream understands psychology in terms of very broad understanding of personality, cognitions, thoughts, emotions, behaviour and social relations. In comparison, Asian Psychologies and particularly the Yoga as well as the mindfulness frameworks focus on what has been now called as micro-phenomenology as integrated moment by moment experience. Mindfulness particularly focuses on moment by moment awareness of behaviour, movements of thought, feelings, emotion, impulses, desires and even physiological drives as a whole. These all constitute the contents of consciousness, moment by ephemeral moment. With this brief background, let us introduce a model of consciousness from a Vedānta text called the Māndukya Upaniṣad and see how it illuminates the study of psychology, particularly for students of psychology in India

These co-mingling cross-currents of world-views and a thoughtful living are slow, and yet a profound shift has affected not only psychology and cognitive neuroscience; but rather other social sciences, law and public policy as well. Instead of accounting for these co-mingling cross-currents of thought, the psychologists in India –academia, research and practitioners have been stuck and stagnated in the outdated notions of psychology, education and health. Dalal and Misra (2010) have discussed the 'front and the bulk' of psychology in India. The front of psychologists in India have done work and contributed (Sinha et al., 2010); the bulk of psychologists in India continue to follow the colonial concepts, frameworks and methodologies, and therefore, their research and practice has merely mimicked the mainstream critiqued for a persistent sampling bias (see, Nielsen et al., 2017). Indeed even today, it is fashionable to be a 'behaviourist' in a university and very unfashionable to talk about philosophy and consciousness! We discussed inter-disciplinarity earlier and mentioned that there is an amazing interdisciplinary work happening in mind sciences in the European and American context. Tragically, in the Indian context, which is a civilizational cradle of systematic enquiries on consciousness, psychologists, Indologists and others are stuck with old frameworks. So, the question is – can we decolonize psychology, which then must necessarily include diverse voices? One of the serious contributions of this decolonized psychology would be a consciousness-based Indian psychology of well-being and liberation from suffering.

Consciousness in Indian knowledge traditions

Psychologists in India have engaged in an academic debate – whether psychology existed in India prior to the British. This is similar to several African psychologists' discussions as well. Such discussions are linked to the stunning impact of colonization. The word 'psychology' as an academic discipline did not exist in India prior to the introduction by the British in the early 20th century. However, it would be interesting to note that the first reference to the word – Manas (for psyche in psychology) appears in the tenth mandala of the Ṛig Veda, in reference to a processing and coordinating mechanism between the five different senses. There are several references to the word Manas throughout the Vedic texts, which also proceed with a conceptualization of the antah-kārana translated as 'the inner instrument'. Antah-kārana, as discussed in the Vedic corpus, comprises of four processes: Citta – the repository of all experiences/memories/actions/impressions/impulses), buddhi – the process of decision making, judgement and reasoning, ahamkāra – the sense of I, me and mine-ness, and Manas- the mechanism of coordination and processing of sensory inputs. Note here that, the Rig Veda is dated to about 5000 years before the Common Era by some estimates. Thus, there clearly existed psychological frameworks; several such frameworks have been very sophisticated, such as the Advaita frameworks, which are then further detailed downstream. All have these key concepts of consciousness, cognition, affect and action in their frameworks as integrated systemic whole, thereby bypassing the legacy traps of European philosophy and psychology.

Now, how do contemporary psychologists define and understand mind? Till about a decade back, it was a moment to watch psychologists themselves getting flummoxed and fumble to define mind! Important to note here is that, there are philosophies of mind, yet, the word mind itself has not been defined in psychology till recently. Contrast this with a very clear conceptualization of Manas as that which is relevant to processing of sensory and physiological data and the coordination between the various senses and cognition in the antah-kārana model.

With the advance in cognitive neuroscience and the great influence of Tibetan Buddhism and especially His Holiness the 14th Dalai Lama, the updated versions of cognitive psychology have defined mind as 'the representation of the external world in the functions of the brain' whereas psychology itself is defined now as 'systematic study of the functions of the brain, the mind and the behaviour' (Matlin, 2006). About 30 years back, psychology was defined as the study of observable behaviour alone. The wonderful irony to emphasize here is that, psychology has a model of the brain functions, but they struggle with a model of mind, frequently confusing the mind with consciousness. This is the reason, perhaps, that contemporary psychology yields to physicalist models which equate the mind with the brain. In comparison, in the antah-kārana model, we see a model of the mind but we do not equate or map it with the activity of the brain alone as IKS assumes the pervasiveness of consciousness. Are the cells conscious or unconscious by themselves? Why, if at all, does consciousness emerge in connections? Why do cells connect with each other?

Similar to the idea of Manas, the term or the notion of the 'body' has also received attention in IKT. Depending on the meaning implied, three concepts of the body can be introduced here, both from Yoga as well as Yogācāra. From Yoga, the first meaning of the body and the word denoting the body is 'Śarira' – which has been defined as 'that which decays'. Characteristics of the body are also defined as that which grows, that which procreates, that which decays and that which dies. The next concept which is used to denote the body is 'Kāyā'. Śarira and Kāyā, in IKT, are not limited to the physical body. The word 'physical body' itself is a particularly amusing Indian construction (what else) precisely because the yogic physiology in the Indian world-view talks of three bodies – Śarira! According to yogic physiology, we have three bodies *interwoven with each other.* The most obvious is the physical body – the Sthula Śarira, the next is the psychological body – the Sukṣma Śarira– and the most subtle aspect is the kārana Śarira, which is the causal, intentional body. Similarly, the Yogācāra Buddhist theorizations also formulate the three Kāyā-s, the nirmāṇakāyā, 'transformation body', the sambhogakāyā, 'enjoyment-body' and the dharmakāyā, 'dharma-body'. Finally, another concept that denotes the body is the word – 'Tanu'. Tanu as a technical concept, in Yoga sutra as 'tanukārana' means the weakening of the pain and distress by manifesting itself materially. This is comparable to 'antah-kārana'; kārana as a word means to process and manifest. Other concepts of body, utilized contextually, which are out of scope for further discussion are Deha, Vigraha and Vapu.

The distinction between the mind and the body is important to re-emphasize primarily because the Greek thought and the Cartesian dualism, which undergirds European and American psychology. Philosophy has been struggling with this dichotomy and dualism between the mind and the body. Almost all the contemporary psychology definitions, concepts, models including the definitions of personality, self and indeed of behaviour have struggled with this dichotomy between the mind and the body. In comparison, the Indian idea of mind and body is level by level *iterations of superset-subset relationships*. The mind is a superset and is assumed to include the body and continue even if the body dies. Sāmkhya texts clearly describe the body as the material manifestation of the mind. As Sāmkhya conceptualizes the body as the material manifestation of the mind, Yoga practices focus on the mind through rāja and Hatha Yoga. The relationship between the mind and the body has been the biggest problematic conceptualization for contemporary psychology, which we will try and understand in the chapters that follow.

After the preliminaries, and disaggregating the conceptualizations of antah-kārana, Manas and Śarira, we come to the central idea of consciousness. Consciousness as a central concept in all the Indian systems is commented upon and noted by several philosophers and psychologists in recent times as they were able to have a dual perspective having either being trained in Indian philosophy and then having worked in American and European universities or vice versa (Chadha, 2015; Ganeri, 2017; Hayes and Timalsina, 2017; Paranjpe, 2012; Ram-Prasad, 2013; Rao et al., 2008; Timalsina, 2008, 2011,2012). Consciousness is a central concept not only in the classical Darśana-s but also in the two heterodox systems of Buddhist and Jain thought. Even the Cāravākas, in their denial of consciousness, were part of this investment of intellectual energy in the investigations on consciousness. In line with this immense enquiry, the word consciousness is named differently according to the particular functional and contextual relevance. Several word concepts that indicate the word consciousness in different functionalities and contexts of use and reference are Ātman, Nija, Vastu, Svarupa, Brahman, Puruṣa and Dharma, Kshetrajna, Dehi, etc. The word 'ātman' means consciousness which is bound/personalized- a Jivātman and a paramātman. The word 'Brahman' means an unbounded, continuous, unbroken consciousness as such, which is not bound by any trace of intentionality. Similarly, there are other words such as nija – which means the most intimate, personal; Swarupa, which means one's own form. This introduction for the word concept suffices for now, yet several volumes have been written on consciousness and can be referred if required.

Do contemporary systems view consciousness, mind and the body in a systemic framework? In the current flow of thought, the dominant perspectives, view the body as the primary, most 'real' and, therefore, 'true'; within the body, the nervous systems as central and the complexity of this nervous system as expressed in the brain that gives rise to the consciousness. Consciousness is also the representation of the external world – which is the 'mind'! There cannot be consciousness as such! Thus, there are three key points for us to note – firstly, consciousness is an emergent phenomenon contingent upon the complexity in the physiological systems. Secondly, consciousness is with content or representational of something; always with content. Thirdly, physiological systems and the body are primary. This conceptual architecture is deeply problematic for several reasons. Firstly, we now know that no meaning exists in the single neuron; indeed, where does meaning exist in the mass of neurons, glial cells and neurotransmitters at the synapse? If you were to ask adrenaline, she would say – this reductionism has damaging consequences! Adrenaline shows action readiness and is seen in marathon running, just as running helter-skelter after spotting a mouse or attending an interview! Poor adrenaline has been demonized for the last 70 years. So it is the reductionism on other neurotransmitters and elements of the nervous system, including the brain. Similarly, for the last 70 years, the hippocampus was the only structure associated with memory; now we know that while the hippocampus is important for memory consolidation, memory is in the architecture of the brain itself; similar is the story with amygdala and unreasonable emotion. The point to ask is –where is the meaning? Does meaning emerge at a level of complexity or is it that pre-existing complexity and meaningful order (dharma) devolve and manifest downstream as specific structures and elements?

Because IKT asserts the latter world-view, scholars and philosophers have also identified three central concepts in the IKT. These have been the pivots of discussion through the history of ideas in the subcontinent. They are the concepts of Dharma, Karma and Mukti/nirvāna. Each has been dealt with extensively in IKT. These concepts are interwoven with the understanding of consciousness as such, where this pre-existing meaningful order and complexity is not related to Abrahamic God, but is experienced as an infinity of intentional possibilities. Similar to the question about the relationship between the mind-body and consciousness in contemporary psychology, what is the relationship between the mind, body and consciousness in the IKT? In the traditions which acknowledge the authority of the Veda, different schools have conceptualized this relationship differently. Primarily, the Vedānta view gives primacy to consciousness, that then acts as a witness and the world devolves as an illusion or in some other views an active, real and continuous transformation. The two heterodox schools have taken different positions as they dialectically engaged on these questions which is seen in current discourse as well. (Metzinger 2020).

Thus, we turn our attention to the concepts that most seekers use – enlightenment, liberation and freedom. What do we mean by enlightenment, and how does it compare with the Indian word – mukti/nirvāna? If we take the contemporary psychology view, then the death of the body or indeed the death of the brain functions is the death of consciousness. If we take the Vedānta view, then even if the body dies, nothing is lost to consciousness – the cluster of experiences trans-migrate, to find a new body and continue this circle of life, death and rebirth till it exhausts its karma and/or gains self-realization. From a physicalist's view, this sounds not only pseudoscientific but delusional! Note, however, freedom in a purely physicalist view of consciousness as an emergent phenomenon is a negative definition; it is only possible with the death of the neurons. This freedom cannot bring joy while living. Thus, a physicalist view is filled with terror and the resultant pressure to predict, plan and control to prolong the neuronal life. In contrast to a positive definition as seen in IP, particularly tantra (Pandit, 2011; Pandit and Misra, 2013; Paranjpe, 2009; Sen and Pandit, 2013; Samadarshi, 2019; and Timalsina, 2007, 2011).

Recently, scholars have commented about how 'modern' and particularly European, the word enlightenment is! While there are several models in the IKT of Mukti, none is modern, most seem to be timeless. How would enlightenment be related to consciousness, which is beyond the category of ignorant/enlightened or renders the word enlightenment quite meaningless? How would Mukti be related to Brahman? The answer to the second question is much easier because of the detailing in the conceptualization and frameworks in IKT, where the Brahman doesn't need any enlightenment and none other to grant it. Brahman is that ownerless consciousness, the consciousness as such; It is only the 'I' consciousness that must travel towards enlightenment (Kristeller and Rikhye, 2008). With this brief introduction to consciousness as Brahman, let us try and introduce a model of consciousness from Indian psychology (IKT) in the next section.

An Indian model of consciousness – Māndukya Upaniṣad

Keeping consciousness at the centre, there are several psychological frameworks of IKT which have been extensively used, notably from Patanjali's Yoga sutra to the Bhagavad Gita. In this chapter, we will start with a model of consciousness most closely associated with the states of awareness in an embodied consciousness. This model is the earliest and most profound; it also easy to start with since it starts with embodied states of awareness and beyond. This Upaniṣad is an explanation of the sacred 'Om' as the four apparent states of consciousness, thus connecting profound philosophy with the embodied nature of listening. Māndukya Upaniṣad is one of the principal Upaniṣad in the Indian tradition. Upaniṣad, in Sanskrit, means to sit next to a teacher and enquire about/engage with reality as it is. Upa – means next to; ni – means with a firm resolve and ṣad – means to enquire about reality. The word 'teacher' or implication of sitting next to teacher is implicit in this word. Upaniṣad form, what is known as the 'section of knowing' – jnāna kānda in the Vedic corpus. They also come at the end of the Vedic texts sequentially and, therefore, are also called as Vedānta. Some scholars have also interpreted the term Vedānta as the fruition or culmination of Veda as well. Since the Veda-s were remembered and communicated orally, the learning teaching method was pivoted on patterning, rhyming, pronunciation and verbal organization of knowledge that *facilitated exact recall*. Each of the four Veda-s and its oral recensions were remembered by specific oral tradition or lineage called as 'shākha' (literally translated as branch). Each of the four Veda-s has several Upaniṣads associated with them. Thus, there are more than 100 Upaniṣads, even as there are four Veda-s. The word 'Veda' itself arises from the Sanskrit root-vid, which means to know/enquire/learn. Scholars have arrived at about hundred and eight major and minor Upaniṣads. Out of these, 12 Upaniṣads are called as principal Upaniṣad. Primarily, as Upaniṣad's are aligned with certain Veda-s and the Veda-s are themselves dated by scholars, the dating of the Veda determines the Upaniṣad. A more important reason is that the Upaniṣads, which have been commented upon by the great masters and teachers in the Indian tradition, are called as Principal Upaniṣads. Māndukya Upaniṣad is one of the principal Upaniṣads which has been commented upon by all the grand masters and teachers of the Indian knowledge tradition.

Even as all the Upaniṣads discuss consciousness as such or consciousness as reality, they particularly focus on certain specialization topics, facets or characteristics that a student needs to enquire about. Thus, Taittriya Upaniṣad is traditionally called as Ānanda Mimāṃsā and focuses on the enquiry into the nature of well-being. Similarly, Iśa Upaniṣad enquires into the pathways of well-being and recognizing consciousness as the reality during the process of dying. Māndukya Upaniṣad, is a short and a profound discussion on the principle that even though it appears that there are different states of awareness in consciousness, consciousness is one, undivided and unaltered. Thus the first point to note in comparison to the contemporary ideas of altered states of consciousness, the Māndukya Upaniṣad states that the alteration of awareness and states of consciousness is an appearance, whereas consciousness as such is undivided and unaltered.

The Upaniṣad discusses three apparent, easily available, cognizable states of consciousness as waking, dreaming and sleeping. It describes the flow and direction of awareness in each of the states. For example, in the waking state called Jāgrata, the direction and flow of awareness is outwards, from the senses towards the manifest world. In the dreaming state called svapna, the direction and flow of awareness is within, yet objects, events and processes manifest in the dream world. And in the dreamless sleep state called Suṣupti, the direction and flow of awareness is confined in itself, there is no manifestation to be aware of. Indeed, the phenomenal lived distinction between the world in the dream and the non-dream state is the most profound to note. How do we know that we are seeing the reality as it is and not as a dream? The purpose of dreaming and sleep is recently getting unravelled. Sleep is the most profound of the embodied phenomena; all animals go to sleep, despite or accounting for their fears of survival. The famous 'Rātri Sukta' in the Veda-s alludes to this fact with wonder and then reveres the night as a Goddess who lets the creation sleep in her bosom!

All of us, know these states of awareness in our day-to-day living; the Upaniṣad further states that the interweave, the background, the surround of these three apparently separate states of consciousness is the constant, unbroken, unaltered fourth – the ever-present, ever new, untouched consciousness as such. In the Upaniṣad, this is called as Turiya – or 'the fourth'. In parallel, the Upaniṣad also maps the three states of embodied awareness with the three sounds of 'A', 'U', 'M' and the fourth as unspoken. Scholars and teachers have compared this unspoken fourth with the silence that pervades and is then expressed as sound, language, text and music. The Upaniṣad states that the Turiya or consciousness as such is like a four-legged creature! In the short twelve Mantra-s of this Upaniṣad, we see the definition of consciousness, states of awareness and a model of consciousness connected to audition-body-mind and indicating to transcendence of awareness. In contemporary psychology, both meditative states and substance-induced states are lumped together in 'altered states of consciousness' as if dream and sleep are not altered states of consciousness to waking, which is assumed as the default normal! In any case, we don't know what is 'altered' as the quality of the waking consciousness itself changes through the day, through reveries, daydreams and other automatic behaviours. Note also that substance-induced alteration of consciousness has damaging effects on body, brain and behaviour over the short and long term, which cannot be said about intentional cultivated meditational practice. These are basic framing errors in the contemporary psychological frameworks, where new names need to be coined to distinguish between these altered states of consciousness.

We can see that the Māndukya model of consciousness is *grounded in but not limited* to the body-mind and brain. The model talks of phenomenal awareness and sense perception moving outwards during waking state. In contemporary psychology, this is easily measured through EEG and even more advanced instrumentation such as fMRI and MRI. Perhaps the quality of the awareness in waking state (such as relaxed attention, to revery to intense attention) may pose a challenge to the current instrumentation. Next, the model talks of the dreaming and dreamless sleep state and discusses awareness and sense perception. This, again, can be studied through neuroscience at a surface level as the 'firing' of the neurons in population or sparse. The key point is that it asserts that there is an unaltered fourth – the inter-weave, surround, base and apex. Given so, IKT overall, and not this Upaniṣad in particular, then unambiguously devolves into specific methodologies and techniques to directly 'recognize' this unaltered fourth during waking states, dreaming states and dreamless sleep states. Therefore, in Indian Psychology, not only do we encounter detailed and specific models of refining phenomenal awareness during wake states but also practices such as Yoga nidra that focuses on the awareness during dream and the in-between states and several pranayam practices that closely follow the relaxation of deep sleep states, while keeping the awareness unaltered.

We discussed the characteristics of consciousness as discussed in mainstream psychology. *Awareness* is an overlapping concept in both contemporary and Indian psychology; however, the key distinction is awareness in IP is not broken into waking awareness, dreaming awareness and sleeping awareness; neither is waking awareness or conscious attention alone conflated with consciousness. This is not a semantic quibble – if learning and memory consolidate during rapid eye movement (REM) and non-rapid eye movement (NREM) and cycles, then clearly, things experienced in waking states are processed in dreaming states and are further available as learning in waking states again (Kahan, T. L., & LaBerge, S.,1994). The profound role of dreaming and sleep augments that awareness as such is unbroken, whether in awake, dreaming and sleep physiological states. The role of conscious attention and unconscious attention, explicit and implicit memory all get emphasized. If attention can be shared, which it can be during intense attachment activities such as mother and child playing, then can non-conscious attention also be shared and known? How do psychologists answer this question? Suffice to say, awareness (of both variety-conscious and unconscious), sense of existence/ownerless witness consciousness and joy,/positive affect are the three characteristics of consciousness according to IKT. They are simply understood as Sat, Cit and Ānanda. Note the definitional nature of affect in consciousness. IKT doesn't discuss characteristics such as qualia or unified field as they are assumed in the sense of – me and the mine-ness of experience. We will keep reviewing these questions in the next chapters on body, affect, cognition and day-to-day living in freedom.

The dot: Conclusions and the movement forward

The practice of rangoli making every morning, also called as alpanā in Bengal or Koḷam in Tamil, usually starts by inserting the dot in the centre as the day-to-day Indian cultural practices. Inserting the dot signifies the awareness of infinite space and time turning into finitude; creation then radiates outwards and also coheres back to the dot. This chapter has inserted the central dot – the bindu, by discussing consciousness. You will agree that there are dots, which are actually whorls, spirals and complex mazes, when looked at closely! Centring consciousness through the model introduced here is important because mainstream psychology is not able to cohere back several points and advances in its research to the foundational questions of being. In line with the intentions of the textbook, the next chapter will start with the embodied consciousness.

References

Asad, T. (1973). *Anthropology & the colonial encounter* (Vol. 6). Ithaca Press London.

Berry, J. W., Poortinga, Y. H., Pandey, J., Segall, M. H., & Kâğıtçıbaşı, Ç. (1997). *Handbook of cross-cultural psychology: Theory and method* (Vol. 1). John Berry.

Bhatia, S. (2017). *Decolonizing psychology: Globalization, social justice, and Indian youth identities*. Oxford University Press.

Bhatia, S., & Priya, K. R. (2019). From representing culture to fostering 'voice': Toward a critical indigenous psychology. In *Asian Indigenous psychologies in the global context* (pp. 19–46). Springer.

Bhatia, S., & Priya, K. R. (2021). Coloniality and psychology: From silencing to re-centering marginalized voices in postcolonial times. *Review of General Psychology*, *25*(4), 422–436.

Chadha, M. (2015). Meditation and unity of consciousness: A perspective from Buddhist epistemology. *Phenomenology and the Cognitive Sciences*, *14*(1), 111–127.

Christopher, J. C. (2014). Putting 'positive' and 'psychology' in perspective: The role of Indian psychology. *Psychological Studies*, *59*(2), 110–112.

Cohn, B. (2020). *Colonialism and its forms of knowledge: The British in India*. Routledge.

Cornelissen, M. (2008.). Consciousness. In *Handbook of Indian psychology* (pp. 414–428). Foundation Books. https://doi.org/10.1017/upo9788175968448.023

Dalal, A. K., & Misra, G. (2010). The core and context of Indian psychology. *Psychology and Developing Societies*, *22*(1), 121–155.

Dirks, N. B. (1989). The invention of caste: Civil society in colonial India. *Social Analysis: The International Journal of Social and Cultural Practice*, *25*, 42–52.

Dreyfus, G. (2011). Self and Subjectivity: A Middle Way Approach. In M. Siderits, E. Thompson, & D. Zahavi (Eds.), *Self, No Self?: Perspectives from Analytical, Phenomenological, and Indian Traditions*, (pp. 114–156) Oxford University Press.

Ganeri, J. (2017). *Attention, not self.* Oxford University Press.

Hayes, G. A., & Timalsina, S. (2017). *Introduction to 'cognitive science and the study of Yoga and Tantra'*. Multidisciplinary Digital Publishing Institute.

Henrich, J., Heine, S. J., & Norenzayan, A. (2010a). Beyond WEIRD: Towards a broad-based behavioral science. *Behavioral and Brain Sciences*, *33*(2–3), 111.

Henrich, J., Heine, S. J., & Norenzayan, A. (2010b). Most people are not WEIRD. *Nature*, *466*(7302), 29.

Jones, D. (2010). *A WEIRD view of human nature skews psychologists' studies*. American Association for the Advancement of Science.

Josipovic, Z. (2010). Duality and nonduality in meditation research. *Consciousness and Cognition*, *19*(4), 1119–1121.

Josipovic, Z. (2014). Neural correlates of nondual awareness in meditation. *Annals of the New York Academy of Sciences*, *1307*(1), 9–18.

Josipovic, Z. (2019). Nondual awareness: Consciousness-as-such as non-representational reflexivity. *Progress in Brain Research*, *244*, 273–298.

Josipovic, Z., & Miskovic, V. (2020). Nondual awareness and minimal phenomenal experience. *Frontiers in Psychology*, *11*, 2087.

Kahan, T. L., & LaBerge, S. (1994). Lucid dreaming as metacognition: Implications for cognitive science. *Consciousness and Cognition*, *3*(2), 246–264.

Kristeller, J. L., & Rikhye, K. (2008). Meditative traditions and contemporary psychology. In *Handbook of Indian psychology* (pp. 506–538). Foundation Books. https://doi.org/10.1017/upo9788175968448.028

Kuhn, T. S. (2012). *The structure of scientific revolutions*. University of Chicago Press.

Matlin, M. W. (2006). *Cognition*. John Wiley & Sons.

McEwen, B. S., Nasca, C., & Gray, J. D. (2016). Stress effects on neuronal structure: Hippocampus, amygdala, and prefrontal cortex. *Neuropsychopharmacology: Official Publication of the American College of Neuropsychopharmacology*, *41*(1), 3–23. https://doi.org/10.1038/npp.2015.171

Meaney, M. J., Aitken, D. H., Bodnoff, S. R., Iny, L. J., Tatarewicz, J. E., & Sapolsky, R. M. (2013). Early postnatal handling alters glucocorticoid receptor concentrations in selected brain regions. *Behavioral Neuroscience*, *127*(5), 637–641. https://doi.org/10.1037/a0034187

Metzinger, T. (2020). Minimal phenomenal experience: Meditation, tonic alertness, and the phenomenology of 'pure' consciousness. *Philosophy and the Mind Sciences*, *1*(I), 1–44.

Moghaddam, F. M. (1987). Psychology in the three worlds: As reflected by the crisis in social psychology and the move toward indigenous third-world psychology. *American Psychologist*, *42*(10), 912.

Moghaddam, F. M. (2009). Commentary: Omniculturalism: Policy solutions to fundamentalism in the era of fractured globalization. *Culture & Psychology*, *15*(3), 337–347.

Moghaddam, F. M., & Lee, N. (2006). *Double reification: The process of universalizing psychology in the three worlds*. In A. C. Brock (Ed.), Internationalizing the history of psychology (pp. 163–182). New York University Press.

Nielsen, M., Haun, D., Kärtner, J., & Legare, C. H. (2017). The persistent sampling bias in developmental psychology: A call to action. *Journal of Experimental Child Psychology*, *162*, 31–38.

Pandit, S. A. (2011). The concept of 'Rasa' in Indian psychology: A preliminary qualitative study. *Journal of Psychosocial Research*, *6*(1), 139.

Pandit, S., & Misra, G. (2013). Emotions in Indian psychology. In *Psychology and psychoanalysis* (Centre for Studies in Civilization, pp. 663–691). Indian Council of Social Science Research ICSSR.

Paranjpe, A. C. (2009). In defence of an Indian approach to the psychology of emotion. *Psychological Studies*, *54*(1), 3–22.

Paranjpe, A. C. (2012). *Theoretical psychology: The meeting of East and West*. Springer Science & Business Media.

Paranjpe, A. C. (2019). The foundations and goals of psychology: Contrasting ontological, epistemological and ethical foundations in India and the West. In *Asian Indigenous psychologies in the global context* (pp. 69–87). Springer.

Parent, C. I., Zhang, T.-Y., & Meaney, M. J. (2012). Epigenetics and the environmental regulation of genomic structure and function: Implications for health. In *Research and perspectives in neurosciences* (pp. 31–53). Springer Berlin Heidelberg. https://doi.org/10.1007/978-3-642-27913-3_4

Popper, K. (2005). *The logic of scientific discovery*. Routledge.

Ram-Prasad, C. (2013). *Advaita epistemology and metaphysics*. Routledge Curzon. https://doi.org/10.4324/9781315029399

Rao, K. R. (2014). Positive psychology and Indian psychology in need of mutual reinforcement. *Psychological Studies*, *59*(2), 94–102. https://doi.org/10.1007/s12646-013-0228-4

Rao, K. R., & Paranjpe, A. C. (2016). *Psychology in the Indian tradition*. Springer India. https://doi.org/10.1007/978-81-322-2440-2

Rao, K., Paranjpe, A. C., & Dalal, A. K. (2008). *Handbook of Indian psychology*. Cambridge University Press India/Foundation Books.

Salagame, K. K. (2014). Positive psychology and Indian psychology: Birds of the same feather. *Psychological Studies*, *59*(2), 116–118.

Samdarshi, P. (2019). Spatial and architectural constructs of Tantric Buddhist Mandalas: A cognitive approach. In *Eloquent spaces* (pp. 69–87). Routledge India.

Sen, R. S., & Pandit, S. (2013). Exploring Vātsalyam: The emotion of love for the child. *Psychology and Developing Societies*, *25*(1), 165–193. https://doi.org/10.1177/0971333613477303

Shweder, R. A., & Sullivan, M. A. (1993). Cultural psychology: Who needs it? *Annual Review of Psychology*, *44*(1), 497–523.

Sinha, J. B. P., Singh, S., Gupta, P., Srivastava, K. B. L., Sinha, R. B. N., Srivastava, S., Ghosh, A., Siddiqui, R. N., Tripathi, N., Gupta, M., Srivastava, S., Mulla, Z., Vijayalakshmi, C., & Pandey, A. (2010). An exploration of the Indian mindset. *Psychological Studies*, *55*(1), 3–17. https://doi.org/10.1007/s12646-010-0001-x

Smith, L. T. (2021). *Decolonizing methodologies: Research and indigenous peoples*. Zed Books Ltd.

Timalsina, S. (2007). Metaphor, Rasa, and Dhvani: Suggested meaning in tantric esotericism. *Method & Theory in the Study of Religion*, *19*(1–2), 134–162.

Timalsina, S. (2008). *Consciousness in Indian philosophy: The Advaita doctrine of 'awareness only'*. Routledge.

Timalsina, S. (2011). Encountering the other: Tantra in the cross-cultural context. *The Journal of Hindu Studies*, *4*(3), 274–289.

Timalsina, S. (2012). Body, self, and healing in Tantric ritual paradigm. *The Journal of Hindu Studies*, *5*(1), 30–52.

Valsiner, J. (2014). *An invitation to cultural psychology*. Sage.

Walsh, R. (2015). Wise ways of seeing: Wisdom and perspectives. *Integral Review: A Transdisciplinary & Transcultural Journal for New Thought, Research, & Praxis*, *11*(2), 156–174.

Walsh, R., & Shapiro, S. L. (2006). The meeting of meditative disciplines and Western psychology: A mutually enriching dialogue. *American Psychologist*, *61*(3), 227.

Weaver, I. C. G., Cervoni, N., Champagne, F. A., D'Alessio, A. C., Sharma, S., Seckl, J. R., Dymov, S., Szyf, M., & Meaney, M. J. (2004). Epigenetic programming by maternal behavior. *Nature Neuroscience*, *7*(8), 847–854. https://doi.org/10.1038/nn1276

3 Deha

Consciousness, embodiment and idli-sambhār

Introduction: Embodied consciousness and the taste and smell of the world

When we say that we are eating and enjoying idli-sambhār, a Khatta Dhokla or a cocktail of flavours in a pāni puri, is consciousness involved in the sensation, perception, working memory, long-term memory and the phenomenal awareness of 'I' awareness OR Is consciousness completely uninvolved? A myth that pervades India and students of psychology in India is that consciousness is not related to psychology and lived experience as such because it is *always* transcendental and otherworldly!

If consciousness is indeed otherworldly alone and not in the day-to-day lived experience of this world, why do even philosophers or cognitive scientists or the Veda/Vedānta even discuss it; what are we doing here? The duality or split between material and spiritual, between this world and the other world, is stark and most damaging in the logical scholarship of mainstream Euro-American psychology. A sequel – the mind-body problem is one of the biggest philosophical and belief questions in current science and philosophy. Let us first set the tone for what the problem is. Clearly, our bodies and minds are linked and they interact with the world. When we eat khatta dhokla, the brain responds to the sensations and continuously updates its perceptions and beliefs, memory traces of the khatta dhokla, to then judge whether it's a 'good' experience or not; this experience, good or bad then gets transferred into and re-consolidated as the continuing new memory of this person. The body cognizes the taste and the mind presumably notes it.

The question that Euro-American philosophy has been wrestling with is – are these two separate categories or the same? What is the relationship between the two? Note that the Euro-American idea of 'dualism' is different from the functional dualism in Sāṃkhya. In Sāṃkhya and the later developments in Indian thought, it is clear that 'Prakriti' or materiality is an expression of the 'Purusha' or the principle of consciousness. Thus, Sāṃkhya in IKS is functional dualism with essential monism. The issues in the philosophy of psychology are different. If one experiences psychological

DOI: 10.4324/9781003336204-3

states, for example, then how do they relate to physiological expression, or do psychological states map with neurobiological correlates? These are the questions that indicate dualism in contemporary psychology.

Some key divergences which explain the predicaments are a consensus on the body as the primary category. Indeed, the general consensus, most surprisingly, at least to an Indian person, is that since physics is the most advanced science, one of the influential proposals has been to 'reduce' all psychology to physical and mathematical laws and expressions! Nagel, in his influential 1961 paper, basically argued that if theories could be reduced to other theories, using bridge principles or bridge laws, then not only all the scientific vocabulary will get standardized and translated into others, but eventually, all theories (of mind and society) could get reduced to physics!! The strongest version of this argument would be a strict physicalist and computational perspective. Therefore, all the theoretical and philosophical attempts would be to reduce and map; in such a scenario, we can clearly see that consciousness would be reduced to neurobiological correlates if that was indeed possible; the rest would be just fantasy, including the philosophers agreeing or disagreeing with each other!

Later thinkers, finding the obvious difficulty with reductionism, proposed the 'idea of multiple realizability' (Fodor, 1975, 1980). This is to propose that the same psychological state can be experienced with different neurobiological structures among other creatures such as bats! For example, does the experience of the fear map with the exact same neurons in rats, humans, and bats? Indians might say, 'the consciousness is the same'! And they would miss the whole point. Indian knowledge systems look at the consciousness *principle* as all-pervasive, and Euro-American philosophers are trying to standardize and reduce the psychological to the physical while completely rejecting the 'spiritual'. Indeed, the word 'spiritual' is problematic from IKT perspective as well and is not cognate with the Sanskrit word – 'Adhyātma'.

Consciousness, in such a circumstance, by most scientists and philosophers, is viewed in the brain or in the realm of imagination or in the form of abstraction or is 'otherworldly' in a theological sense. When Indian students and people doing Yoga practice say, consciousness is 'otherworldly', they are mindlessly transferring the binaries of the Abrahamic religions about 'this' world and the 'other' world. Indeed, Indian traditions talk of 14 worlds, and the term 'loka' refers to the world as much as a state of consciousness.

Several of these binaries that Euro-American psychology has hypnotized itself into including the subject-object and the material-spiritual create a particular difficulty both ways – one, for scientific understanding of psychology and consciousness, and two, for a non-stereotypical, non-esotericized understanding of Indian knowledge traditions (IKT) as well!

Perhaps a more direct illustration of an upward integration of *body-mind-consciousness* in IKT would be to start from auditory senses of patterns of sounds, of music, which is perceived, cognized, and enjoyed by the body-mind to then immerse the person into deep absorption and possibly momentary experiences of no-thought, just awareness or choice-less conscious attention, such that at points of time, consciousness is 'altered' into meditative states. In this upward integration example, there would be no awareness of the body, as well as conscious thought, at the weakest 'realization'. Thus, we need to re-examine the embodied consciousness of the person in the Indian psychological traditions. In the IKT, the body is conceptualized as the materialization of consciousness, and therefore, the body is *the pathway* to access altered states of consciousness, recognize self-nature and transcend the body awareness as well.

Transcendental and embodied consciousness: Pan-psychism, challenges to physicalist and functionalist theories

In the earlier chapter, we introduced the Indian idea of consciousness that pervades and is interwoven with all the states of awareness – awake, dreaming, and dreamless sleep and yet transcends or 'overflows' it. According to the model of consciousness given in the Māndukya Upaniṣad, consciousness pervades the three states of awareness and remains before and after as well. In recent years, a similar-sounding proposal has been offered by the American philosopher, Ned Block (2007), who argues that consciousness 'overflows' conscious awareness. Block, along with philosophers such as Fodor and Putnam, launched a philosophical proposal and argued against the reduction in the understanding of consciousness from the physicalist perspective. Pan-psychism's argument of consciousness means that all objects, including physical objects, instantiate consciousness (Bruntrup & Jaskolla, 2016;Goff, 2015; Nagasawa & Wager, 2016). This argument, in its strong version, means that consciousness exists prior to the physical objects and all objects have a micro-consciousness in them! The 'panpsychist' proposal has been controversial. In recent times, Information Integration Theory has been proposed (Tononi, 2004), which states that consciousness is an inherent aspect of reality, where the integration of information exchanged itself constitutes consciousness. The key critique of pan-psychism is that it is not able to explain the all-pervasive consciousness (called macro consciousness) with consciousness among creatures (called micro consciousness) and how and why these gradations in consciousness occur. Further, pan-psychism is not able to propose an empirical way forward, and therefore, Euro-American philosophers and psychologists cannot find new insights about mind-body-dualism as well as the reduction of mind into body or body into mind!

Perhaps, the ideas of pan-psychism and related proposals of cosmo-panpsychism (which is a better proposal than panpsychist monism), remind us of similar debates among the three schools of Vedānta – the Advaita school of Adi Shankara, the School of Viśiṣṭādvaita and the dualists (Dvaitins); noting that these debates happened at least a thousand years ago. Another key translatable concept from Euro-American philosophy, for Indian students, is the proposal of P-consciousness and A-consciousness. P-consciousness or phenomenality is broadly understood as 'feeling', which is distinguished from psychology, or A-consciousness, which informs us how a human access element from experience – access consciousness. There are several philosophers who question this proposal of P and A-consciousness as well. The questions are still open, with huge research projects raising their stakes and claims on what reality should be prior to then run these research programs! At least, through these proposals of consciousness as a priori and overflowing, a possibility exists that the Indian knowledge systems may not be dismissed as superstitious. Notwithstanding these debates, consciousness *is* embodied as experienced, whichever argument the student might agree or disagree with; those disagreements relate to the consciousness prior and later to the boundaries of the body and the brain. In reference to Māndukya Upaniṣad, the consciousness not only pervades and transcends the waking state where one may or may not be consciously attending to each and every aspect of one's experience but also pervades and transcends dreaming and dreamless sleep states – *phenomenologically*. Thus, the first point to note is that when we are talking about transcendence in the context of Indian philosophical traditions, nowhere are we implying that transcendence is the opposite or contrary to the embodiment. At the same time, we are also not trying to 'reduce' samādhi to body awareness or the limited embodied consciousness alone.

As Ram-Prasad, a British philosopher of Indian origin, has said in his paper on saving Indian philosophical assumptions from physicalism (Ram-Prasad, 2001), Advaita Vedānta asserts – the experience that the non-embodied consciousness of samādhi is *the same/Identical* as the consciousness embodied as a person (called as Jivatma) is the central and profound, no doubt, because it illuminates the whole of embodied consciousness as experienced by the person, in their waking, dreaming and non-dream sleep states. For all 'practical' purposes of the embodied consciousness of waking, dreaming, and sleep states; this interwoven 'fourth' can always be accessed through contemplative practices called – adhyatma sadhana. In this chapter, we will focus on the particular manner in which Indian psychology has addressed embodied consciousness in variance with mainstream psychology.

A positive theory of mind-body consciousness is given in the Sāṃkhya tradition, which has been further developed in the non-dual schools of IKT. Indeed, in the IKT, great detailing is done on the idea, experience, and the processes of embodiment, which is seen as a downstream devolvement as opposed to the process of integration, which is conceptualized as upstream evolution. In the Yoga-Sāṃkhya system, the upstream process from the body to awareness consciousness is called a Nivrtti marga, and a downstream process from phenomenal and awareness consciousness to body is called the Pravritti marga. Pravrtti marga or the downstream devolution is seen as the pathway to the world and its multiplicity. During the downstream process from pure awareness as consciousness to body awareness, embodiment takes place, not just for humans, but all creatures of this animate and sentient world, and thus, phenomenal awareness becomes increasingly specified. In the process of embodiment, 'multiple realizations' occur at different levels of consciousness in the body. Some of the word concepts utilized for embodiment are Śarira, Tanu and Tanukarana, Vapu and Kāyā and Deha, Kalevaram, Murti and Vigraha. Each word has been defined specifically in terms of its contextual and functional relevance. This functional relevance is called 'pravritti nimitta'. For example, the word śarira denotes bodies and the 'en-mind-ment' of the body. This concept first occurs in the Brahrdāranyaka Upaniṣad, one of the oldest Vedānta texts, where the concepts of three bodies – Sthula, sukśma and kāraṇa śarira are explicitly delineated. The Sthula Śarira is understood as a gross body or a manifest body, the second is understood as the psychological body or the body in mind and the third is understood as the causal body or the deepest aspects of the psyche which give rise downstream to expressed explicit ideas, desires, thoughts and aspirations; feelings and other contents which are amenable to conscious attention at least in part; a student of Indian psychology traditions is trained to access and feel these as conscious awareness.

Similarly, the Ayurvedic texts have consistently used the word – 'Deha' for body and have detailed sections on what are the constituents of this body. For example, some Ayurvedic texts explicitly specify the role of the nutrition, malnutrition of the mother, and the genetic material inherited from both the father as well as the mother as a constituent of what is called the 'Deha Prakriti'. Third, the particular word 'Tanu' and its process signifying the word 'Tanu kārana' is found in Patanjali's Yoga Sutra (PYS) in the second Sutra of the second chapter.

The key point to hold on from this brief discussion is that – we recognize that consciousness is all pervasive and can be known as such during advanced meditative states; this meditative experience, which overflows the body awareness, will profoundly affect all the embodied states of consciousness.

The idea of transcendence as an opposite to embodiment arises from the Euro-American Cartesian dichotomy. Note that it is true that advanced states of meditation must necessarily include awareness where there is no conscious awareness of the body as such. This means that there are no conscious thoughts of 'I', no awareness of breathing, and keeping the body posture for an extended period of time. In almost all states of advanced meditation, non-dual awareness as well as immersion, we do lose a sense of body consciousness just as we lose a sense of 'self' consciousness. For example, the sense of body consciousness emerges and becomes important for our conscious attention as we age. We attain mastery in dance, we lose the sense of body consciousness as a separate sensation in conscious attention while performing dance. However, in these 'flow' states, we continue to hold the sense of 'I' consciousness. Therefore, transcendence in Indian psychology does not mean immediately losing of body consciousness like a switch. It also means a graded loss of access and phenomenal consciousness.

The first level of understanding body and consciousness is that phenomenologically we may lose the sense of the body as conscious attention requires action from us many times during our state of being awake. At the next level are states of meditation or sports or any kind of sensory-motor mastery, where we lose the sense of body awareness during immersion into any act. The third layer of meaning is those advanced states of meditation, particularly where we are minimally aware of the body. These are called *minimally phenomenal states* (Metzinger, 2020). To finally, come to the most subtle layer of losing even those minimally phenomenal awareness states in meditation. Even if most of us are not meditators or interested in meditation as such as a subject matter of psychology or as students of psychology, we still would be experiencing the first three layers of losing the states of body consciousness or awareness while doing or enacting day-to-day activities in our waking states.

Point of transition between two states of consciousness to recognize the interwoven fourth.

Body in the mind! Consciousness and dreaming states

During dreaming states, psychologists of contemporary times have been able to identify some critical characteristics that distinguish the dreaming state from the state of being awake. The first characteristic is that for almost all states of dreaming, with the exception of particular disorders such as somnambulism or sleepwalking, the motor functioning of the body is absent and body awareness is minimal. We say minimal because, even while in a dream, we are aware of our body such that it doesn't fall off the bed or such that it doesn't topple over someone else by our side. Phenomenologically, we do have an experience of ourselves as embodied with an 'I' consciousness; we experience ourselves walking, talking and interacting with people around us in the dream world, called Swapna Sriṣṭi in the IKT. It is a phenomenological – a 'lived' world as is experienced. Physiologically, while the motor functions are mostly switched off, the body does respond to a mosquito bite or a sudden change in the temperature, etc. the sensory *functions* are experienced internally/phenomenologically, while the sensory *organs* are minimally operating in the body. Clearly, we do not operate the physiological visual systems, but we do see and experience sight internally in the Swapna Srishti. Similarly, while the auditory system of the body is minimally present, we do experience sound. Thus, we see that, if we take awareness as such as the central pivot to organize consciousness and locate awareness as a legitimate subject matter of psychology, the IKT seem to have a much-refined subjectivity framework about dreaming states. They indicate an alignment to the idea of a lived dream world. Following this line, are several methods proposed in the IKT to change or regulate these dream worlds and interpret the content of the dream world awareness – non-psychoanalytically. The yogic practice of Pratyāhāra, which stands at the fuzzy borders of external Yoga practice up to Prāṇāyāma (Bahiranga Yoga sadhana) and the internal Yoga practice starting from conscious attention till non-dual awareness in samādhi (Antaranga sadhana) *precisely addresses to these states of consciousness which are at the graduated sliding scales of an embodied awareness with body consciousness to an embodied awareness with minimal body consciousness*. In the practice of Pratyāhāra, using systematic relaxation, body consciousness is minimized, and lived experience of the body (phenomenologically) is leveraged for better insight, interpretation, and recognition. In recent years, the practice of Yoga nidra has been gaining a lot of popularity (Dwivedi, 2016; Moszeik et al., 2022).

Minimized body consciousness results in mild to deep relaxation as an outcome – the principle of Yoga nidra. Several contemporary practices of relaxation are accused of being taken/lifted/inspired from Yoga without honouring the lineage; however, we can say that the same principle of relaxation as minimal body discomfort to letting go of a separate sense of body awareness is a feature of all relaxation states. The same logic of reduction in body consciousness can be claimed to result in better performance in creative tasks such as sports, dance or creative pursuits that require sensory-motor coordination, where a minimized body consciousness is a separate awareness and, therefore, increased psychological/mental flexibility results from the mastery/skill in preparation and action (Gold & Ciorciari, 2020; Sinnott et al., 2020), according to research in flow and eastern traditions such as Zen, Tai-Chi and of course Yoga. In the particular context of Yoga nidra, minimized body consciousness enhances the awareness of the body as a lived experience in the dream and dream-like awake state. In traditional contexts, people who follow and consistently practice Yoga-nidra report richer dream content, with greater self-awareness and, therefore, a better ability to change or regulate one's dreams. Neuro-physiologically, contemporary psychology report evidence of learning and memory consolidation during sleep and dream states in the hippocampal regions of the brain (Wamsley, 2019).

To understand embodied consciousness in the waking state from an IKT perspective, we have more than 100 years of mainstream research evidence that has now been accepted as the applied psychology of the east. The first is the lived experience of body and body consciousness through the practice of Hatha Yoga and āsanas. Second, awareness through the sensory self in Tantra, where the assumption of the sensory self, as it engages with the ecosystem will question contemporary psychology's notions of the self as largely social. Is self-social? Several philosophers are argued that it is not. If self is not social and also not transcendental then, what is it about? (Zahavi, 2009). The idea of self as social, quite prevalent in mainstream psychology, is neither here (anchored in the body) nor there (anchored in a transcultural insight of Vedānta). Buddhists denied the transcendental self as illusory and empty, but Tantra would propose that a 'pure' sensory self is directly intimated in the body consciousness. The practice of non-dual Tantra enhances the sensory self and yet reveals deeper insight through an equally powerful 'witness consciousness'.

Mind in the body! Body consciousness in the psyche

The specific practice in Pratyāhāra – Yoga nidra minimizes the body consciousness as such phenomenally. Another particular method in IKT leverages the mind *in the* body through the practice of āsana. The word āsana, which is superficially translated as body postures by the commodified milieu of today, means much deeper than that. Āsana comes from the root word in Sanskrit, 'as' which means 'to be'. This profound root word or dhātu, brings forth several related words such as 'asti' (existing), 'asmi ("I" consciousness)' and 'asmita' – all related to existential being. Thus, āsana implies being phenomenally aware of the body. The foundational Yoga text, PYS, mentions the word āsana in the second chapter of the text. The fact that it mentions it sparingly, implies that the word āsana is a much-understood word and practice that does not require deeper elaborations. The commentaries on this foundational text elaborate on certain āsanas and suggest specific practices. In the later Hatha Yoga texts, of Hatha Yoga Pradeepika and Siva Sutra, one finds deeper elaboration of aligning the mind with the body!

In recent years, there have been a number of research studies that evidence the result that a regular āsana practice results in better physiological and mental health outcomes (Wiese et al., 2019). In fact, the popularity of Hatha Yoga in contemporary times is precisely because it aligns the mind with the body as mind *in the* body. Several physiological mechanisms have been proposed to explain the positive outcomes that research reveals. Physiological mechanisms, going with the best traditions of physicalism, focus on physiological explanatory variables such as blood pressure, heart rate variability, deep tissue relaxation, lower oxidative stress, better oxygen absorption, and better muscle control. Lifestyle disorders such as asthma, hypertension and coronary heart diseases, diabetes, sleep disorders, and endocrine disorders have shown a statistically significant result due to not just Yoga practice but indeed all body-mind practices from the Asian context such as Tai-Chi. Most research studies actually do damage to theory as the explanation is reductive and physicalist and does not possibly look at the strengthening of a conscious connection between the different motor – the sensory-perceptual systems of the body and the phenomenal awareness of an embodied self. It is possible that the explanatory variables become more nano such as cellular and sub-cellular biochemistry and biophysics and that would be the future research direction.

Apart from and in addition to addressing diseases, the mind in the body is also leveraged for positive health through Yoga practice and is shown to result in better immune response and a stronger sense of being embodied. *Since IKT assumed a non-anthropocentric world-view, āsanas teach embodiment not only in human but in non-human forms as well* (Radha, 2006).

Does the body alter as the states of consciousness alter? Very few studies in Euro-American psychology have noted alterity in the body. One notable exception would be Walsh (Walsh, 1993), who compared and mapped shamanic, Buddhist yogic, and schizophrenic experiences of body awareness. Sadly, this was published in a journal on religious studies and did not see its implications in Euro-American psychology, much less implication in Indian consciousness-based psychology (IP).

Polarities and the body-mind

Traditional Yoga practice and teaching follow methods to align several polarities in the body, where the aim of the practice is to review these polarities and transitions from one to another towards a higher integration, better regulation of body physiology is a mere by-product. The first polarity is the right and left polarity in the body. All Yoga practices address the right and left polarity in the body phenomenologically. The second polarity is the above the stomach and below the stomach polarity in the body; all Yoga practices as traditionally taught to address this polarity through standing and sitting and lying down practices. The third polarity that Yoga practices traditionally address is the polarity between movement and rest. All traditional Yoga practices transition systematically between movement and resting into the āsana that is practised. By resting in the āsana, the purpose is to enhance the body awareness in short and medium term and minimize the body consciousness as such eventually. This concept of polarity is called 'dvandva' in PYS and is shown in the Sutra of the second chapter of PYS that asserts that through āsana and body, one gains an insight into the infinite (ananta-samapattibhyam) indicating minimizing the body consciousness as such that juts out and disturbs deeper phenomenal insight. This is the particularity of the process of the āsana practice, wherein the first step is to *ground the mind in the body* and enhance body awareness to experience relaxation, *to then* transcend body awareness and minimize body consciousness. This cannot be found in any of the texts of phenomenology in the European and American traditions. This is a lived experience of transcending the body consciousness as such after grounding the mind in the body is a particular and unique aspect of Yoga practice. The Hatha Yoga practices, esp. the practice of āsanas is a unique embodied practice of consciousness and a step towards transcendence of the body, where by 'body', we mean the conscious and non-conscious awareness of the body. Similar principles can be hypothesized for understanding of music perception and immersion in both music as well as augmented reality and virtual reality (AR and VR) in contemporary neuroscience.

As mentioned earlier, in contemporary Euro-American psychology, the self is generally understood as a largely 'social self'. Indeed, Dan Zahavi, a pre-eminent phenomenologist philosopher, has been working on social ontology and *precisely argued against* the conception of self as social in one of his papers (Rochat & Zahavi, 2011; Zahavi, 2009; Zahavi & Rochat, 2015) as well as written with Phillipe Rochat, another pre-eminent developmental psychology researcher, working on the emergence of self-awareness, for *a re-view* of the conventional explanation of the self-awareness among infants through the mirror test.

In Yoga, we are asking this question – Can we think of a self, if all the sociality is stripped away either through a kind of a hypothetical situation where one grows without or consciously strips away the social context and, therefore, there is no 'implied, imagined and actual presence of others' – *just plain unmarked awareness*? A situation where the sociality could be stripped away would be through the process of meditation in Yoga-Sāṃkhya and Advaita, which Paranjpe calls as a 'successive deletion of cognitive content' (Paranjpe, 2010, 2021). The Yoga Sutras assert and Yoga practitioners validate that during the practice of Yoga, there is a process of stripping away of the sociality from consciousness. This process starts with the surface-level sensory-motor impressions and then moves towards imagery, working memory and long-term memory– all the phenomenal experiences in body as well as thought to finally stripping away of the 'potentialities' towards sensory awareness called as *tanmātra*. Indeed, yogic texts claim that this process of stripping away of the contents of consciousness is how meditation becomes *more and more advanced*. At the final level, Yoga states that all sensory potentialities are completed/closed, and thereafter the awareness *that remains is without any content or representation or trace*. This state of non-representational, non-content awareness would still have the potential to 'sprout again' and is, therefore, called as the final edge frontier before the state of complete liberation, which is the most advanced state of 'nirbija samādhi' or seedless samādhi. In nirbija samādhi, there appears to be no possibility of the sprouting of the impressions of the content of consciousness. Note that meditators do return back to the same body after experiencing nirbija samādhi. How do they engage with the world then? This is discussed in later chapters as – 'Can there be no mind', which seems to imply that though sensory awareness could be the true essence of body awareness, in lived experience, it is transcended completely in nirbija samādhi.

Therefore, the first point to consider is that – even if one were to entertain the possibility that all the social contents of the consciousness were stripped away linguistically, there would still be a question of stripping away of all the five senses in a particular order before one reaches the nirbija samādhi as stated in the yogic texts. If we were to look at it from an empirical neuroscience perspective, an interesting way to study this, would be in case of dying and death in which one of the sensory systems would close down sequentially and which sensory system would continue to show some activity even after the body has 'died' or is hypoxic.

Now, similar to the dual process as seen in practice of āsana, where we ground the mind in the body *so as to* then in the second step, transcend the 'body awareness'; *pratyahara* in yogic meditation focus on grounding and increasing the acuity and sensitivity of the five sensory systems to then presumably transcend it. This is seen in the lifelong practices of traditions such as Baul, which focus on *Deho and Mano-Sadhana* – a set of unconventional spiritual bodily practices (Bhattacharyya, 1993; Hanssen, 2006; Knight, 2011; Lorea, 2013).

Even in non-meditation contexts, we still lose the sense of body awareness or transcend the actions of the body by counter-intuitively leveraging and grounding our sensory awareness. The five sensory systems in āyurveda are called as the jnānendriya. Jnānendriya is a compound word of knowing (jnāna) and organs (īndrīya) and through these jnānendriya, the self is conceptualized as 'reaching out' and know the world. *According to Āyurveda, the health of jnānendriya is central in defining the body-mind health.* This is measured through sensory acuity and sensitivity and assessed clinically through case history taking. Āyurveda proposes that the overuse or the dysregulation of the jnānendriya will result in the loss of embodied mental health. This seems to be much nuanced view for body and mind in psychology beyond the mechanics or functioning of sensory systems. Going beyond the obvious fact that loud noise, for example, can result in loss of acuity and sensitivity to sound in the ears, āyurveda and Yoga propose that the training of listening/not listening to certain quality of the sound can affect the acuity and sensitivity of the auditory system and the mind-body as such. This training of the sensory system is part of the systematic step to transcend it. This principle of understanding sensory systems as constituting embodied mental health is relevant to the understanding of health psychology as defined in Yoga and IP.

The training of the sensory systems in understanding embodied consciousness in IKT is fundamental to find joy in life experiences, whether meditative or not. In the IKT, there are detailed pedagogies developed based on the refinement of subjectivity and inter-subjective shared understanding. In music, which requires training in auditory perception and production, for example, the first stage, requires the students to learn the notes in actual and concrete comparison with the base note *cognitively* and not through a written form. At the second stage, students are taught to sing the note on demand with a *mental comparison* to the base note and identify whether the person is singing *in tune* with the base note or not. In these first two steps, the student is able to listen in and distinguish between the two notes as compared to the base note mentally, and thus the acuity and the sensitivity to the quality of the note are enhanced. At the third level, the student is taught to assess and perform to the quality of the note by connecting one note with the nearby notes in the octave with a particular nuance, emphasis, sequence and speed to arrive at a particular 'sound and musical quality' of experience and performance. Finally, the student is trained to distinguish between micro-notes (Shruti) and get the right frequency. This tedious yet ultimately fulfilling process, requires a constant validation of the perception in a shared intersubjective space. This process is purely sensory, not yet layered with meaning/songs, etc. Similar diligence is followed in the training of dance, sculpting, painting and other pursuits. Obviously, even if a physicalist view is taken for an AI-driven music, one recognizes the gigantic work requirement to reach anywhere near a novice's music sensibility, what to say about a genius such as Pandit Ravishankar, Menuhin or Beethoven.

In summary, two points are important to note are that firstly, in Yoga and taṇtra, the dual process of grounding the sensuousness of the sensory experience, is broadened to include a range of perceptual-cognitive experiences, which is to be accomplished *without sexualizing* all sensory experiences. Therefore, you see a structure and yet a bewildering mindfully cultivated diversity of experiences for all the senses – taste, fragrance, cloth/touch, audition/sound, vision and activity. The grounding of body awareness and embodiment, is purposively utilized to transcend it. Interesting to note here is that just as the 'flow state' as proposed by Cziksentsmihalyi and colleagues (Mirvis, 1991) indicates to a loss of self-consciousness and the integration of action and awareness(mind/body); researchers have found that 'sexual objectification' of the body, *arrests the flow* experience (Guizzo & Cadinu, 2017; Guizzo et al., 2017). All spiritual seekers across the world would agree! This is esp., a challenge for women or transgendered mystics and seekers, and even male seekers, to remove the performativity associated with their bodies. All bodies are relentlessly objectified, such that a meditators task is to then strip away this internalizing and identification to body and yet ground it in pure sensory awareness. Similar, would be the plight of In Pratyahara, first step of this dual process would be when the mind is grounded in the sensory experience and the body.

In the second step process, through this grounded immersion, the experience either transcends or steps out of the initiating modality, spontaneously or is trained to transcend it. In mundane life experience, the sensory self is tied/neurally associated with repetitive worldly associations mostly sexual objectification; whereas, in āyurveda, the question of taste and cultivation of taste in the embodied sensory self, is discussed in reference to the guna-s or the outcome principles of sattva, rājas and tamas, to encompass not just sexuality, but every detail of the waking experience. Such refined embodied subjectivity practiced in āyurveda and Yoga is utilized in Tantra or the śāktādvaita as well as bhakti traditions, such that vulgalization and sexualization, which is mindlessly super-imposed on the body is removed. Can you see the body as it is? – the grounded-ness of 'flesh', as Merlau-Ponty, a French philosopher, indicated to in the Euro-American context is the first and an important part of an embodied experience of the sensory self and the transcendence in the next step is an important part of the practice that must inevitably lead to the recognition of consciousness.

Āsana, Prāṇāyāma and Pratyāhāra are specifically related to embodiment and act as bridges between the social, ethical commitments of the externalized Yoga in the aśtānga Yoga, that is yama and niyama and the internalized aspect of Yoga that is Dharana, Dhyāna and samādhi. Note that in the discussions related to mukti or nirvāna, which is commonly translated as transcendental freedom or liberation, there are two important word concepts in Advaita relating to embodiment and liberation. They are the concepts of Videha-mukti and Jīvan mukti. In Jīvan mukti, there is a post-realization living and life of the teachers/masters who remain embodied. Many modern Jīvanmukta-s have been discussed by scholars of religious studies and philosophy and some scholars have written extensively about Jīvan mukti. Recall that the great master, Siddartha Gautama, arose from his 3 days and nights of meditation under the sacred Bodhi tree and embodied that knowing called as sambodhi till he was extinguished about 40 years later. We will discuss Jīvan mukti in the later chapters of this book as a profound and a radical Indian psychology (Pandit, 2021), way beyond the current frontiers of Euro-American psychology.

Body and sensory awareness *changes and alters* through the typical states of awareness in waking and dreaming states of consciousness just as it becomes altered in meditative, drug-induced or disturbed states of consciousness such as schizophrenia. In general, the concept of Pratyāhāra locates embodiment in sensory modalities including proprioception and is much sharper/subtle than the idea of 'flesh' in the conceptualization of Merlau-Ponty when he discusses embodiment within the European continental phenomenological tradition.

The limb or anga above āsana in aśtānga Yoga is Pranayāma. Prāṇāyāma practice bridges *this concrete body with the body in the mind*, bi-directionally. In contemporary times, for lack of word in English, masters have called prana (bridge between the three bodies as the 'vital or the energy' body in attempts to translate the yogic idea of a body; subtler than prana, in Aśtāṇga Yoga, the anga above prāṇāyāma is Pratyāhāra, another bridge of the sensory self towards cognition, which is the ambitious focus of Euro-American psychology efforts. Senses create perception but do they create the correct perception? This leads us to the next section on cognition and what has been called as the 'monkey mind' by the IKT.

Sensory self: Minding the mind – cognition, affect and behaviour

Conjoint to the dual process of transcending the sensory self, a foundational concept in the PYS-s that helps in practices of transcending the mind-body through the modality of senses is the concept and practice of Vairāgya. Vairāgya is generally understood in religious terms and wrongly translated as 'detachment' which doesn't throw any light and, in fact, throws darkness on the psychological concept of Vairāgya. The definition of Vairāgya in PYS illuminates, making Vairāgya a verb as much as a noun! Yoga Sutra defines Vairāgya as, 'Drṣta-anuśravik vaśikāra saṃjnā' which means knowing (saṃjnā) that arises from mastery (vaśikāra) of seeing (Drṣta) and hearing (anuśravik). Note the keywords here – 'seeing' and 'hearing' which relate to the sensory self. The word – vaśikāra, implies complete mastery. Complete mastery denotes three-step process of understanding, regulating and, thereafter, mastery of the sensory processes. The third keyword – Saṃjnā – knowing, relates to cognition, based on senses and recognizes that unregulated and also, more importantly, ungrounded sensory processes lead to wrong knowing. The word concept – Saṃjnā is used as sensory knowing, considered as unrefined in the early Buddhist conceptualizations as well (Lindahl et al., 2017; Premasiri, 2008).

Vairāgya, therefore, is a practice of three steps: firstly, becoming aware of the sensory processes; second, learning to regulate them according to one's motivations, including both the so-called 'spiritual' and 'secular' motivations! Third step, is to have complete mastery over sensory processes. Therefore, as I have argued earlier as well (Pandit, 2021), Vairāgya as a practice is quite amenable to contemporary neuroscience research. Becoming aware of sensory-driven knowing, regulating the sensory processes that construct this knowledge and developing insight into deeper cognition based on that knowing and cognition, could illuminate the theoretical understanding about the embodied consciousness of long-term meditators, who would likely have unconventional brains, due to neuroplasticity.

Vairāgya is such a foundational practice component in PYS-s, that in the first chapter of PYS-s, only two practice components are centred – Abhyāsa and Vairāgya. Vairāgya starts from the sensory modalities and moves towards deeper cognitive processes of imagery and memories that arise from the tagging through sensory modalities and currently muddle up theories on 'knowledge representation' in contemporary Euro-American psychology. In IKT, imagery and memories that arise from sensory modalities are part of what are called as samskāra (impression formation and recording) and vāsana(residue, usually of desire). Concepts of samskāra and vāsana, represent knowledge in the psyche, comparable to the contemporary concepts of schema and scripts. However, we have a theoretical framework in Yoga, where samskāra, vāsana and karma are first experienced and lived in the body, through the senses, and thereafter get recorded as a *residue* in the reservoir consciousness called as Citta. Indeed, in the philosophical school of mimāṃsā, karma and the emotion that precedes karma is called as Bhāvanā, which is constituted of embodied intention – action and, thereafter the expectancy from the action. When we discuss karma as recorded in citta, we imply the embodied intention action and expectancy from the action in the reservoir consciousness, which then needs to be stripped clean, forever, and not just in flow states or limited time periods of samādhi states.

Consciousness as ownerless awareness is dialectically contrasted with 'ownered' consciousness of Prakriti; the ownerless consciousness is called as the principle of 'true' intelligence. According to Ayurvedic conceptualization, there are 22 elements/principles of mind-body relationship as it engages with the mirroring principles in the ecosystem. The 23rd element is the *Puruṣa* – the principle of consciousness and awareness. Note, here, that in casual conversations in the Indian cultural context, the word *Puruṣa* implies a man. However, technically the word Puruṣa is not associated with any gender and implies the principle of non-agentic, ownerless awareness or consciousness. The other 22 elements arise from the principle of materiality and manifestation known as *Prakriti.* Prakriti has three Guna or qualities which lead a process of transformation and manifestation downstream into the rest of the 21 elements of a creative sequence of world-making. These sequential transformations include the materialization of the body. Manas which is usually translated as mind in this particular context of sequential transformations again refers to the sensory-motor coordination. Thus in the prakriti puruṣa conceptualization in Yoga-Sāṃkhya, both the mind and the body are part of a principle of consciousness which materializes and changes material forms. Thus, body and mind are intimately connected and are the transformations of the same elements arising and circulating from the three guna-s laterally and vertically (upstream and downstream). Within the domain of prakṛti and the three guna-s, Sattva, Rājas and Tamas, *the body-mind keeps transforming through* karma, samskāra and vāsana; the world making keeps happening – getting expressed, enacted, intended, remembered and recorded. In all this, the ownerless consciousness, which is Puruṣa – does not get transformed or change substantially. Awareness is embodied only due to association with Prakṛti and yet remains transcendental, and thus, 'overflows'!

Another automated binary is the understanding of the embodied self as separate from the collective ecologically embedded self. While we do discuss concepts such as a self, relational self and collective self (Sedikides & Brewer, 2015), in social psychology textbooks, the body is seen as separate from nature. Some of these corrections in mainstream psychology have been instantiated by the discovery of mirror neurons and advanced understanding of attachment relations, shared attentional processes, etc. (Adamson & Bakeman, 1991; Shteynberg, 2015, 2018). Notwithstanding this advance, a key meta-theoretical aspect that remains a work in progress has been the understanding of physiological or bodily responses to non-body environmental and situation demands. The case of physiological drives is interesting from consciousness and embodiment perspective. Earlier, psychologists studied only the fight and the flight response of animals and their cognition-behaviour affect nexus, which is, broadly mapped to high alertness and vigilance cognitively, fight and flight as behaviours and fear and anxiety as affect. However, in recent decades several biologists have enlightened us with rich and insightful descriptions of animal behaviour in the threatened context (Eilam et al., 2011). Similarly, psychologists studying human behaviour have also recognized that there are several neurotransmitters and hormones involved in at least three pathways to respond to an external event. Human response to an external trigger stimulus is based on the interpretation of what that stimulus means. In reference to fight and flight, adrenaline is often implicated, not only is adrenaline alone triggered but the human body also releases several other complimentary neurotransmitters and hormones based on the complexity of the interpretation by the mind. For example, while completing a marathon – adrenaline and dopamine along with endorphins are likely to be released. This points to the reductive, linear lines of thought in research designs till now, even when it comes to concrete body! Thus, Taylor (Taylor et al., 2000) has proposed at least three more responses in addition to the fight and flight response of the human body in reference to an external threat event or a stimulus. This is important because drives and motivations related to physiological motives may include threat but are not exclusive to threat perception. Survival aspects such as hunger, sleep, the first and sexuality which were earlier thought to be primary drives and involuntary in nature, we now recognize that these aspects of the embodied consciousness are quite amenable to a bewildering diversity across cultures. For example, in certain communities in north-western India, such as the Jain community, fasting is an important part of lifestyle and even young children are taught to fast for long periods of time and regulate their food and thirst cycles. Similarly in several cultures and communities across the world, fasting and further on regulation of food types of foods preferred the seasonality and the local production of foods and their diversities are all the factors that determine the lifestyle, the microbiome in the gut of the human intestine and thereafter the interactions of the microbiome with the nervous system and neurotransmitters such as serotonin(Berk et al., 2013; Bravo et al., 2011; Ramnani et al., 2015; Romijn et al., 2017; Tillisch et al., 2013). There is a *gut-brain axis*, which has been recently 'discovered' and this gut-brain axis interacts with the bacterial microbiome in the gut, where the choice of foods including fermented foods such as buttermilk, curd/yoghurt and other fermented food products interact and keep redesigning the microbiome throughout life. Indeed, new research has discussed this intriguing possibility that the gut microbiome is significantly affected and disturbed years prior to a clinical diagnosis of depression (Limbana et al., 2020).

If food and hunger motivation is largely culturally and behaviour related, so are other physiological drives also regulated by cultures and behaviour. For example, sexuality, in principle, from an evolutionary perspective is responsible for adaptation and transfer of genes for the survival of the species. Having said that, across all cultures and societies we find multiple, diverse pathways of regulation of the sexual drive from celibacy choices to intensive sexual engagement behaviours; we find bewildering variation in the stimuli that trigger a sexual response to varied sexual practices. Similarly, the other physiological drive – sleep and wake cycles which are part of the circadian rhythms of the body are largely moderated and regulated in response to the cultural and contextual features throughout the lifespan. In summary, the idea of drives as automatic motives towards behaviours is a very simplistic reduction of the physiological patterns of the body and lifestyle of the body-mind. It is true that the body of the human and indeed all creatures have circadian rhythms, and yet, these circadian rhythms are moderated by cultural and lifestyle factors. Micro-organisms and the biome interact with the body throughout life, and indeed, cultures encourage certain kinds of interactions of the micro-biome with the body. Additionally, it is important to note that, the drives and the motives related to physiological drives themselves are regulated and contextualized with socio-political processes and events such as famine and droughts, long-term deprivation and malnutrition, that then transfer inter-generationally; a point relevant for psychology in the global south/third world and India as well. In recent years, researchers in health psychology have noted the 'social bodies' (Freund et al., 2003) – markers on the bodies that arise from mental illness, deprivation, poverty and malnutrition, all structural and political issues, similar to the markings on the body through physiological processes such as sudden loss of weight or creases due to ageing.

These advances in contemporary Euro-American psychology imply that we need to look at the *body itself not as a rigid fixed entity,* rather body may be viewed as a dynamic process that changes minute by minute and appears as a fixed entity only in terms of *an illusion or a concept best discussed in old school terms.* This is completely in line with Yoga-Sāṃkhya and the Yogācāra schools! In Yoga, body is part of the prakriti and is undergoing constant and dynamic change representing a big illusion in a substantive sense! Indeed, according to Yoga, that is the reason why no truth may arise out of body awareness alone. In Buddhist practices, meditation and contemplation on the nature of body is given to monks and nuns to drive home this learning that body and body awareness is concrete and looks real, but is not real. This Indic insight and contemplative practice, resonates with current contemporary Euro-American psychology research as an advance and not reflected in the colonized psychologies as taught or researched in India, where there is a synergy to this idea. In the IKT, and the folk psychologies of India, including the indigenous traditional knowledge systems, the humans interact with ecosystem in a non-extractive world-view. In a non-extractive world-view, the ecosystem is as important as the humans themselves.

Not only is the body continuously evolving and is not a fixed entity, but it is co-evolving with the micro-context and the environment (which is always changing). Thus, the dichotomy between the self and the environment in the self; the collective in the self and the other as in non-self needs to be critically reviewed. Now, if we were to now agree that the ecosystems are part of the body dynamically making and remaking the body throughout the lifespan, then in this chapter itself, we have arrived at a radical review of the body! If we agree to this review, then we must be open to re-view if consciousness is limited to the functions of the cerebral cortex alone or emergent upon the body processes! Note that, the cells of the whole body interact with the molecules, the bacteria, viruses and the physical elemental aspects of temperature, air, water and space dynamically, moment by moment, while the bodies are fashioned and refashioned throughout the lifetime. Beneath the appearances of the 'body' or beyond appearances of a 'stable body', indeed, what is clear is the weave of a constant systemic interaction; beyond a conscious 'body-mind' awareness. The conclusion that can be drawn, at the very least, is a sense of humility for our limited understanding of the networks of information that are unseen, unobserved, unmeasured and yet inferred in the web of life.

In the Euro-American context, there is a legacy of an Abrahamic God, the premium on faith and the idea of 'intelligent design', which the Indian historical context, doesn't inherit. Without getting into the muddled debates on God (as a male, human) as an entity or 'intelligent design', this chapter, continues to focus on the fundamental question that has been asked in the taught philosophy of mind as well as IKT. What is matter and what is the relationship between matter and consciousness? Can mind be either equated with matter, and therefore considered inert, or consciousness? Can body be equated with matter or consciousness? Is all consciousness, assuming the illusions of form and name, as Advaita says? Several philosophers and cognitive scientists in the current times have debated this question; Scholars such as Chalmers, Tononi, Koch and Block have problematized the unquestioning proposal that consciousness emerges out of matter, which is defined as insentient. A philosopher such as Strawson has flipped the argument and framed the 'hard problem of matter' rather than the hard problem of consciousness as such. In the Indian traditions of philosophy as well, the relationship between matter and consciousness has been discussed and debated in great detail. Indeed, this question remains open for all thinkers of psychology as well. In general, this book is biased towards the Advaita view that consciousness pervades, and at moments of recognition, it is awareness alone; matter doesn't exist at all in the awareness.

Clearly, the 'boundedness' of material substances gives an appearance of fixity; from a molecular, cellular and biochemical perspective, there is fixity, no doubt, but there is *porosity* as well. *Hard* bounded-ness of substances is problematic because these boundaries are fuzzy even in material substances, albeit in a varying degree of porosity. Since the Euro-American academic context looks at body as central in its assumptions of reality and empirical knowing; its ontology and epistemology, a peculiar question in the European and American traditions of philosophy, especially the philosophies of mind, needs to account for this porosities in body-mind and therefore, the question whether minds or consciousness can spill out of or overflow the body! Since this is the legacy of the Euro-American meta-theoretical assumptions, it is a problem, they will need to solve. The Indian intellectual context can become familiar and remain a peaceful witness to this churn! In line, with the assumptions of IKT, position that this book takes, the psyche is much broader than the 'mind', just as the mind is much broader and is inclusive of cognition affect and behaviour of the self-other porosity. As Advaita says, it is only the raw sense perception which gives us the illusion of a separate body-mind.

In recent years, cognitive scientist-Donald Hoffman along with his collaborator Chetan Patel have proposed precisely the idea that our sensory perceptions are not veridical. In the IKT, it is agreed that our conventional sense perceptions do not reveal the truth! Beyond conventional and consensual knowing, our sensory perceptions are not veridical since they are not able to go beyond sensory reality which hides or is unable to be known beyond the limitations of our senses. Hoffman has taken another interesting line of reasoning; Hoffman (Hoffman et al., 2015) has proposed an *interface theory of perception* which suggest that reality is prior and the sensory-motor system tied to the brain acts as a **user interface**. According to Hoffman and Patel, this user interface of the senses, body and brain is geared to optimize the survival of the body. In another provocative proposal, Hoffman also seems to seriously examine the idea that consciousness is a network of several conscious nodes. This idea, to resonate with the Indian idea of Iswara and satsanga. Satsanga, in the Indian tradition, is a network of fully conscious and compassionate agents/nodes. The discussion on interface theory again begs the question – Is it possible that consciousness is central to psychology rather than a cognitive emergence; Can we re-examine the meta-theoretical assumptions of consciousness as such?

Ageing and preparing for death

The assumption of consciousness as central to psychology, is sharpened in our enquiries on life and death. Clearly, there is no death of the body, when we look at it from a molecular point of view; indeed bacteria, viruses and fungi keep collaborating as well as feasting on our bodies –throughout the lifespan. What is death is central to the illusion of a separate body-mind.

What are the intersections of life and death? A hard bounded-ness between life and death is similar to a hard bounded-ness between consciousness and matter: of this self and the other? These questions are central in our understanding of consciousness and psyche in both the contemporary Euro-American psychology, neuroscience and IKT. Scientists do empirical research on accident victims, coma patients and patients under anaesthesia and are increasingly showing an openness towards IKT frameworks of consciousness. If we accept the understanding and the meta-theoretical assumptions that consciousness is prior to and overflows the mind-senses-body complex while pervading it, a particular applied orientation to the questions of ageing, dying and death follows. This applied psychology orientation is seen in the IKT, starting from the Vedāntic corpus. In the Yogic conceptualization of the three bodies – Sthula, Sukśma and kārana śarira, the idea of exhaustion, decay and extinguishing of these is implicit, where the exhaustion, decay and extinguishing of the physical body results in the death of the physical body and the possibility of extinguishing of desires implies the death of the causal body.

In recent decades, biologists and lifespan human development psychologists have discussed and debated the theories of ageing and indicated several interesting facets. Firstly, it appears that there is a certain moderation possible to ageing process based on lifestyles and behaviours, particularly through the yogic, mindfulness, dietary and Āyurvedic practices. In the earlier section, we discussed lifestyles and behaviours in terms of fundamental physiological drives of food/hunger, sleep and wake cycles and sexuality, where, now mainstream psychology acknowledges the role of behavioural regulation or dysregulation facilitated by cultural practices. In recent years, several new theories based on oxidative stress, which is moderated or impacted through Yoga practice and ayurvedic lifestyle have been proposed to understand ageing and variations in cellular ageing, which appears as death to the empirical 'eye'.

In the IKT, specifically in Āyurveda and Yoga-Sāṃkhya, the concepts of behavioural regulation and dysregulation of the body have been discussed in detail since the last at least 3000 years and explicitly connected to rejuvenation and longevity. The behavioural regulation and/or dysregulation of the fundamental physiological drives of the body seem to moderate the ageing processes in the body, the senses and the mind in so far as, the mind is defined as a sensory-motor coordination mechanism within the Yoga-Sāṃkhya framework. Thus, the karma, samskāra and the vāsana of the jīvātman, which it enacts, through the trajectory of its lifespan affects the ageing process. Indeed, cells may continue to show activity up to a particular point of time even after the body as such has been pronounced as clinically dead. Research also shows that, in the nervous systems, the auditory sensory system is last to get extinguished during dying and death. This insight from neuroscience confirms, at least to a limited extent, the phenomenological insight and the living practices in the IKT which prepare the person for death and help the person and the social networks to transition from life to death.

Several texts starting from the Iśa Upaniṣad, the Bhagavad Gita to folksongs, bhakti literature and other sources of cultural transmission continue to articulate and emphasize on the healthy transition from being a phenomenologically living person to a dying and dead person, the key learning from an Indian applied psychology from a consciousness-based perspective would be to prepare the mind and the body as it starts the process of dying and death.

In this preparation, the focus is on preparing and optimizing cognitive resources, regulating senses and preparing and accepting suffering during the process of dying and death as an inevitable part of *leaving or dropping the body*. Even if one does not have an empirical proof or a validation of the claims of the existence of consciousness beyond the body, *one also cannot empirically conclude otherwise*. The preparation of the body, mind, and senses towards peaceful and surrendered death would still be an important aspect of psychology as it is practised. This preparation and an acceptance of death can come through a belief structure such as 'leaving the body'. In the Indian context, the preparation for acceptance of dying and death as a transition is far easier as a lived experience if there is a consistent consciousness-based practice through the lifespan lived earlier. Given a lack of lifespan practice of meditation and regulation of senses, body and mind, as well as the illusion of immortality that humans seek to nurture, the news of death and dying, even though theoretically always seen as a possibility, comes across as a great shock, resulting in denial, grief, depression and a non-acceptance of the dying and the death process.

Going further, in the IKT, there are discussions on specific conditions, when a person may voluntarily plan and *design one's own death*. In certain communities such as the Jain and the Buddhist communities, the practice of planning and preparing for a voluntary death is engaged in till this contemporary day, where laypersons consult their spiritual and religious teachers and design, plan and prepare for their voluntary death, in the presence of the community. This can only be attributed to the enduring influence of a consciousness and not body-based psychology. A body-based psychology cannot lead to an acceptance of death, as the struggle would be to arrest it. In IKT, it is a transitional process on the larger canvas of consciousness.

Sacred bodies: The four-door mandala to jnāna, rāja, bhakti and karma Yoga

A rarely discussed, possibly unknown facet of the IKT, is the idea of sacred bodies! In contemporary times, Swami Vivekananda, expressed his message of making sacred, the mind-body through a lifetime practice. 'Through practice comes Yoga, through Yoga comes knowledge, through knowledge love, and through love bliss', so wrote Swami Vivekananda (Saradananda, 2015). Similarly, the Divine Life Society's motto also refers to these four pathways of the transformation of consciousness while being awake, during dreams and in a deep sleep. Can a body-mind be sacred, through the lifetime? The contemporary IKT teachers and masters have emphasized the use of all the four Yoga paths to sacralize the body-mind through the lifespan. In this manner, the day-to-day lived experience of the seeker is sought to be transformed through the transformation of the now embodied consciousness. Indeed, the four Yoga pathways use the metaphor and imagery of entering the model plan of a traditional Indian home or a temple to internalize the external correspondences and vice-versa, externalizing internal correspondences. For example, the map of the temples is typically internalized through visual maps which are located in the body in certain practices such as Nyāsa.

Normatively, seekers and practitioners usually follow one primary path and two or three supportive paths. For example, seekers may start with Yoga practices and then find supportive practices such as chanting, singing or voluntary service. Similarly, other seekers may start with voluntary service as the main practice and then follow it up with singing, chanting, meditation and Yoga practices as well. Other seekers might start with Rāja Yoga and directly address and seek to understand the nature of the psyche and find supportive practices in terms of voluntary service, music, reading philosophical texts, etc. It is important to note that, right from the 14th century onwards, in the IKT, a movement to integrate these four Yoga paths is seen in the teacher-student taught transmissions. In the South Indian tradition of meditations, tantra and vedānta was integrated with Hatha and Rāja Yoga, these four Yoga paths have been delineated using the metaphor of four doorways to a traditional Indian home. The first doorway on the north, as depicted through a mandala or a visual map, is the doorway of knowledge and insight. This is called as the jnāna Yoga. The second doorway, which is in the East of the mandala, is the doorway of immersion and absorption and this is called as laya Yoga or Rāja Yoga. The third doorway, shown through the south in the visual map/mandala, is called as bhakti Yoga and is the pathway to towards transformation of consciousness through relationships and emotions. The fourth pathway which is in the West of the visual map/mandala is that of selfless service or action and work without reward motivation (including the rewards of enlightenment). This is called as karma Yoga.

In recent years, Timalsina, from a religious studies disciplinary perspective (Timalsina, 2007, 2011, 2013, 2016), has written extensively on these advanced frameworks and conceptualizations of the Indian Tantra – both the Hindu and the Buddhist Tantra. The Tantra or the practices of consciously tying and tightly enmeshing – the body through senses, motor movements through gestures and cognition through Mantra are particular aspects of an applied psychology that is embodied but systematically applies cognitive and affective processes towards the transformation and transcendence of the body-mind. As Timalsina has rightly mentioned, systematic use of the Hindu and Buddhist Tantra allows us to transform and transcend the embodied nature of consciousness while being embodied! In this manner, during advanced meditative states, and at all times during waking, dreaming and sleep states, it is possible to re-make every moment of life sacred; the seeker thus consciously divinizes the body without requiring to torture and emaciate the body-mind.

In this manner, we have turned the full circle; we have seen that the idea of transcending the body consciousness is only an instantiating time-limited strategy such that we are able to systematically cognize and live a conscious life. Having experienced a conscious awareness, which is not limited to a conscious attention to body and body processes, including the processes of brain and cognition, the meditator consciously now uses the body as the most concrete symbol and externalizes the internal awareness and processes. This advance in an applied Indian psychology, which has been practised since millennia, albeit in small communities, is quite a lot of stretch for the edges and the frontiers of current mainstream Euro-American psychology and its methods which are body centred, holding on to the idea of a body and mind! One would imagine, that we would still need about another 100 years for the mainstream psychologists and the meta-theoretical assumptions to grasp and appreciate this profound applied psychology, with appropriate honouring of the lineages of the teachers of IKT, who lived this, most times as silent, unknown masters guiding their students through the lives.

Conclusions: Body as text

We started this chapter with a discussion on the tangy and spicy idli-sambhār or pāni puri. The lived worlds and the embodied consciousness that perceives them are filled with colours, sounds, music, melody rhythms, tastes, fragrances and varieties of touch. By themselves and isolation, each of the sensory modalities means nothing; even if the sensory modalities are connected to cognition, they would still mean nothing unless the self and its relatedness with the worlds is involved in this core 'construction' of reality. Thus, we see that in the later and more advanced practices of meditation, grounding, enhancing, healing the body and thereby transcending the body awareness is seen as sacred and a concrete expression of that consciousness.

In recent years, especially in reference to artificial intelligence and systems, the questions of emotion, self and cognitive capacity such as attention has been debated and discussed by philosophers, cognitive scientists and psychologists. Ganeri (Ganeri, 2017), one of the most brilliant logician philosophers of current times has argued in his book, 'attention, not self' that attention alone is key in explaining consciousness and not self. Building the position taken in this book, we might want to examine the possibility that the central nexus between body-mind and consciousness is *emotion*, which is directly connected with the sense of self. Is it possible to say that transformation of attention is brought about through the transformation of emotion? Indeed, untransformed raw emotion is viewed as one of the biggest obstacles to the attention as such and the quality of attention and absorption. Thus, in the next chapter, we travel to another fascinating radial of the integrative framework of Indian psychology.

References

Adamson, L. B., & Bakeman, R. (1991). The development of shared attention during infancy. In R. Vasta (Ed.), *Annals of child development* (Vol. 8, pp. 1–41). Jessica Kingsley Publishers.
Berk, M., Williams, L. J., Jacka, F. N., O'Neil, A., Pasco, J. A., Moylan, S., Allen, N. B., Stuart, A. L., Hayley, A. C., Byrne, M. L., & Maes, M. (2013). So depression is an inflammatory disease, but where does the inflammation come from? *BMC Medicine*, *11*, 200. https://doi.org/10.1186/1741-7015-11-200
Bhattacharyya, B. (1993). *The path of the mystic lover: Baul songs of passion and ecstasy*. Inner Traditions/Bear & Co.
Block, N. (2007). Consciousness, accessibility, and the mesh between psychology and neuroscience. *Behavioral and Brain Sciences*, *30*(5–6), 481–499.
Bravo, J. A., Forsythe, P., Chew, M. V., Escaravage, E., Savignac, H. M., Dinan, T. G., Bienenstock, J., & Cryan, J. F. (2011). Ingestion of Lactobacillus strain regulates emotional behavior and central GABA receptor expression in a mouse via the vagus nerve. *Proceedings of the National Academy of Sciences of the United States of America*, *108*(38), 16050–16055. https://doi.org/10.1073/pnas.1102999108
Bruntrup, G., & Jaskolla, L. (Eds.). (2016). *Panpsychism: Contemporary perspectives*. Oxford University Press.
Dwivedi, M. (2016). Yoga Nidra as a stress management intervention strategy. *Purushartha*, *9*, 18–25.
Eilam, D., Izhar, R., & Mort, J. (2011). Threat detection: Behavioral practices in animals and humans. *Neuroscience and Biobehavioral Reviews*, *35*, 999–1006. https://doi.org/10.1016/j.neubiorev.2010.08.002
Fodor, J. A. (1975). *The language of thought* (Vol. 5). Harvard University Press.
Fodor, J. A. (1980). Methodological solipsism considered as a research strategy in cognitive psychology. *Behavioral and Brain Sciences*, *3*(1), 63–73.
Freund, P. E. S., McGuire, M. B., & Podhurst, L. S. (2003). *Health, illness, and the social body: A critical sociology*. Prentice Hall.
Ganeri, J. (2017). *Attention, not self*. Oxford University Press.
Goff, P. (2015). Against constitutive Russellian Monism. In Alter, T. & Nagasawa, Y. (Eds.), *Consciousness and the Physical World*. Oxford University Press. 370–400.
Gold, J., & Ciorciari, J. (2020). A review on the role of the neuroscience of flow states in the modern world. *Behavioral Sciences*, *10*(9), 137. https://doi.org/10.3390/bs10090137
Guizzo, F., & Cadinu, M. (2017). Effects of objectifying gaze on female cognitive performance: The role of flow experience and internalization of beauty ideals. *British Journal of Social Psychology*, *56*(2), 281–292.
Guizzo, F., Cadinu, M., Galdi, S., Maass, A., & Latrofa, M. (2017). Objecting to objectification: Women's collective action against sexual objectification on television. *Sex Roles*, *77*(5), 352–365.
Hanssen, K. (2006). The true river Ganges: Tara's begging practices. In *Women's renunciation in South Asia* (pp. 95–123). Springer.
Hoffman, D. D., Singh, M., & Prakash, C. (2015). The interface theory of perception. *Psychonomic Bulletin & Review*, 22(6), 1480–1506.
Knight, L. I. (2011). *Contradictory lives: Baul women in India and Bangladesh*. Oxford University Press.

Limbana, T., Khan, F., & Eskander, N. (2020). Gut microbiome and depression: How microbes affect the way we think. *Cureus*, *12*(8), e9966. https://doi.org/10.7759/cureus.9966

Lindahl, J. R., Fisher, N. E., Cooper, D. J., Rosen, R. K., & Britton, W. B. (2017). The varieties of contemplative experience: A mixed-methods study of meditation-related challenges in Western Buddhists. *PloS One*, *12*(5), e0176239.

Metzinger, T. (2020). Minimal phenomenal experience: Meditation, tonic alertness, and the phenomenology of 'pure' consciousness. *Philosophy and the Mind Sciences*, *1*(I), 1–44.

Mirvis, P. H. (1991). Flow: The psychology of optimal experience. *Academy of Management Review*, *16*(3), 636–640. https://doi.org/10.5465/amr.1991.4279513

Moszeik, E. N., von Oertzen, T., & Renner, K. H. (2022). Effectiveness of a short Yoga Nidra meditation on stress, sleep, and well-being in a large and diverse sample. *Current Psychology*, *41*, 5272–5286. https://doi.org/10.1007/s12144-020-01042-2

Nagasawa, Y., & Wager, K. (2016). Panpsychism and priority Cosmopsychism. In G. Brüntrup & L. Jaskolla (Eds.), *Panpsychism: Contemporary perspectives* (pp. 113–129). New York: Oxford University Press.

Pandit, S. A. (2021). Advaita: Oneness as a lived reality – examining aspects of a profound and a radical psychology. *Psychology and Developing Societies*. https://doi.org/10.1177/09713336211038814

Paranjpe, A. (2021). What is Yoga psychology and where does it stand in contemporary psychology? *Psychology and Developing Societies*, *33*(2), 155–174. https://doi.org/10.1177/09713336211038809

Paranjpe, A. C. (2010). Theories of self and cognition: Indian psychological perspectives. *Psychology and Developing Societies*, *22*(1), 5–48.

Premasiri, P. D. (2008). Varieties of cognition in early Buddhism. In K. Ramakshishna Rao, A. C. Paranjape, & A. Dalal (Eds.), *Handbook of Indian Psychology* (pp. 105–129). Cambridge University Press.

Radha, S. S. (2006). *Hatha yoga: The hidden language*. Timeless books.

Ramnani, P., Costabile, A., Bustillo, A. G. R., & Gibson, G. R. (2015). A randomised, double-blind, cross-over study investigating the prebiotic effect of agave fructans in healthy human subjects. *Journal of Nutritional Science*, *4*, e10–e10. https://doi.org/10.1017/jns.2014.68

Ram-Prasad, C. (2001). Saving the self? Classical Hindu theories of consciousness and contemporary physicalism. *Philosophy East and West*, 51(3), 378–392.

Rochat, P., & Zahavi, D. (2011). The uncanny mirror: A re-framing of mirror self-experience. *Consciousness and Cognition*, *20*(2), 204–213.

Romijn, A. R., Rucklidge, J. J., Kuijer, R. G., & Frampton, C. (2017). A double-blind, randomized, placebo-controlled trial of Lactobacillus helveticus and Bifidobacterium longum for the symptoms of depression. *The Australian and New Zealand Journal of Psychiatry*, *51*(8), 810–821. https://doi.org/10.1177/0004867416686694

Saradananda, S. (2015). *Sri Ramakrishna-The Great Master*. Lulu Press, Inc.

Sedikides, C., & Brewer, M. B. (2015). *Individual self, relational self, collective self*. Psychology Press.

Shteynberg, G. (2015). Shared attention. *Perspectives on Psychological Science*, *10*(5), 579–590.

Shteynberg, G. (2018). A collective perspective: Shared attention and the mind. *Current Opinion in Psychology*, *23*, 93–97.

Sinnott, J., Hilton, S., & Wood, M., & Douglas, D. (2020). Relating flow, mindfulness, cognitive flexibility, and postformal thought: Two studies. *Journal of Adult Development*, *27*, 1–11. https://doi.org/10.1007/s10804-018-9320-2

Taylor, S. E., Klein, L. C., Lewis, B. P., Gruenewald, T. L., Gurung, R. A. R., & Updegraff, J. A. (2000). Biobehavioral responses to stress in females: Tend-and-befriend, not fight-or-flight. *Psychological Review*, *107*(3), 411–429. https://doi.org/10.1037/0033-295x.107.3.411

Tillisch, K., Labus, J., Kilpatrick, L., Jiang, Z., Stains, J., Ebrat, B., Guyonnet, D., Legrain-Raspaud, S., Trotin, B., Naliboff, B., & Mayer, E. A. (2013). Consumption of fermented milk product with probiotic modulates brain activity. *Gastroenterology*, *144*(7), 1394–1401.e14014. https://doi.org/10.1053/j.gastro.2013.02.043

Timalsina, S. (2007). Metaphor, Rasa, and Dhvani: Suggested meaning in tantric esotericism. *Method & Theory in the Study of Religion*, *19*(1–2), 134–162.

Timalsina, S. (2011). Encountering the other: Tantra in the cross-cultural context. *The Journal of Hindu Studies*, *4*(3), 274–289.

Timalsina, S. (2013). Imagining reality: Image and visualization in classical Hinduism. *Southeast Review of Asian Studies*, *35*, 50–70.

Timalsina, S. (2016). A cognitive approach to tantric language. *Religions*, *7*(12), 139.

Tononi, G. (2004). An information integration theory of consciousness. *BMC Neuroscience*, *5*(1), 1–22.

Walsh, R. (1993). Phenomenological mapping and comparisons of shamanic, Buddhist, yogic, and schizophrenic experiences. *Journal of the American Academy of Religion*, *61*(4), 739–769.

Wamsley, E. J. (2019). Memory consolidation during waking rest. *Trends in Cognitive Sciences*, *23*(3), 171–173.

Wiese, C., Keil, D., Rasmussen, A. S., & Olesen, R. (2019). Effects of Yoga Asana practice approach on types of benefits experienced. *International Journal of Yoga*, *12*(3), 218–225. https://doi.org/10.4103/ijoy.IJOY_81_18

Zahavi, D. (2009). Is the self a social construct? *Inquiry*, *52*(6), 551–573.

Zahavi, D., & Rochat, P. (2015). Empathy ≠ sharing: Perspectives from phenomenology and developmental psychology. *Consciousness and Cognition*, *36*, 543–553.

4 Conceptualizing Bhāvanā

Emotions and well-being[1]

Introduction: Consciousness and affect

There are more than 150 (grand and micro) theories of emotion. The discourse on emotion is monopolized by the biochemical idea of emotion, where mainstream Euro-American psychology largely views emotion and affective processes as primarily automatic or non-conscious, even as European phenomenological perspectives do mention self and agency, frequently in relation to the cognitive process. Another key aspect of Euro-American theories of emotion is that these theories are topographically flat, thus, getting muddled with concepts of transformation of emotion relevant for contemplative practices. Arising out of the conceptualization of emotion as largely non-conscious, we see a struggle with interventions for transforming hedonic and aggressive emotions in the social, personal, interpersonal and situational contexts towards harmony, peace and a sense of well-being. Emotion is conceptualized as positive and negative, leaving aside the possibility of equanimity *or śānta/peace* as an emotion – a basis of Indian Hindu thought and a contribution of the Indic civilization to the world. Second, the substantive possibility of re-emotion or experiencing and articulating a pure emotion – Bhāvanā as a methodology towards well-being is not well-articulated. In this chapter, I draw upon the vast traditions of contemplation from the Hindu Śāktādvaita to make two points. First, I identify and elaborate on the possibility of Śānta as a powerful emotion of equanimity and peace, which is beyond the topographically flat idea of positive and negative emotions, defined as they are, in terms of the traps of personal pleasure and pain. It is critical that we foreground the possibility of foundational peace in the psyche as conceptualized and experienced by the Indian knowledge traditions. Second, building on the foundation of peace or equanimity and Śānta, is the Śāktādvaita concept of Bhāvanā, which is understood as 'experience and articulation of pure emotion'. Bhāvanā can only be possible if it is consciously experienced and articulated on the foundational emotion of peace. In all other cases, substituting one emotion with another will be a cosmetic change. I build the conceptualization of both Śānta and Bhāvanā from the Indian traditions

DOI: 10.4324/9781003336204-4

and propose that these concepts and models educate and inform psychology theory and applied practice.

Contemplation and affective processes in Indian knowledge and wisdom traditions

Contemplative sciences have been focused on in recent years in psychology due to increased awareness and the honouring of applied psychology from Asian and Indian knowledge traditions (Oman, 2013, 2019; Oman & Lukoff, 2018; Varela et al., 2017). In contrast to the earlier held, European-American idea that philosophy originated *only* in the West and that Asian and Indian civilizations did not have a philosophy! (Frazier, 2011, 2020). It is now revealed (yet still being discussed and grudgingly accepted) that Indians not only did have a philosophy and a rich system of metaphysics, logic and rationality but also had the philosophical underpinnings translated themselves into applied psychology which were practised through the millennia. Some of the applied psychologies and practices that emanated from the IKT philosophical perspectives are Yoga, āyurveda, taṇtra, Bhakti and advaita vedānta. Each of them has made a contribution to contemporary life.

In the earlier chapters, we have mindfully followed a sequence that starts from the embodied consciousness, continuing to centre on consciousness and Indian psychology as *an integrated form of a knowledge tradition*. The justification is in the availability of a treasure trove of experiential manuals, manuscripts of experiential manual texts (called *prayoga granthas*) as well as philosophical texts (called *prakarana granthas*) available in several traditions of the Indian knowledge systems. These are available not just in Saṃskrit, Pāli and Ardha-magadhi scripts but in other Indic languages and scripts as well. Since the conceptual and applied discussions are available in the Indian languages as well as oral traditions, the chapter uses the term 'tradition' in Indian knowledge traditions (IKT, hereafter), mindfully recognizing that many of the practices and lived experiences have been documented but may not be fully accepted as part of formal philosophical systems or applied psychologies in the academic sense.

As mentioned earlier, there are more than 150 (grand and micro) theories of emotion (Fox, 2008; Hillman, 2013; Lyons, 1999; Strongman, 1996). Paranjpe called for the rasa theory as an integrated consciousness-based Indian theory of emotion (Paranjpe, 2009). The mainstream Euro-American views conceptualize emotion in a scattered form. For example, emotions have been emphasized as 'real' and further understood only in terms of positive and negative emotion even in the constructivist schools (Barrett, 2012; Barrett et al., 2011; Barrett & Wager, 2006; Izard, 1991a, 1991b). Primarily, affective processes have been framed in terms of not one but several dichotomies that fragment and splinter the understanding of affect and its transformation. Rasa theory, as an Indian theory of emotion, not only identifies the integration between the body-mind, reason-affect but self-other and stage-audience as embodied, enactive and embedded form of being and becoming.

Arising out of the inadequate, splintered and inchoate conceptualization of emotion and its interconnection with body, senses, breath and mind, how do the psychologists then view well-being and affective components of meditation states? Emotions are defined as responses that consist of subjective phenomenological and cognitive states, physiological reactions and expressive behaviours. All psychologists agree on three factors central to emotions – a subjective phenomenology and cognitive appraisal, the physiological/bodily response and an expressive behavioural (relational/social) response. Different theorists have focussed on these to derive a cross-cultural understanding of the construction and expression of emotion.

In terms of method, Husserl (c-1900), a key philosopher of continental phenomenology, distinguished between two parts of first person experience; first as a formal act of theorization and second as a cognitive act of experience. Among Indian philosophers, Mohanty as well as Ramprasad (Gupta, 2021; Kasturirangan et al., 2011; Mohanty, 2001; Ram-Prasad, 2018; Siderits et al., 2011) have recognized this particular distinction between Indian philosophy and applied psychology and the continental tradition of phenomenology as formal philosophy. Ramprasad identifies the theoretical school of phenomenology with a 'P' (in caps), whereas the cognitive discipline and commitment of bracketing and non-judgemental awareness, essential in contemplation, is used with a 'p' (small caps).

In the current chapter, taking the views of Mohanty and Ramprasad forward, the chapter emphasizes that the cognitive discipline and commitment of first person experience is the necessary condition for the applied psychological frameworks that emanate from IP/IKT. Indeed, the cognitive act or the discipline in the first person experience then yields to a refinement in subjectivity, a re-conceptualizing of an 'Indian cognitivism' and only thereafter, the philosophical framework. In contrast to the Euro-American tradition of philosophy as analytical speculation leading to psychology, Indian psychology is based on lived experience, which then leads to philosophy on one hand and application in teaching–learning on the other. Secondly, the cognitive discipline of the first person experience has also led to the possibility of systematization of a refined and 'rigorous subjectivity', which Cornelissen identified as a key step in IKT (Cornelissen, 2003, 2007, 2016). Several philosophical IKT practices identify and enact these step-by-step refinement processes of subjectivity in their applied psychological practices.

If one person's subjectivity is different from the other person then, how do we generalize 'theory' – the psychological insights from these applied psychologies? The Indian knowledge traditions do not wish to generalize the learnings of one system over all the human beings in contrast to the assumptions of the philosophy of science in Euro-American tradition. To the extent that the motivation of the human beings are similar and their eligibility (adhikāra) and preparation are fulfilled, the results and the insights of these systems are generalizable. Indeed, there are no classifications according to social factors such as class, race, caste or gender in the IP/IKT.

We discussed the centrality of consciousness in IP/IKT right from the first chapter. A Critic may look at the theoretical differences between schools in IKT. Without papering over these differences, this chapter distils the key insights from different schools of thought as relevant to the transformation of affect.

Two features are central for our discussions in this chapter: Prakāśa, understood as self-reflexivity/self-knowing and saṃkalpa, understood as intention. In the Indian knowledge traditions, reflexivity (sva-prakāśa) and intentionality (saṃkalpa) are central in defining consciousness. In the non-dual advaita tradition of Ādi Śankarācārya, reflexivity is emphasized, whereas in the non-dual Kashmiri Śaiva tradition, both reflexivity and intentionality are emphasized as the defining features of consciousness. The practices that move from Yoga towards Ādi Śankara's advaita focus on the non-intentional self-reflexive nature of consciousness as recognized and realized through advanced meditation states of saṃādhi. The śāktādvaita perspectives in IKT have focused on the practice of a free and liberated nature of both intentionality in and as consciousness; never clouding reflexivity. Indeed, it is un-reflexivity that clouds intentionality, which is the essential nature of consciousness, according to non-dual trika Śaiva thought.

IKT assumes that self-awareness recognizes its own reflexive-intentional consciousness every time affective transformation and refinement of subjectivity takes place. It is also understood that this transformation is not immediately accessible to all humans, and therefore a series of practices are prescribed and derived to arrive at this 'recognition' of the nature of consciousness. In recent years, Timalsina has illuminated extensively on this aspect of meditation and healing practice from the religious studies and Hindu tantra perspective, which we will discuss later (Hayes & Timalsina, 2017; Timalsina, 2008).

Positive psychology and contemplative practices in Euro-American psychology have largely focused on cognition, mind, brain functions and behaviour. The central role of affect and affective processes-emotions, feelings and sentiments has not been focused upon even though feeling relaxed, happy, compassionate and joyous is a very frequent lived experience of well-being. Indeed, in the current social psychology from the Euro-American tradition, affect and affective processes are at best viewed as 'primes' and, at worst, looked at as sources of bias! This is a profound distortion of knowledge and has significant implications for well-being. In this chapter, the focus is on understanding affective processes and well-being from four distinctive yet overlapping models available in the Indian knowledge traditions.

Affective processes: Four IKT perspectives based on motivation and maturity

With a more than past 100-year history of intellectual exchange between East and West, several profound transformations have occurred in the Euro-American mindset about psychology, consciousness and well-being as part of academic and research psychology. A series of masters from the east visited Europe and the Americas and have influenced the discipline of psychology. Starting from the discussions between Swami Vivekananda and William James to the series of experiments conducted at the Menninger Institute, Topeka, Kansas, where Swami Rama, as a subject, showed voluntary control over involuntary physiological responses, to Sri Mahesh Yogi, from whom the TM (Transcendental Meditation) movement inspired the understanding of the relaxation response, to the profound influence of His Holiness, the Dalai Lama on the current cognitive psychology; eastern thought has radically influenced psychology as a discipline away from its mechanistic behaviouristic leanings. The influence of the East on European, esp. continental philosophy always existed, but this exchange has hastened in the last 100 years (Cornelissen, 2014; Walsh, 2015; Walsh & Shapiro, 2006).

Cognitive neuroscience and psychology today are deeply influenced by the knowledge traditions of the east – as the phenomenological method utilized by the contemplative traditions informs and educates the interpretations of the neuroscience findings, which are meaningless by themselves. Mindfulness, first utilized as a specific interpretation of the Buddhist practice of Sati (smriti/memory), is currently used in a fairly broad manner to indicate a variety of body-mind processes which leverage conscious attention.

Aligned with the general assumptions of a Euro-American meta-theoretical lens, there is a mapping of cognition and cognitive processes rather than self and affective processes while theorizing about consciousness. Self, itself, is a matter of debate, especially in cognitive psychology and consciousness studies and is conceptualized in terms of social and cognitive processes. Attention has been conceptualized in feature binding for sensory-perceptual coupling and Ganeri, recently has argued that it is attention and not self, which binds psyche (Ganeri, 2017). However, the paper is proposing that a higher order binding is provided by affect for transformation and recognition of self. Therefore, affective transformation and the role of affect as a binding process in self-realization and post-realization embodiment/living in freedom, is the next building block from the earlier chapter on embodied consciousness. If we define meditation as the transformation of self and self-understanding, then affective processes and transformation of affective processes are central in transformation and re-creation of self and being in the world.

Affect, body, self and drives

Contemporary psychology has spent a lot of time, energy and investment in negative emotions. The key insight from IKT is that negative emotions bind the self-awareness to the body, while positive emotions free the self-awareness of body awareness! For example, fear binds the self to the body and its survival. A tangentially similar theorization is seen in Fredrickson's 'broaden and build' theory, which proposes that positive emotions arising out of day-to-day events broaden the cognitive field and allow for flexible actions (Fredrickson, 2001, 2004). The role of positive emotions in the body-mind complex is fairly well-known, but the nuanced idea of body-mind in the Indic traditions is still not understood and appreciated. How can we say that?

In Ayurvedic texts, 'Manas' is taken as *bhautika*, that is material and bodily and intimately connected to the body. 'Manas' is generally translated as 'mind'. In technical terms, however, Manas refers to the sensory-motor coordination aspects of the psyche. In Indian knowledge traditions, the term – *antah karana chatushtya* broadly denotes the psyche. *Antah-karana* has four mental structures/processes – *Citta*, *Buddhi*, *Ahamkāra* and *Manas*. *Citta* – refers to the deepest structure/process of a reservoir and record of all the experiences the person has gone through. *Ahamkāra*, refers to the sense of ownership and 'I' consciousness. *Buddhi* refers to cognitive processes and *Manas* – refers to sensory-motor coordination. So, the question arises – where are affective processes? Indeed, all the affective processes are aligned with the self, which is denoted by different functional terms – *Ahamkāra*, Ahambhāva and Asmitā. In indicating the stages of advanced meditation as identified by Patanjali's Yoga sutra, affective well-being – sānanda samādhi (immersion with happiness) and 'I' awareness in sāsmita samādhi (immersion with pure 'I'/phenomenological awareness) occur very close to each other. This is seen again in Vedānta, where it is mentioned that the first awareness, according to the Vedas, was self-awareness and the next moment, this self 'felt' a keen sense of being singular and decided to become many! Therefore, the awareness of self was accompanied with the awareness of loneliness and the desire to be abundant! Thus, affect is intimately connected to the self-awareness itself. How are Ahamkāra, Ahambhāva and Asmitā different? In the concluding comment, this will be briefly indicated to.

The Yoga-Sāṃkhya perspective locates both the body and mind in the domain of *Prakṛti* or the principle of change and materiality. The question of drives and affective processes related to physiological drives are most obvious and need to be understood first. Ayurvedic texts say that there are two kinds of drives that have concomitant affective experiences. These physiological drives are called 'forces' or vega-flows, broadly understood as biological motives or drives. One categorization of the *vega* is the *śāririka vega* or the physiological drives, with their associated affect. In a body and health affirmative stance, āyurveda says that these drives **should not be controlled or denied/stopped**, rather they should be expressed. Some of the *śārirka vega* are yawning, burping, urinating, defecating, passing wind, feeling hunger and sleep. Serious Yoga practitioners do eventually regulate even these physiological processes, but the route is always through understanding the affective response of the body-mind complex. In the IKT, broadly, there is a socio-cultural emphasis on lifespan regulatory practices such as fasting, selecting certain foods for certain occasions and 'intentional not sleeping' (*jāgarana*).

In parallel, āyurvedic texts emphasize that the *mānasika vega* – affective-physiological drives, which have some possibility of regulation need to be regulated, channelled and disciplined. A clear example would be – to not suppress or stop a yawn or a burp or a defecation but to regulate the sexual or aggressive drive. Āyurveda says that suppressing the śāririka vega causes disease. Whereas affect related physiological drives such as sex or aggression and, to some extent, hunger and sleep – **called as *ṃānasika vega* need to be understood and expressed mindfully and with regulation.**

So, at the first level, Ayurvedic texts recognize the dual nature of physiological drives and how they can affect the affective process in the psyche, particularly self-awareness-behaviour nexus. As the texts say that if *śaririka vega,* such as burping, passing wind, and urinating are suppressed, diseases are caused in the body. On the other hand, if *mānasika vega* are *not* regulated, then diseases are caused in the body-mind complex. Even though, early traditional research in Euro-American psychology focused on the drives from a clear stimulus-response conditioning perspective, we know now that even the physiological drives such as hunger motivation are complex and related to affective processes such as desire, disgust, comfort, satiation and embedded in social-cultural factors such as portion size, availability of and preference of food materials, advertisements and access to healthy food, etc. Thus, in a dual approach through a tightly body enmeshed link to affective processes, we see body affirmation for *śāririka vega* and regulatory perspective of *mānasika vega* such as sex and aggression. It is amazing to note that, in contemporary times, we see the opposite in practice and social behaviour – people are quite judgmental about passing wind and tend to suppress it, but unmindful of sexual desires! Fear is a survival-oriented affective process, tightly enmeshed with the body, and indeed, is seen along with other emotions such as pain, distress, anguish and suffering as the beginning of mindfulness towards the self-affect-cognition-behaviour system.

Thus, we see a clear line of refined awareness associated with affect and body, with due respect to both, even as the mechanism orientation in contemporary psychology through neurotransmitters, etc., is not seen. Early research in cognitive neuroscience located the survival-oriented emotions with amygdala as a seat of uncontrolled passions! Recent neuroscience research does identify the role of insula, amygdala and hippocampus in survival related emotions and affect. However, the dichotomy between cognition and affect as well as the Cartesian dualism of psyche and body still persists. More importantly, the affect related to bodily satiation needs better empirical understanding and discrimination from a generalized 'relaxation response'. The question is – what does the mind feel when the stomach is full or hungry – Is it relaxation? Can we train the mind-body to remain relaxed while starving? In the Indian contemplative traditions, experiences of equanimity or peace are seen as more relevant than the modern ideas of 'positive emotion'. Equanimity and peace are associated with satiety in the physiological, bodily sense and contentment in affect. If we look at the framework of positive and negative emotions, or 'subjective well-being' it stands on weak conceptual grounds for a variety of reasons, as we don't have a complete theory of positive and negative emotions, even as we do see correlates in terms of brain activity.

Transformation of emotion and meaning making

When the body is satisfied, satisfaction doesn't last for long. So, affective transformation must mean a deeper practice of reframing emotion. In IKT, fragmentation of experience into disaggregated incoherent parts is a fundamental aspect of distress and illness; coherence and integrity in body-mind are seen as a sign of health. Thus, stronger the fragmentation, the more dogmatic and frozen, the cognition, the more automatic the emotion: Such a person is called as 'bound', stuck/constrained – '*Baddha*'. The first step in IP/IKT is to recognize this automaticity, brought along due to three factors – (a) Karma: past intentions and actions, (b) Samskāra: past experiences and their associations and (c) Vāsanā: residual and unfulfilled/incomplete desires, impulses and needs. The person is Baddha – bound due to these.

The recognition of this insight on the automaticity of affective processes triggers the contemplative practice and leads to a successive re-framing and meaning making of emotions. Broadly, the 'raw' automatic affective components of the self-awareness in psyche have been accepted as a block or a constraint towards *self-recognition* in the IKT and the transformation of emotion and meaning makings leads to integration and well-being. Note, however, that this freedom and well-being are not 'otherworldly' and are embodied in this world as well (Fort, 1998, 1999; S. A. Pandit, 2021; Rukmani, 2005).

Emotions in IKT are called 'raw' when they are not deliberated upon, consciously experienced and arise from automaticity of karma-samskāra-vāsana. At the beginning of the chapter, the point about the seeker's motivation and eligibility was made. If the person is motivated to understand *the raw emotions*, which bring distress and anguish, then, in that contextual space, emotions are conceptualized as 'enemies'. There are six such raw emotions, also called, 'ṣad ripu-s'. They are Kāma (lust), Krodha (rage), Mada (arrogance/pride), Moha (delusion), Matsara (envy) and Ahamkāra (a sense of 'I' as egotism). These six enemies are widely understood in the Indian socio-cultural contexts, even among those in non-contemplative communities. The ṣad ripu-s are very close and overlap with the mānasika vega, as discussed earlier. For these emotions, which are considered as raw, unmindful, conditioned and automatic, a particular methodology is prescribed in the Yoga-sutra-s for those who seek affective transformation. The methodology is captured in two words, with their opposites – Āsakti and Anāsakti in generic IKT approach and Rāga and Vairāgya in the context of affective processes. In this essay, we will limit the discussion to *Rāga* and *Vairāgya*.

In Patanjali's Yoga Sutra's (PYS, hereafter), which is one of the foundational texts of Yoga Sāṃkhya, the cognitive-affective concept – *Vairāgya* is utilized. The term Vairāgya is connected to an important word concept – Rāga in the Indian knowledge traditions. Rāga is directly translated as attraction but in a much broader sense can be understood as emotional or affective approach-ing towards objects/processes and events. We see this broader understanding of Rāga in Indian music, for example. Rāga, Anurāga, Ranjana are word concepts associated with 'a positive approach-ing/attraction and a broader sense of indulgences in moods, thus, emphasizing on the healthy nature of desire; a euthymic response. In Yoga Sutra-s, the concept Rāga is used as attraction and approach-ing action *towards* an internal or external object/event/person or process. Rāga in PYS is contrasted with Dveṣa – or repulsion/moving away from an internal/external object/process/event/person. Note that Vairāgya is not the opposite of attraction and repulsion. Similar to our clarification of samatva/equanimity or peace/śānta as experienced substantively different from positive and negative emotions and subjective well-being in contemporary Euro-American frameworks, Vairāgya is not about attraction (Rāga) or repulsion (Dveṣa) but the next step in vertical practice spiral. It is, indeed, one of the fundamental practices to transform *the dichotomy* of attraction and repulsion, which are automatic and unmindful cognitive-affective-behavioural states and tie in an automatic raw self-awareness. In the context of ṣad-ripu-s or the six enemies – automatic affective responses based on karma-samskāra-vāsanā, Vairāgya, is a particular affective transformation method to derive insight, transform raw emotion, and thereby, be free of their grip. Vairāgya thus represents an embodied transcendence from automatic affective processes. Vairāgya is particularly amenable for neuro-science investigation possibilities from sensory level to imagery, working memory and implicit memory (S. A. Pandit, 2020).

In the PYS, *Vairāgya* is related to the embodied sensory inputs in its very definition. Yoga sutra defines *Vairāgya* as '*Drṣta-anuśravik vaśikāra saṃjnā*' – which means the insight that arises from mastering visual and auditory processes. Note that *drśta* (visual) and *anuśravik (auditory)* refer to sensory, attentional, working memory, imagery and bodily processes associated with vision and audition, inside and outside the body-mind. *Vairāgya* has four milestone levels as described in the commentaries on PYS, a detailed discussion of these four levels is outside the scope of this essay.

Till now, we have seen a layered approach. The drives which are connected to involuntary physiological processes are required to be expressed without suppression. The drives which are closely connected to social and emotional behaviour are required to be regulated, disciplined and channelled. At the third layer, the automatic social emotional affective processes based on *karma-samskāra-vāsana* are called as *ṣad-ripu-s* or six enemies. They are called so because they are automatic and unmindful of relational and collective self-awareness. The sad-ripu-s/raw emotions arise automatically and bring suffering and pain, and therefore, *Vairāgya* is a practice to process automatic affect and find insight, thereby transcending them towards a transformation of self-awareness.

The ṣad ripu-s denote the basic fundamental self-other duality where the other is looked at not as a subject but as an object. This subject-object fragmentation brings us to another framework of transforming affective processes through IP/IKT.

Bhāva and rasa: Duality, transforming affect and relational well-being

Can we look at the 'other' as a subject and not as an 'object'? Certainly, human beings can and do approach and look at the 'other' as a 'subject' in healthy relational contexts. Indeed, some of the most fundamental ideas of both dysfunction and well-being are associated with this question. In the current times, the philosopher Monima Chadha has compared the distinction between self-reflexivity that brings self-awareness on and in itself, called sva-prākāśa, along with reflection of the self in self-other dynamic, called para-prākāśa (Chadha, 2011). The Indian knowledge traditions, including Buddhist thought, view the self as knowing itself (*Sva-samvedanā*) without necessarily viewing itself as an object. Non-dual perspectives and applied psychologies, such as Advaita and Kāshmiri Śaiva frameworks, conceptualize 'self' and consciousness as the only noumena or ontological categories that reveal themselves in their own light. Note that this 'self' is not the conventional social self. As Chadha, convincingly argues, self-reflexivity and reflectionism in self-other dynamic are not as oppositional or dichotomous as framed in formal philosophical arguments. However, this is only in reference to a deeper self and not conventional self, which is largely socially constituted. In any case, the point is that – can there be transformation of affective processes in relationships and duality, as well? Certainly, there can be a very elegant model, as IKT would educate us!

In the IKT, the default assumption of non-self is not an object but an animated self, which is a conventionally constituted self (with small 's').

Aligned with this meta-theoretical assumption in IKT, are cognitive-affective and behavioural concepts and practices such as Karuṇa (compassion), Ahimsā (non-injury/violence), Dharma (ethical order), Śīla (ethical and affective commitments). All these are required for the self (small 's'). Therefore, the first point in self-other is that the other is a non-object. We arrive now at a fairly well-known and accepted cultural psychology of emotions and emotional transformation based on inter-subjectivity and dialogue – the rasa theory.

Rasa theory has been much discussed in the last few decades, from anthropological and religious studies perspectives and psychologists have also commented upon it (Deutsch, 2021; Higgins, 2007; Lynch, 1990; Mitra, 2016; Nair, 2013; L. Pandit, 2004, S. A. Pandit 2011; Sen & Pandit, 2013; Shweder et al., 1993). Paranjpe has proposed that rasa theory as an Indian psychology of emotion presents several unique contributions to understanding emotions, its expression and its transformation towards well-being.

In a very brief background, it is reiterated that rasa theory in the context of emotion is first elucidated in the sixth chapter of Nātyaśāstra called as the Rasādhyaya, while the term 'rasa' as such is found in the Vedic literature to mean variously as essence, sap, fluid (S. A. Pandit & Misra, 2013). There are two key concepts relating to affective processes in the rasa theory. First, is the concept of *Bhāva* or Bhāvanā and the second, the concept of *rasa*. Let us first take the concept of *Bhāva*.

Bhāva is translated as emotion/feelings in most of the Indian languages spoken in India today. Technically, the word *Bhāva* emerges from the root word – *bhu*, which means to exist or manifest. One of the words for Śiva-Natarāja is *Bhāva* which means 'as manifested'. *Bhāva*, then, implies the subtle intentions of the Bhāva in the manifestation of the concrete sensorially accessible world. The word Bhāvanā has been discussed in Yoga, Sāṃkhya, mimāṃsā as well as in Trika Śaiva thought in IKT.

In PYS, the foundational text of Yoga, which has more than 50 extant commentaries in Indian languages as well as in English, the word *Bhāvanā/Bhāvanam* occurs in major sutra's. In the first chapter, Samādhi Pāda, the word – Bhāvanā, occurs in the sutra on the description of 'Om'. Immediately after describing the word indication for Puruṣa, Iśvara as Praṇava(Om), the next sutra states that the yogi needs to do the japah (reflection) and the Bhāvanā of Om! In this sutra, commentators and masters have interpreted *Bhāvanam* as 'consciously cultivating the *affect of being* Om'!

The next important sutra where the word concept – Bhāvanā occurs is when the discussion is about negative affect–cognition nexus (*Vitarka*) arising in the contents of consciousness. The sutra is *Vitarka Bādhane, Pratipakśa Bhāvanam*. The meaning of the sutra is that in case and whenever the mind is constrained/disturbed with Vitarka (negative affect-cognition nexus), the yogi needs to cultivate the opposite cognition-affect-self nexus. Therefore it can be said in the meaning implied, from PYS, *Bhāva/Bhāvanam* is a conscious mindful cultivation of cognition-affect-self-awareness.

In the context of rasa theory of emotions, Nātyaśāstra identifies *eight Bhāva-s* or primary emotions set in a dialogical context (S. A. Pandit & Misra, 2013). Each of the *Bhāva* has been tied to a concomitant rasa. The relationship between *Bhāva* and rasa has been debated intensively spanning over a few thousand years. Briefly, scholars have translated Bhāva or Bhāvanā as a personal and a particularized emotion, whereas rasa has been understood as the transformation of a particular individual emotion towards a universal affect and insight/compassion. Rasa as a transformed affect is a unique contribution of Indian knowledge traditions and, therefore, closest to the idea of fluidity of consciousness – Cid-rasa (Bansat-Boudon, 2014).

How do we experience this transformation of emotion into rasa? How does Bhāva translate into rasa experience (rasa niśpatti). According to the Nātyaśāstra, rasa is experienced in interconnected elements:

- *Sthāyi-bhāva*-predominant emotion felt emotion,
- *Vi-bhāva* – the contextual triggering factors,
- *Anubhāva* – the embodied, behavioural expressions and actions and
- *Sancāri and Vyābhicāri bhāvās*, which are the transitory emotions.

One of the greatest Śaiva masters – Ācārya Abhinavgupta, in his text – Abhinavbhārati gave a process mechanism of the transformation of the *Bhāva* – a personalized emotion into a transformed affect, leading to compassion and insight called as *rasa*. He theorized this in the context of a dramatic performance, esp. dance. Ācārya Abhinavgupta introduced a step-by-step process of dialogical transformation of affect, which is followed in Indian performance traditions to this day. The first step, according to practising teachers of dance, is the presentation of a familiar emotion through the selection of a song. The next step, called *'carvaṇa'*, involves reiteration and re-interpretation; enacted and communicated to lead to a subtle and unfamiliar interpretation of the emotional experience and presentation. At this point, the audience/viewers get immersed (*tallīnata*) and mirror the emotional experience and expression vicariously as the performer presents them. This paradoxical state of seeing and mirroring the emotion and its experience was called a paradox-*'camakāra'* Finally, Ācārya Abhinavagupta introduced the term *sādharanikaraṇa* (shared empathy/universalization) to identify the point at which a personal emotion becomes a transpersonal, collectively processed affect and leads to compassion (S. A. Pandit, 2011).

Sādharnikaraṇa is a particular transition point that allows for the rasa to be experienced together as a group, in the context of a dance or an aesthetic performance, so that the viewer becomes a *sahṛdaya* (shared heart) and accepts and recognizes even the most unpleasant and disturbing emotions as performed and presented on stage as part of the personal and transpersonal psyche. According to Ācārya Abhinavagupta, the viewer recognizes and accepts all the emotions, pleasant and unpleasant as part of the universalized consciousness/psyche and thereby experiences insight-*samvid*.

In this way, Ācārya Abhinavgupta emphasized on the modality of distance between the audience and the performance to arrive at compassion and acceptance even for unpleasant emotions performed on the stage. This is a profound theorization, which was then utilized in the context of meditation with the correspondence to the inner stage and the detached, choice-less internal attention and insight. The self-other and stage-viewer are especially identified and emphasized in contemplation and meditation states, where a correspondence is drawn between the inner and outer stage, internal and external attention and a dialogue between inner and external presence of others.

Acārya Abhinav Gupta, in his Abhinavbhārati, also contributed, thus, to a foundational rasa-*śānta rasa or the affective immersion in peace.* Nātyaśāstra originally only identifies eight *Bhāva*-s and their concomitant rasa's. According to Ābinavaguptācārya, *śānta* is the foundational rasa. Indeed, it is the *śānta* which is the ground of all seeing and insight – internal as well as external and arises from a *camatkāra*! *Camatkāra* in conceptualizing peace is a paradoxical state of a non-emotion emotion; a stability and quietude, where emotions are conventionally always experienced as volatile and non-quiet! In contemporary Euro-American psychology, we use the term 'peace', but we have no conceptual grounding of affective and cognitive processes in and of peace. According to rasa theory, peace is experienced when the person is able to watch and see, be immersed and recognize cognition-affect self choicelessly and with equanimity.

Parā Bhakti and the Śānta rasa

Śānta rasa becomes a base and foundation for Bhakti (immersion in love) rasa as a sādhāna/practice for love as a contemplative and active practice in duality and multiplicity of the social and relational self. Particularly in the domain of love even for the adversary and enemy. Even as Bhakti finds mention in the Śvetaśvatāra Upaniṣad and in the Bhagavad Gita, the connection between Bhakti and rasa was first drawn by a Marathi philosopher Vopadeva in 12th century CE. In their framework and practice of contemplation on relationships and well-being, the Bhakti practitioners, show an intentional cultivation of a particular relationship style and intensity towards embodied consciousness, with form, name and qualities. In some schools of Hindu thought, the contemplative approach of relating to consciousness with form, name and qualities was accepted and encouraged as an intermediate step before re-cognizing the consciousness *as not limited by* name, form and qualities.

During the 14th, 15th and 16th centuries, India was suffering through tumultuous times and a new wave of thinking arose across the sub-continent to address and process suffering at individual, relational and social/societal levels. Bhakti, as a historical movement, represents a landmark culmination and integration of the various perspectives of contemplation and spiritual realizations in the Indian historical context. The Bhakti movements starting from 12th century onwards, engulfed the whole of India and the bhakta masters, wandering minstrels travelled across the sub-continent, using social, psychological and aesthetic methods, singing and dancing songs of love and fellowship and bringing the suffering multitude together in relational and social well-being.

In the development of Bhakti, several masters were poets and singers, many were philosophers and authors of deeply philosophical texts and most integrated several schools of thought and engendered a deep literary, social and cultural transformation in the Indian sub-continent. The Gaudiya or the Bengali Vaiśnava philosophers, radically reframed the concept of rasa and Bhāva and utilized this re-conceptualization for relational well-being. Firstly, the definitions of Bhāva and rasa were proposed in the text – *Bhakti Rasamṛta Sindhu,* which is translated as the 'boundless ocean of love'. In this text, going with the metaphor of an ocean, the chapters were written and titled as waves. The definitions of Bhāva and rasa occur in the fifth wave, southern quadrant, canto 132 and 133. *Bhāva* was defined as 'an intentional and focussed state of contemplation and relationality towards a consciousness with form, name and qualities'. These could be the forms of Saints, Gods, Viśnu (or even the prophets such as Jesus). However, Bhāva, the authors say, are always mediated through deep experience and its cultivation (samskāra). Thus, here we see, Bhāva as cultivated intentional, affect-based contemplation that requires and leverages cognitive processes of memory and sustained attention/flow and immersion.

Rasa was defined as 'an experience of amazement and joy/relish *beyond* contemplation'. Firstly, in the conceptualization of Bhāva, we see a coherence of cognitive processes of experience, memory and sustained attention/immersion, processes of intention and selection of the intentionally chosen principle for attention/immersion. While Bhāva is a conscious cultivation, in the definition of rasa – we see 'overflow' in the affective processes of joy and relish/savouring as well as the experience of amazement, pointing to the unpredictability and non-fabrication of the self-recognition of consciousness!

The Bengali Vaiśnava philosophers, proposed that only and only in reference to a relationship with the divine (which is a chosen principle of consciousness with name, form and quality), intensity of raw emotion can lead to transformation of the self-cognition-behaviour nexus into well-being. In his text, Bhakti-rasāmṛta-sindhu, Śrila Goswami, identifies five relational modes that one can *intentionally* assume for a lifelong role and a relationship with the divine. Amazingly, Śrila Gosvāmi, places śānta bhakti as the lowest ladder! For details on Bhakti rasa, see, translated by Haberman (Haberman, 2001, 2003); also see in reference to Vātsalya (Sen & Pandit, 2013).

Śrila Goswami, in his text says, how can one remain quiet and peaceful in the mesmerizing and bewitching awareness of the divine! Next ladder above śānta bhakti, is dāsya (servitude) and sakhya (friendship), where the human intentionally assumes the lifelong role of a servant and a friend, respectively. The highest levels of love/Bhakti rasa are *vātsalyam* and *sṛṅgāra*, which are understood as intentionally viewing the divine as a child to be cared for and/or as a lover, respectively. Thus, we see in this elegant and sophisticated theorization, some resonances from all the contemplative traditions in the world in terms of practice. For example, in mystical and contemplative traditions across the world, meditators do intentionally take a role in relation to the divine. What makes this profound theorization unique is the conceptual sophistication and its unbroken practice in Indian contemplative traditions till this day.

Indeed, śānta bhakti is foundational for a meditator's journey! The meditating masters may or may not choose to embrace the 'insanity' of an intense life-long romantic relationship with the divine, such as many spiritual masters have done. In conclusion, we can say that Śānta rasa is the transformational milestone, from seeing emotional and dramatic content on stage to seeing dramatic and emotional content on the internal stage; From enacting the drama of life with multiple 'others' to enacting the drama on the stage of life, with the *one and only 'other'* – the relationship with the divine.

Āchārya Abhinavgupta's contribution to the foundational rasa-śānta rasa, the rasa of śānta/śānti, is a contribution to a global psychology of the world. Śānta or peace arises from a transformed affect and insight into the compassionate acceptance of emotions.

The understanding of Bhāva and rasa in IKT, with a theorization of emotion and its transformation to insight and peace is in the context of *human inter-subjectivity*. In comparison to the earlier model of Vairāgya, this model of rasa and Bhāva specifies the modality of self-other, identifies distance, enacted through stage in the context of a dramatic performance as well as relational distance in social context. Recall that we defined *Vairāgya* as a mastery of the visual and auditory processes. While, *vairāgya* in the meditative context is purely psychological, Bhāva and rasa in the context of nātya or performance are relational, socio-emotional and dialogical. Rasa framework initiates with a concrete stage, projected outward, which then is consciously projected inward for a *witness consciousness* that accepts the inner emotional dramas with compassion. Developments in the Indian historical context show a transformation of the world rasa itself with an additional layer of meaning of relational well-being or unadulterated love as Bhakti, where Bhakti is a particular system of relating to the world and 'loving' the one and the only 'Other' unabashedly, with several ethical-cognitive and behavioural commitments. Does the insanity of passion mean, bypassing the social? Well, IKT educates another perspective on affect and action.

This brings us to another perspective on affective processes as triggers to action. How do affective processes tie to action in contemplative traditions? In the Mimāṃsā perspective in IKT, the focus on action and its intentions, utilizes Bhāvanā as affect/emotion that is an instrumentality for contemplative intentional action. Very briefly, Bhāva/Bhāvanā is that emotion which triggers action and is thus connected to ethics and Dharma/Vidhi. In this perspective, Bhāvanā is associated with an ethical intentionality and arises from transformed affect, associated with deontic and dhārmic action (Ollett, 2013). As we have mentioned earlier, the IKT are diverse, but six classical Darśana-s have been well discussed. Among the six classical Darśana-s, the school of purva-mimāṃsā, has not been much discussed in the psychology scholarship. Purva-mimāṃsā primarily focuses on actions, intentions and consequences, thereby, refers to several central concepts of Dharma, Karma and Samsāra. In the context of purva-mimāṃsā, the word concept – *Bhāvanā/Bhāvanam* is central and refers to three internal *affective* states – expectancy, means and outcome of action, that trigger ethical action. More detailed discussion is out of scope for this chapter.

Intentional cultivation of affect-thought-action: The self-awareness is complete

Finally, we come to the apex of the sophistication of non-dual Vedānta perspective in the Kāshmir Trika Śaiva tradition. In the Kāshmir Śaiva tradition, we find the use of the word Bhāvanā as a pivot in reference to contemplative immersion and recreation of a new world! Here, in several texts, the word Bhāvanā overlaps with the word concept Dhāraṇa (meditation/immersion). The great Śaiva masters Utpaladeva, Somānanda, Abhinavagupta and Kshemarāja, through their profound writings, appear to have radically integrated all the earlier schools of thought and practice as well as the different meanings associated to the word *Bhāva/Bhāvanam.* For details, see Timalsina's scholarship on tantra, where Trika Śaiva scholarship is also referred as Hindu tantra or, more specifically – Hindu Śāktādvaita. Writing from a 'religious studies' perspective, Timalsina has tried to 'excavate' the applied psychology and contemplative practice from the 100 odd years of sensationalism and a pile of mystification and vulgarization of tantra as such (Hayes & Timalsina, 2017; Timalsina, 2007, 2012, 2015, 2016).

In the Śāktādvaita/Hindu tantra, Kāshmiri Śaiva thought, *Bhāva*/ Bhāvanā reflects the self as active, intentional, self-luminous consciousness. Consciousness is not an inert, passive witness alone! It is filled with intentionality and play, and therefore, self-recognition, which we started the chapter with, includes an integrated and transformed self-awareness – cognition, affect, body and behaviour to re-create the world anew every day!

In the Kāshmiri Śaiva framework, the consciousness with name, form, quality and intentionality is organized as the eternal union of śiva and śakti. This removes the presumed duality and discussions on Prakrti and Puruṣa in Yogā-Sāṃkhya, as both śiva and śakti are principles of consciousness. In the same line of thought, the difficulty of aligning māyā with Brahman, a discussion point for intellectual scholars in Śankarācārya's advaita is also resolved, where śakti, now is the creative manifesting aspect of the same consciousness/Brahman *and is not* unreal. With all the conceptual issues resolved, the Kāshmiri Śaiva framework is, thus free to organize and conceptualize a step-by-step process of emotional transformation as *recognition* of the non-duality between consciousness with name, form and quality and consciousness as such – Both as one's own self. Indeed, it is Bhāvanā of the consciousness that creates the world and its plurality. When the consciousness is immersed in the Bhāvanā of 'let me be', it 'becomes'.

In the text, Vijnāna Bhairava, the Kāshmiri Śaiva master – Śri Kshemarāja identifies 112 Bhāvanā for the individuated consciousness/self to *recognize* one's own true non-dual nature as delight, joy and astonishment (Lakshmanjoo, 2015; B. N. Pandit, 1977; Singh, 1990). Such is the immersive process of Bhāvanā, that minute by minute, moment by moment, the practitioner continues to recognize the non-duality of self-nature as consciousness along with the multiplicity of the world as 'play of the bhāvanā' of the consciousness. In this manner, the silos and dichotomies of material and spiritual, work and meditation/relaxation, emotion and cognition are all effaced in the self-recognition of consciousness as self and the world. In advanced meditators, with their aligned cognitive-affective-behavioral processes, Bhāvanā 'recreates' the world. It is emphasized and can be seen that this intensity and immersion of Bhāvanā in advanced practitioners must necessarily come from intense and immersive training as well as transformation of affective processes from āyurveda-Yoga-Sāṃkhya and Bhakti to finally fructify into a Bhāvanā that *intentionally creates and recreates* the phenomenal as well as inter-subjective worlds.

Thus far, we have travelled a long journey and landscaped models of contemplation and transformation of affective processes in Indian knowledge traditions. It is clear that Indian knowledge traditions have recognized and detailed a series of contemplative practices for the transformation of affect depending on the preparation and eligibility of the practitioner. We also see that affect is recognized at all levels from physiological processes and body as seen in āyurveda, sensory processes in Yoga, self-other processes and aesthetic processes in rasa theory and relational socio-emotional processes in Bhakti.

In all the frameworks, raw affect must be sequentially transformed and re-cognized. This process of transformation leads finally to fruition of Bhāvanā – an intentional cognitive-immersive-affective and behavioural response and engagement with the world to create and recreate the world.

The understanding of Bhāvanā and contemplation use emotion as a central instrumentality and prescribes specific and customized pathways towards well-being. The sequencing of the models in this chapter moves from the most concrete to the most profound radical self-recognition.

We started with this essay with the claim that affect is the binding feature in the IKT and is intricately tied to self as Ahamkāra, Ahambhāva and Asmitā. In general, Ahamkāra is understood as a self-awareness with a sense of ownership (Siderits et al., 2011), Asmitā in Yoga-Sāṃkhya refers to the first non-reflexive separative awareness, which forms the sense of ownership and a large social self. Vairāgya, therefore, is one of the transformative methodologies to understand the Asmitā. Finally, it is only with the transformed affect, that one arrives at Ahambhāva – an intentional and recreated self – arising from the recognition of non-duality between consciousness with name, form, quality and intention and consciousness as such, *unbounded* by name, form quality and intention. Thus, self-transformation means emotional transformation and vice-versa.

As several commentators have noted, consciousness is central to Indian thought and the Indic civilizational heritage is seen through this tremendous intellectual energy invested into questions of consciousness, validity of cognition, affect, action, social and relational worlds and well-being. We also mentioned the philosophical debates about the nature of consciousness in the current context, with Ganeri arguing that it is attention, and not self, that binds the living systems. Ganeri's argument is philosophically interesting, no doubt, but does nothing to inform living practice in pre- and post-meditative episodes, where the self emerges and must then relate to the environment. In so far as Ganeri brings the Indian contributions in focus, it is indeed important, but the dichotomy of this world and the other world, inherent in the Euro-American idea of 'transcendence' is perpetuated by focussing on attention, which is a mere instrumentation of self as consciousness. In the Kāshmir Trika Śaiva Śāktādvaita thought and practice, the fruition and culmination of the wisdom of contemplative traditions, show that instead of merely focusing on the role of affective processes as subservient to cognition, affect and its transformation is central in the understanding of self – which is well-being in embodied living and becoming.

Note

1 This chapter has been published in the SAGE journal – *Culture and Psychology*, with the title, 'Conceptualising Bhavana: How do contemplative Hindu traditions inform understanding emotions and well-being?' The link is DOI: 10.1177/1354067X221118919. journals.sagepub.com/home/cap

References

Bansat-Boudon, L. (2014). On Śaiva terminology: Some key issues of understanding. *Journal of Indian Philosophy*, *42*(1), 39–97.

Barrett, L. F. (2012). Emotions are real. *Emotion*, *12*(3), 413.

Barrett, L. F., Mesquita, B., & Gendron, M. (2011). Context in emotion perception. *Current Directions in Psychological Science*, *20*(5), 286–290.

Barrett, L. F., & Wager, T. D. (2006). The structure of emotion: Evidence from neuroimaging studies. *Current Directions in Psychological Science*, *15*(2), 79–83.

Chadha, M. (2011). Self-awareness: Eliminating the myth of the 'invisible subject'. *Philosophy East and West*, *61*(3), 453–467. https://www.jstor.org/stable/2301535

Cornelissen, M. (2003). The need for the Indian tradition. *Psychological Studies*, 48(3), 38–52.

Cornelissen, M. (2007). In defence of rigorous subjectivity. *Transpersonal Psychology Review*, *11*(1), 8–18.

Cornelissen, M. (2016). Types of Knowledge and their Use in Psychology: Towards Rigorous Subjectivity. In A. Dalal, & K. Ravi (Eds.), *Qualitative Research on Illness, Wellbeing and Self-Growth: Contemporary Indian perspectives*. Routledge India, 45–58.

Cornelissen, R. M. M. (2014). A commentary on 'positive psychology and Indian psychology: In need of mutual reinforcement'. *Psychological Studies*, *59*(2), 103–104. https://doi.org/10.1007/s12646-014-0248-8

Deutsch, E. (2021). Studies in comparative aesthetics (Monographs of the society for Asian and comparative philosophy, no. 2) (pp. 1–23). University of Hawaii Press.

Fort, A. O. (1998). *Jīvanmukti in transformation: Embodied liberation in Advaita and neo-Vedānta*. State University of New York Press.

Fort, A. O. (1999). On Destroying the Mind: The 'Yogasūtras' in Vidyāraṇya's 'Jīvanmuktiviveka'. *Journal of Indian Philosophy*, *27*(4), 377–395.

Fox, E. (2008). *Emotion science cognitive and neuroscientific approaches to understanding human emotions*. Palgrave Macmillan.

Frazier, J. (2011). Reason and rationality in Hindu studies. *Journal of Hindu Studies*, *4*, 1–11. https://doi.org/doi:10.1093/jhs/hir014

Frazier, J. (2020). 'The view from above': A theory of comparative philosophy. *Religious Studies*, *56*(1), 32–48.

Fredrickson, B. L. (2001). The role of positive emotions in positive psychology: The broaden-and-build theory of positive emotions. *American Psychologist*, *56*(3), 218.

Fredrickson, B. L. (2004). The broaden–and–build theory of positive emotions. *Philosophical Transactions of the Royal Society of London. Series B: Biological Sciences*, *359*(1449), 1367–1377.

Ganeri, J. (2017). *Attention, not self*. Oxford University Press.

Gupta, B. (2021). *An introduction to Indian philosophy: Perspectives on reality, knowledge, and freedom*. Routledge.

Haberman, D. L. (2001). *Acting as a way of salvation: A study of Rāgānugā Bhakti Sādhana*. Motilal Banarsidass Publ.

Haberman, D. L. (2003). *The Bhaktirasāmṛtasindhu of Rūpa Gosvāmin* (Vol. 4). Motilal Banarsidass Publ.

Hayes, G. A., & Timalsina, S. (2017). *Introduction to 'cognitive science and the study of Yoga and Tantra'*. Multidisciplinary Digital Publishing Institute.

Higgins, K. M. (2007). An alchemy of emotion: Rasa and aesthetic breakthroughs. *The Journal of Aesthetics and Art Criticism*, *65*(1), 43–54.

Hillman, J. (2013). *Emotion: A comprehensive phenomenology of theories and their meanings for*. Routledge.

Izard, C. E. (1991a). Defining emotions and their relations to cognition, action, and personality. In *The psychology of emotions* (pp. 27–57). Springer US. https://doi.org/10.1007/978-1-4899-0615-1_2

Izard, C. E. (1991b). *The psychology of emotions*. Springer Science & Business Media.

Kasturirangan, R., Guha, N., & Ram-Prasad, C. (2011). Indian cognitivism and the phenomenology of conceptualization. *Phenomenology and the Cognitive Sciences*, *10*(2), 277–296.

Lakshmanjoo, S. (2015). *The manual for self realization. 112 meditations of the Vijnana Bhairava Tantra*. Lakshmanjoo Academy Book Series. Lakshmanjoo Academy, USA.

Lynch, O. M. (1990). *Divine passions*. Oxford University Press.

Lyons, W. (1999). The philosophy of cognition and emotion. In T. Dalgleish & J. Power (Eds.) *Handbook of cognition and emotion* (pp. 21–44). John Wiley and Sons.

Mitra, R. (2016). Decolonizing immersion: Translation, spectatorship, rasa theory and contemporary British dance. *Performance Research*, *21*(5), 89–100.

Mohanty, J. N. (2001). *Explorations in philosophy: Indian philosophy* (p. 229) (Edited by B. Gupta). Oxford University Press.

Nair, S. (2013). Rasa theory and neural mechanism. *New Zealand Online Journal of Interdisciplinary Studies*, *1*(2), 1–27.

Ollett, A. (2013). What is Bhavana? *Journal of Indian Philosophy*, *41*(3), 221.

Oman, D. (2013). Defining religion and spirituality. *Handbook of the Psychology of Religion and Spirituality*, 2, 23–47.

Oman, D. (2019). Introduction to the special section: Psychology of Indian spirituality and religion, emerging perspectives. *Psychology of Religion and Spirituality*, *11*(2), 87–90. https://doi.org/10.1037/rel0000256

Oman, D., & Lukoff, D. (2018). Mental health, religion, and spirituality. In D. Oman (Ed.), *Why Religion and Spirituality Matter for Public Health. Religion, Spirituality and Health: A Social Scientific Approach*, vol 2. Springer. https://doi.org/10.1007/978-3-319-73966-3_13

Pandit, B. N. (1977). *Aspects of Kashmir Saivism*. Utpal Publications.

Pandit, L. (2004). The psychology and aesthetics of love: Sringara, Bhavana, and Rasadhvani in Gora. In P. Hogan & L. Pandit (Eds.), *Rabindranath Tagore: Universality and Tradition* (pp. 141–174). Fairleigh Dickinson University Press.

Pandit, S. A. (2011). The concept of 'Rasa' in Indian psychology: A preliminary qualitative study. *Journal of Psychosocial Research*, *6*(1), 139.

Pandit, S. A. (2020). Viveka and Vairāgya: Empirical possibilities for cognitive concepts in Indian psychology. *Journal of Psychosocial Research*, *15*(2), 497–507.

Pandit, S. A. (2021). Advaita: Oneness as a lived reality – examining aspects of a profound and a radical psychology. *Psychology and Developing Societies*. https://doi.org/10.1177/09713336211038814

Pandit, S., & Misra, G. (2013). Emotions in Indian psychology. In G. Misra (Ed.), *Psychology and psychoanalysis* (pp. 663–691). Centre for Studies in Civilizations.

Paranjpe, A. C. (2009). In defence of an Indian approach to the psychology of emotion. *Psychological Studies*, *54*(1), 3–22.

Ram-Prasad, C. (2018). *Human being, bodily being: Phenomenology from classical India*. Oxford University Press.

Rukmani, T. S. (2005). Revisiting the Jivanmukti question in Samkhya in the context of the Samkhyasutra. *Studies in the History of Religions*, *110*, 61.

Sen, R. S., & Pandit, S. (2013). Exploring Vātsalyam: The emotion of love for the child. *Psychology and Developing Societies*, *25*(1), 165–193. https://doi.org/10.1177/0971333613477303

Shweder, R. A., Haidt, J., Horton, R., & Joseph, C. (1993). The cultural psychology of the emotions. In L. Barrett, M. Lewis, & J. Haviland-Jones (Eds.), *Handbook of emotions* (3rd ed., pp. 409–431). Guilford Press.

Siderits, M., Thompson, E., & Zahavi, D. (2011). *Self, no self?: Perspectives from analytical, phenomenological, and Indian traditions*. Oxford University Press.

Singh, J. (1990). *The doctrine of recognition: A translation of the Pratyabhijnahrdayam with an introduction and notes, by Ksemaraja*. SUNY Press.

Strongman, K. T. (1996). *The psychology of emotion: Theories of emotion in perspective*. John Wiley & Sons.

Timalsina, S. (2007). Metaphor, Rasa, and Dhvani: Suggested meaning in tantric esotericism. *Method & Theory in the Study of Religion*, *19*(1–2), 134–162.

Timalsina, S. (2008). *Consciousness in Indian philosophy: The Advaita doctrine of 'awareness only'*. Routledge.

Timalsina, S. (2012). Body, self, and healing in Tantric ritual paradigm. *The Journal of Hindu Studies*, *5*(1), 30–52.

Timalsina, S. (2015). *Tantric visual culture: A cognitive approach*. Routledge.

Timalsina, S. (2016). A cognitive approach to tantric language. *Religions*, *7*(12), 139.

Varela, F. J., Thompson, E., & Rosch, E. (2017). *The embodied mind, revised edition: Cognitive science and human experience*. MIT press.

Walsh, R. (2015). Wise ways of seeing: Wisdom and perspectives. *Integral Review: A Transdisciplinary & Transcultural Journal for New Thought, Research, & Praxis*, *11*(2) 157–175.

Walsh, R., & Shapiro, S. L. (2006). The meeting of meditative disciplines and Western psychology: A mutually enriching dialogue. *American Psychologist*, *61*(3), 227.

5 Pramā

Consciousness and valid cognition

Introduction: Consciousness and cognition

Do we see reality as it is? What do cognitive science and Indian psychology say about this? Indian philosophy even with the focus on lived experience as in Buddhism, granted more to sensorially accessed reality. This differentiates the Buddhists from the empiricists of Europe. If we don't see reality as it is, then the question is – Are there means to 'valid cognition'? If we don't perceive reality as it is, then all existing knowledge, reasoning, and logic based on senses and sense-based instrumentation are put into question. Can we perceive reality with grounded body awareness, a transformed affect and valid cognition? In the last two chapters, the driving point about the organization of Indian knowledge traditions was that grounded body awareness and a transformed affect, lead to Pramā – valid cognition. It is easy and trendy to map consciousness with cognition as such, but as the book has been emphasizing again and again, in Indian knowldge tradition (IKT), we look at the integration of all processes with consciousness – recognized self. If so, can we then recreate the world that we see, consciously and mindfully? These are the three questions, which this chapter discusses in an Indian Psychology of cognition.

I teach a course that tries to bridge understanding of contemporary psychology with a Yoga curriculum – where my students are Yoga and meditation teachers and students. The bridging is relevant because Yoga teachers in contemporary times routinely get referrals for people who are experiencing distress in both body-mind. Many Yoga teachers make efforts to secure formal qualifications in psychology, but many do a casual form of counselling! So, the objective of this course is to delineate both the worldviews such that appropriate boundaries of what can be done or not can be identified in their practice. There are no 'integrative health' courses or programs in India as such. Many Yoga students, both from 'east' and 'west', would like to include Yoga in their daily practice and yet might also work with counsellors or psychiatrists. Most times, people struggling with distress have been advised by all systems – mainstream and 'alternative' simply because of the immensity of distress and desperation thereof. People

DOI: 10.4324/9781003336204-5

and families in India meet counsellors, psychologists and therapists along with Yoga teachers, Vaidya-s, Homeopathy, and everything else. Most people who seek to integrate these two helping paradigms from a background of psychology, may not have a clear understanding of how different paradigms work. Similarly, traditional teachings of Yoga-Sāṃkhya do not include contemporary psychology perspectives. When students study psychology, the bridging of concepts, theories, and frameworks from two different world-views is not available to them. Thus, they may choose one perspective over the other as a binary without looking at possible 'integration'. My courses, which attempt this integration, are a great learning experience for me – I am able to refine my own understanding as mirrored through student questions.

While discussing the conceptual relationship between consciousness, cognition and self, particularly in the Vedānta, the frequent issues related to consciousness as 'God', consciousness as immaterial, and consciousness as emergent from cognition or brain process come up. After the discussions on the consciousness as self – Advaita Vedāntic perspective, Yogacāra – a Buddhist view that is tilted towards consciousness as cognition (Vijnāpti mātra) and therefore cause of suffering and the Yoga-Sāṃkhya view that acknowledges consciousness *in interaction* with materiality, one of my students asked me this question which has triggered this chapter.

The student asked, 'even if we are not able to experience that we (self) are "that" consciousness, which is God, don't you think the *sheer belief* that we are God is an excellent and a good enough belief'.

De-cluttering cognition, religion, God and consciousness

Since the advances in mind sciences, as mentioned in the earlier chapters, consciousness is conceptually tied to the brain processes and the body in mainstream psychology. Indeed, the recent advances in cognitive psychology have flipped several earlier held notions which arose from the behaviourist paradigm about concepts such as memory, attention and learning. Earlier experiments were divorced from the body and brain, leaving aside cultural contextual facets such as language, thinking and creativity in their proclamation of knowledge. Be that as it may, now cognitive scientists across the world are acutely mindful of these limitations of early psychology theory and consistently attempt to theoretically factor in the body, language, motivation and other contexts. Research on attention, for example, has shown that attention circuits are not limited to executive attention alone and change in quality according to the function and task, including emotional regulation in children (Rothbart et al., 2011). Posner and Rothbart (2007) have shown that there are three distinct attentional pathways in the brain, *orienting* being one of the pathways, and *alerting* and *planning* are the other two pathways. The quality of attention, neurotransmitters and disorders are differently implicated in each pathway.

Second, research has shown that reaching and grasping actions have different attentional processing, and objects placed near the hands can have an impact on attentional processing. This intriguing finding shows the role of intention prior to attention. Attention as a cohering and executive process is also well-reviewed (Pratt et al., 2015). Researchers (Pratt et al., 2015) have noted that 'intention to perform' itself changes attentional orientation and processing. Similarly, postures which have been tested, only standing and sitting till now; no yogic postures as yet! Postures seem to have an impact on attentional processing. There is some evidence of hand grip bias in attentional processing and that has been connected to the magnocellular visual system. The immediate questions that arise here from an IP perspective are related to Hatha Yoga/āsana and neurophenomenology, esp. the postures that have been qualified as 'good' for meditation. It seems amenable to both neuroscience and phenomenology that we can examine the alignments of the meditative postures as preparatory steps of attentional training and regulation. Attention now refers to a broad range of processes that tie in contents of consciousness, provide gain of function and are central to the survival of the body-mind – as a set of processes which focus, filter, gain/amplify and cohere with external and internal awareness – sensations, perceptions and cognition. Scientists now are able to primarily derive their results from visual attention but acknowledge that more work needs to be done on auditory and other sensory circuits for understanding attention. Attention, as can be immediately recognized, is the initiating point in all Yoga and Yogācāra practices. As we discussed in the chapter on embodied consciousness, Patanjali's Yoga sutra (PYS), Hatha Yoga practices, Rāja yoga, and indeed the yogic method as such is premised on attentional processes in the transformation of the contents of consciousness and the automatic untrained, cognizing that has been the base for most psychology till now. On the other side, there has been a substantial body of research that now has shown consensus that attentional regulation, particularly using Yoga, has a significant impact on cognitive and physiological processes and affects regulation as well as broader concepts such as health. In the IKT, the objective and intention of attention regulation is the process of immersion and transformation of conventional body-mind ways of being rather than affect regulation or relaxation. The question – why should the body relax when *attending* Yoga practice runs contrary to the idea of survival related vigilance! The positive impact mechanism of attentional regulation on health as such, documented in studies, is a welcome side effect not the main effect. The main effect and object of leveraging attention are self-knowing (which includes self-regulation) and self-abiding. Earlier assumptions in psychology research were riddled with corrosive dichotomies such as the Cartesian dualism, and therefore, several books and well as research papers spend a considerable amount of time, in the current context on 'embodied cognition, situated cognition' or enactivism – which attempt to theoretically link cognition and body and/or cognition and the context and cognition and action. These can be considered as advances, given the background of Euro-American psychology.

When it comes to body awareness, attention as 'conscious' attention, with allocation of cognitive resources, embodied cognition as well as the relationship between attention and action have been most revealing, showing the blind spots in research till now. This attentional process is most clearly seen in working memory function, sensory perception and action bi-direction loops. Studies identify key points from experiments. Firstly, attention is used as an adaptive capability based on current needs/tasks. Attention and visual systems are bi-directionally interlinked; eye movements show the direction/orientation of attention. Recall that Posner and Rothbart (2007) have shown that there are three distinct attentional pathways in the brain, 'orienting' being one of the pathways. In the IKT, the word *antardriṣti* has been used to 'change the flow of prāṇa'. Antardriṣti or changing the focus of inner gaze through Yoga nidra or āsana-s is clearly linked with attentional training in the traditional texts as well. Another question is – in what stages of attention or immersion can specific mudrās or gestures cause and sustain attentional shifts – as this has been stated in the traditional taṇtra and hath-yoga texts? This, as we shall see later, is closely related to the tantric practice of visualization of Nyāsa, Mudrā, Yaṇtra and Mantra. IP has other questions as well – in what stages of attention or immersion can specific mudrā-s or conscious hand-face gestures *cause and sustain* attentional shifts? To emphasize, research in attention now acknowledges the basic embodied nature of visual attention and the position of the body or objects or the world as such. Psychologists in India need to pay attention to these new results!

The question Indian psychology is asking is – Is it possible to be aware and attentive without an object of awareness or a task/intention? In this condition, does attention become 'choice-less'/'Witness' or 'Sākśi'? Is choice less objectless ownerless attention a step closer to consciousness as such, which then plays and decides to attend specifically?

Note also that very few experimental studies have been done on shared attention. Attentional processes in real life and situated in contexts also account for actions of others, inferences and shared attentional processes. Frequently, experimental studies create experimental situations which were divorced from action and varieties of possible actions by the single subject. Recall the classic definition of social psychology by Allport about the imagined, implied and actual presence of others. Are single subjects also attending to the implied and imagined presence of others in their experimental tasks? Researchers identify these constraints with specific references and yet then proceed to identify the specific relationship between eye saccades and perception and action, say. Action is understood as a series of unfolding neural events that require cognitive slices of planning, control and initiation, maintenance and stopping. What about awareness of others in this dynamic? Theories need to explain feature binding and changes in attentional processing for these series of steps. Indeed shared attentional processes are central in the Indian context, with its focus on a relational and a collective self, esp. the guru-disciple or the rasa tradition. This is clearly seen even now in training for Indian music and dance, martial arts like Kalari, for example.

Finally, the relationship between consciousness, attention and conscious attention is fascinating when viewed from the perspective of empirical evidence. Some theories have been proposed to claim that attention and consciousness are two distinct dissociated concepts in several conditions! The attention-consciousness relationship is put on a theoretical spectrum – from those theories that look at attention and consciousness as identical to those which look at these as completely dissociated under some conditions. The key question here is – How are the researchers and authors defining consciousness? In other chapters, a similar debate on how are scholars defining 'self' is indicated (Ram-Prasad, 2010). As mentioned, there is no clear agreement, but those theories that look at consciousness as dissociated from attention, can either look at consciousness as the 'overflow' – which many Euro-American philosophers argue for. Note that this understanding of 'overflow' or the panpsychist argument, as discussed by Block, Tononi, Koch and several scientists and scholars, may not be similar to the framework of consciousness in Upaniṣads and Vedānta, as these scholars are speculating one mind, multiple consciousnesses as compared with one consciousness, multiple minds. This is in addition to the fact that Advaita and Vedānta arise from a very subtle lived experience of oneness of consciousness as self and mind as appearance!

Notwithstanding, some Buddhist schools view consciousness as arising from the cognitive process and, therefore, place attention at the centre of consciousness (see 'Attention, not self' by Ganeri, 2017). Similar to this brief discussion, mainstream concepts in psychology can be reviewed (Harre, 2006). Concepts such as memory, esp. working memory have been shown to expand due to visualization meditation (Buttle, 2011); research has taken an alt route and looked at 'mind wandering' (Hasenkamp et al., 2012) creativity and flow with meditation (Yang et al., 2019) and non-dual awareness (we saw research by Josipovic in earlier chapters), etc. At this point, it suffices to note that at a conventional level, this framework of research works with meditators and looks at the possibility of cognition and consciousness, which feeds mainstream psychology knowledge production. Does it illuminate the Indian Psychology framework as it is specified? Well, the answer is clearly negative. Thus, this route, even when it uses the first person experience of monks, does not present the completely original perspectives that arose in the Indian context.

Most psychologists in India, have pretended to be blind of the interconnections between religion, God, spirituality and consciousness as organized in the Indian mindset, which otherwise would be an important subject of enquiry given the diversity in the Indian context; psychologists and philosophers across the Euro-American world have addressed this recently with a lot of care and rigour (Belzen, 2010; Dy-Liacco et al., 2009; Evans & Manis, 2010; Kaplan, 2009; Mickey, 2015; Oman, 2013). This blind spot is particularly damaging because stereotypical errors abound, even among academicians in India, quite at odds with social and cultural investment into these ideas in the Indian context. This also demonstrates the propensity of psychologists to play safe or remain insular in their quest to follow the largely Euro-American mainstream psychology in India and secure tenures. The historical fact of a painful partition on religious lines might have set the tone in the immediate aftermath of independence. Across the world, the conflations of religion, God, spirituality and well-being were addressed insufficiently till about 40 years ago.

In the recent 40 years, there has been a surge of interest and possibly a pathway to look at these interconnections from a psychologist's lens. Religion and the idea of God, have largely been studied as cultural beliefs and world-views. Recently, religion and the ideas of God, have been discussed among cognitive scientists and psychologists from an evolutionary perspective. It can be argued that God is a good belief and affects our behaviour in a positive way, as a lot of research on religiosity, spirituality and psychology shows, in terms of cognition, affect and behaviour, giving positive results when it is associated with values and strengths. At the same time, the opposite is also true that God and religions constitute belief clusters that can play havoc in cases of dogma, delusions and 'religiosity/dogmatic religiosity' and lead to further dogma, stereotypes, religious persecution, radicalization, hatred, discrimination and violence. At different levels of analysis, all the above are true and no single and reductive direction of argument can explain the rich psychological phenomena of religious thinking adequately. For example, religiosity and magical beliefs are more likely to be found in the contents of consciousness in disorders such as schizophrenia or bipolar disorders. Therefore, a disambiguation of authentic religious spirituality and mental illness is a serious task for psychologists, esp. in India, where the cultures frequently provide both dogmatic as well as healing pathways to express and resolve psychological conflicts. An example of this cultural framework of embodying, expressing and healing psychological conflicts or states of well-being is the ritual practices of *Theyyam* in the Southern state of Kerala in India. For the unaware, Kerala temples diligently follow the tantric practices of a systematic embodying of states of mind – including the violent and aggressive Demi-Gods and Gods! In a shared sense making cultural context, a systematic preparation is done for a conventionally constituted self through changes in diet/food, meditation, changes in costume and music, such that the person is inducted into an altered state of consciousness, to become that God! The specific psychological (cognitive, affective and behavioural) *persona* of the Demi-God or God/Goddess is evoked/instantiated. This ritual continues for a limited period of time and during this altered state of consciousness, both for the individual who is 'performing' the Demi-God, God/Goddess and the collective, which is witnessing and participating are provided *the altered space-time* to resolve their psychological conflicts and experience individual as well as collective well-being. Thus, note the cultural complexity and richness of the Indian knowledge traditions and the inadequacy of the contemporary psychologies of conceptualizing such and similar interconnections between religion, God, spirituality and consciousness.

Mainstream psychology considers God and religion as a cluster of beliefs or as schema and scripts in a strictly isolated sense. Consciousness seems to be difficult to be accommodated here. Clearly, consciousness is not a belief or a cluster of beliefs or integrated beliefs, affect and behaviours. Even among Yogācāra, consciousness arises as a cognizing process – an existential malady! Consciousness, at least as has been understood in recent years and studied in psychology through neuroscience is a lived experience – both embodied and transcendental. With this narrow limited definition and large gaps in a research-based understanding, only dogma of the scientific kind can abound. In any case, belief *in* God and God *as a* belief/not 'real' have two different meanings. A belief in God necessarily entails a world-view about the sense of sacredness, nature of the world, relationships and the kind of God/Goddess/s, moral action, prescriptive, proscriptive and injunctions, etc. Indeed, in reference to the current discourse on environment and sustainability, research has looked at sacred ecologies that arise from indigenous world-views (Johnston, 2006; Khisty, 2006; Singh, 2017). Thus, it is imperative that even while discussing 'belief', we need to differentiate between the Abrahamic religious world-views and the Hindu/Buddhist/Tantric view in specific, where Demi-Gods, Gods and Goddesses are all expressions of consciousness and happily co-exist with the Advaita Vedānta realization of 'awareness' alone. Anthropologists and increasingly psychologists have studied the culturally agreed-upon pathways of healing through temple rituals (Ranganathan, 2018; Smith, 2010). Even within this non-judgemental shared sense making, note that pathology is identified and dealt with by the communities; their methods of recognition and healing are different. Another example, which has been studied in reference to psychopathology and cultural pathways of healing by invoking the idea of God/Goddess in a particular context of embodied consciousness and spiritual well-being are the studies conducted on ritual exorcism in the North Indian State of Rajasthan and the town of Mehendipur through the Deity called Balaji (Nathawat & Menon, 2018; Pakaslahti, 1998; Sood, 2016). Critical theories, psychologists and anthropologists have particularly focused on cultural pathways of recognizing and healing psychological disorders through these cultural world-views, cognitive frameworks and practices (Nathawat & Menon, 2018; Sax & Weinhold, 2012; Smith, 2010; Timalsina, 2012).

It is sufficient to note that a narrow idea of religion and its imposition on the Indian context has played havoc. The broader Indian world-view, in general, allows for multiple beings who, in Hindu and Buddhist metaphysics, represent states of consciousness embodied through particular forms, names and qualities! This can be seen in abundant textual references as well.

The key point to emphasize here is that at the most general level, the mainstream Euro-American psychology has yet to connect the diverse facets of being and becoming through an authentic body centred psychology, where the idea and lived experiences of body and embodiment itself are *still not* adequately detailed out to describe, explain and theorize on aspects of human psyche and behaviours, including positive pathways to healing through altered states of consciousness. Therefore, this first task for a Euro-American psychology would be to resolve its inner contradictions on body, mind and consciousness itself before becoming worthy of exporting psychology to the third world. In contrast to a physical body and computational mind centred psychology, the Indian organization of knowledge proposes that *only* and only a consciousness-centred psychology can best describe and theorize on human psyche and behaviours including pathways to healing and well-being. True that the Indian framework of consciousness is difficult to accommodate in the current philosophy of science. Be that as it may. Finally, a consciousness centred psychology will alone be able to adequately theorize embodied and transcendental, cognitive and trans-cognitive, cultural and trans-cultural aspects of experience as such, being and becoming for all being through the detailed frameworks of psychologies at different levels of consciousness and their concomitant cognitions, affect and ways of relating to the world.

In social psychology, an influential theory – the terror management theory (TMT) – proposes that there is a fundamental terror that all beings encounter and the psyche develops a variety of beliefs, actions and affective responses to counter this terror. God as a belief or a belief in the just world is developed to counter this terror. In the Indic perspective, this terror is accepted as valid at certain levels of awareness and the culture supports an acceptance of death (Inbadas, 2016, 2017, 2018). However, Indic perspective would map other states of awareness to question *the absolutist* premise of TMT since it would present several documented instances of meditators who have conquered that fear of death, experientially and even without constructing the belief of an anthropomorphic saviour 'God'. A recent example of this would be the documented instance of Sri Ramana (Kamath & Ramanasramam, 2003). As a young boy, Sri Ramana was gripped with the intense anxiety and fear of death. Instead of denying the fear of death or finding some symbolic immortality as TMT would suggest, the young teenager, accepted the fear of death and *proceeded to actively seek the experience of death* and examine what happens. He experienced that the awareness continued to calmly observe the body as dead. After some time, he was able to 'enter back into' the body and experience bodily awareness. Some may argue that Sri Ramana had a 'depersonalization' experience. That is not the point. The point to note here is – not all people or all cultures deny the intense fear of death through terror management or symbolic immortality or God as belief. Second, is there indeed a profound transformation in the psyche – cognition, affect and behaviour, through addressing the terror of death; then it follows that the role of psychologists would be to ask *why*?

The fundamental divergence from other philosophies and IKT is – Is God a belief or is it an experience of recognition/awareness of consciousness alone? This question gets a diverse set of answers in the Indic worldview. Whatever, may be internal differences between different perspectives in the Indian knowledge traditions on conceptualizing 'God', God as 'consciousness holding name and form' is fundamentally a matter of a profound experience and thereafter of reasoning *and, lastly, belief*. It is amazing that psychological theory is the opposite to this sequence and probably remains at the belief level. In IKT, belief is not denied but is also not separated from action and lived experience. Experience, realization and recognition are the first principles and an anthropomorphic God/Goddess and related cluster of beliefs is one of the many frameworks of God as such of a consciousness centred psychology.

What about fake Gurus and God delusions or delusions of grandeur, frequently seen in clinical psychology practice? It is clear that true and lived consciousness-based well-being is separated from delusions by at least one criterion – the presence of self-acceptance, acceptance of mortality and compassion for self and others. Delusions of grandeur, as seen in clinical work, arise from a disjunction. In the Indian context, several people, esp. gurus are treated as 'living Gods'. It is sufficient to note that the self-recognized/realized person is not 'otherworldly' or transcendental as commonly understood. The Jivanmukta has been studied in the context of contemporary Gurus such as Swami Vivekananda, Sri Aurobindo and others. Contributions by Fort to the embodied practice of liberation is worthy of note for a detailed examination (Fort, 1998; Fort & Mumme, 1996; Rukmini, 1981). The Indian conceptualization of a lived freedom – stems from an unbroken history of documenting first person experiences through a life trajectory and not episodes of altered state of consciousness; not just of a single lineage but multiple lineages; both with and without a formal rigorous training.

Finally, students have asked, is meditation and God some kind of brainwashing or hypnosis? Certainly, sometimes, people have gone into states of consciousness which were different from their usual awareness due to various factors such as drugs, radical food and temperature shifts, sleep deprivation, stress, etc. In several indigenous cultural traditions, systematic and formal 'induction techniques' are used similar to the case of hypnosis. Even accounting for these episodes, it is important to note that, self-recognition/realization in the IKT is not an altered state of consciousness, although it may look like such in the beginning! Certainly, self-recognition/realization cannot be hypnotized for long periods of time. 'Realization' means abiding in knowing the nature of self as consciousness, without doubt or confusion. Having glimpses of altered states, seeing visions and listening to sounds are great experiences, no doubt; they are certainly not the realization and abiding in the knowing of *self as consciousness*. The dystopian idea of a breakdown of a psyche and then its reclamation, which seekers frequently visualize, as they are influenced by the Campbell and Jungian idea of a 'Hero/Heroine' may be relevant in case of torture victims; the case of meditation practice is far away. Whatever trauma might have happened, meditative practice is a healing pathway which recognizes and accepts all experiences rather than an unfortunate breakdown of self.

In summary, two points are noted: One, the conceptualization of God is not a person but recognition and abiding of self as consciousness, which makes IKT psychological and not social or philosophical. We may or may not use the word concept God or we may use multiple Gods/Goddesses/Demi-Gods! Second, recognizing that consciousness as self in first person, is different from the mundane experience of 'I' consciousness; Undoubtedly, refining of cognitive processes such as attention, working memory, thinking, reasoning and examination of beliefs lead to a subtle and rigorous subjectivity. This needs training. IKT emphasizes this training as 'jnāna yoga'. These points make the idea of God in Indian psychology as remarkable and linked intrinsically to consciousness as such. Consciousness alone is seen as sacred and obviously is different from the idea of 'spirituality' as well as 'religiosity' as commonly understood.

With a broken understanding of the body-senses-mind as a system, inadequate instrumentation to study the brain-senses-body-society and a wonderfully complex social context, do we see the reality as it is – in lived reality? Recently, Cognitive scientists such as Hoffman (Hoffman et al., 2015) have proposed that perhaps we don't see reality as it is! Hoffman and colleagues propose that the body-brain-mind act as an 'interface' and is 'hacked' towards ensuring survival and not the truth of reality. Thus, to ensure survival, the body-senses-brain *bend*/revise/obfuscate/hide reality. Hoffman proposes that the purpose of sensory processing – which is a pivot for a positivistic empiricist research, is to just identify survival benefits rather than see reality as it is. Indeed, Hoffman goes on to propose that the purpose of what we sense through our sensory modalities is to *hide reality and conjure a reality fit for survival!* This should not surprise us at all; it is known that both dreams as well as hallucinations conjure a reality, with full or partial sensory experiences in order to cope and process our interaction with the reality.

What is striking is that it fundamentally questions the premises of positivism and empiricism in the philosophy of science. This fascinating proposal, using simulation research, puts a challenge on the Euro-American idea of casual empiricism. As is well-known in the Indian context, advaita proposes that the world as it appears to us, including the body-mind that we inhabit, the relationships that we engage in and the beliefs, including the beliefs of God/religion and consciousness that we indulge as 'truth', are all obfuscating the reality of consciousness; IKT further states that the only way we can recognize this obfuscation or 'superimposition' is through refined awareness alone. *This 'fundamental cognitive error' is called 'adhyasa' in the IKT texts and the pathway to recognize this fundamental cognitive error is through the cultivation of attention. Thus, the question of cognition is better framed as the question of valid cognition, regardless of the advances in experimentation, instrumentation and all other concerns in mainstream psychology.*

We started this section with the student questions – a muddle of beliefs in and about God/consciousness/religion. We abstracted research on attention as a set of cognitive processes, and we close with attention alone. Indian Psychology, including the Buddhist Yogācāra and Hindu frameworks, then focus on attention alone as a pathway to refined awareness. Hoffman and others are further examining the idea that consciousness could be a network of conscious agents (Fields et al., 2018). At this point, discussions become speculative and not taken as questions of psychology. The point to hold on here is that clearly, there is more to consciousness as such than cognition and that the body-senses-cognition system as it exists is probably not geared to examine the reality as it is, empirically. Yogācāra in the Indian tradition was precisely interested in this question through the analysis of cognition-consciousness-perception nexus while pivoting on attention. We will briefly understand that in the next section.

Indian psychology: Examining valid cognition

As many have suggested, Yogācāra is often wrongly translated as subjective idealism/solipsism due to their fundamental tenet of – 'vijnāpti mātra', which is variously translated as cognition alone, consciousness alone or mind alone. It is obvious from these variety of translations that the mistakes are due to the confusions about mind, consciousness and cognition in English or in the philosophical understanding in the Euro-American mainstream. On a broader level, as scholars have stated, In the IKT, the central question was of epistemology – of we know, what we know as real, rather than ontology and metaphysics, which are seen as primary concerns in the Euro-American philosophy and therefore, seep in through the philosophies of sciences and humanities. Indeed, scholars of Yogācāra Buddhism make three important points. One, their analysis starts from the analysis of suffering, which is lived experience; in the next step, Yogācāra School intensively focusses on the *cognizing process* that is central to psychology of suffering/misery as well as liberation from misery/suffering. The logic of Yogācāra school, gives the profound insight that *ordinary* cognitive operations cause suffering. This is similar to the Vedāntic idea that we do not cognize the reality as it is and this mis-perception called 'Avidya' causes misery and suffering. Thus, moment by moment perception of the body-senses-changing context and the process *that cognizes all as real,* was seen as cause of suffering. If so, then valid cognition is object of enquiry than any cognition that goes in fragmented variables in cognition. This is important to grasp and appreciate.

When we cognize something as real, we have now formed a cluster of words, forms, concepts, and beliefs around that experience; Thus, the process of concept formation and concept continuation among humans is central to understand. Finally, in the non-dual Kashmiri Śaiva and Tantra, we see a radical flip! A radical psychology of intentionally cultivating or **making of the mind – manasikarana, esp., after the recognition that the world that we perceive is not the reality as it is.**

In an interesting paper on what the authors term as 'Indian cognitivism', Kasturirangan, Guha and Ramprasad (Kasturirangan et al., 2011) trace the **process of concept formation** as studied by psychologists. Contemporary psychologists have done some very interesting studies on concept formation and before we go further, let us briefly revise the tradition. This tradition starts with Piaget and Vygotsky. Piaget was a French cognitive psychologist and a pioneer of those times – he developed a stage wise, culturally invariant model of cognitive development among children. Post-Piagetians significantly revised several aspects of his original theorization, esp., culturally invariant staging of cognitive development as well as acknowledging post-formal thought. The details of Piaget and Vygotsky's theories of cognitive development are taught to all and can be seen elsewhere. Point to note: If we are interested in valid cognition, then clearly, we need to move beyond linear hypothetical thinking conceptualized by Piaget at the apex of human thought! Wisdom researchers have recently gone further and identified three key aspects of wisdom as 'advanced cognitive constructs' – values contextualism (not relativism, please note), comfort with uncertainty and love for learning and reflection (Grossmann, 2017). Researchers have noted that wisdom is an integration of cognitive, affective and reflexive characteristics that is not enhanced by medicines or substances but is earned through experiencing life. Piaget, stopped his cognitive development model at formal linear logical thought around adolescence. However, his contributions are immense for formal discipline of psychology and one of them is the use of the word 'schema/ cognitive schemes'. Piaget theorized that children learn and develop cognitive schemes about the world as well as to make sense of and engage with the world. These cognitive schemes are flexible and, over a period of time, get clustered into related cluster schemes. Three points – Piaget looked at the symbolization of the world in a typical body-mind as well as body-cognition-affect binary; symbolization was purely cognitive or at least he did not explicitly account for concurrent changes in affective process as well as its embodiment. Second, schema if understood in this way, then tend to become solidified over a period of time. This solidification gives way to a frozen nature of cognition from other psychological processes, the siloes between attention, learning and memory research in contemporary psychology, for example.

The power and elegance of Kasturirangan, Guha and Ramprasad's paper and especially the reference to an 'Indian cognitivism' is that they are able to show that a concept formation is an act of embodied reasoning, logic and experiencing affectively at the same time while negotiating with the situated context. The dynamicity of concept formation includes active (as in body), reflective, logical (as in cognition and self), affective and situated processes. *Since there is no concept in current psychology that integrates these four aspects – embodiment, situatedness, logic and affective-relational response, therefore, the authors use the term –Pramā to indicate these together as an integrated four.* Pramā is the basis of cognition in Indian psychology and is much more direct, immediate and meaningful than the ideas of schema and scripts or concept formation. Pramā, a central concept in Indian epistemology, is linked directly to *pramāna* – reasoned, situated, logical, knowing-being proof as well as *Pramāta* – the embodied, experienced, logical, situated knower self!

To summarize, attention is the first cognitive concept in psychology of valid cognition and *Pramā* – integrated knowing is the second concept of the Indian psychology of cognition. The rest of the details studied by psychologists across the world – memory/working memory, thinking, reasoning, logic, creativity and decision-making are all dependent on these two. As mentioned above, there is no concept in current psychology, to examine valid cognition in basic perception-cognition-consciousness nexus. Wisdom from positive psychology cannot be considered as a candidate here, as it is too loose a conceptualization andcurrently unconnected to the body-senses-mind framework. As mentioned, Researchers (Pratt et al., 2015) have noted that several dichotomies have abounded in attention research, in reference to attention and action, attention and intention as well as shared or group attention. Clearly, we do not know what valid cognition is, leave alone questions of consciousness and self, even in an embodied reductive sense. It is emphasized that in the IKT, reality as it can be accessed only through a cleansing process, as mentioned in both the chapters on embodiment and emotion. A cognitive concept used in Indian knowledge traditions for the sensorially processed phenomenal world is – 'nāma-rupa' – world of name and visual form, thus, implicating language and sensory processing in symbolization of the world. Nāma-rupa is a reality that we engage with but is not the reality as it is (for details, see Falk, 2006).

If we don't see the reality as it is and engage with the sensorially accessed reality throughout life, then can humans ever engage with reality as it is? Thus, we arrive at the central cognitive concepts of accessing valid cognition – 'Viveka' and 'Vairāgya'. As written elsewhere (Pandit, 2020, 2021), Viveka and Vairāgya are the methodologies to refine cognitive processing. Viveka is a decisional process, with underlying reasoning, thinking and memory processes to recognize and decide what is 'real' and 'unreal'. Vairāgya is the cognitive-affective-behavioral pedagogy to address the bias that arises in human cognitive processing through the raw, unprocessed affect. As discussed in the last chapter, Vairāgya is the method to process affective processes that automatically bias human thinking and stop human beings from seeing reality as it is! Note that, it is precisely, this point that Hoffman makes when he proposes that sensory perception is a 'hack' given by evolution for survival and adaptation of the body-mind and not an aide to perceiving reality as it is.

Ganeri (2017) as mentioned earlier, writing on attention and self in Buddhist philosophy of mind, emphasizes that Buddhists viewed the self as a system centred on attention and not necessarily as an entity. This is similar to some models in contemporary cognitive sciences, where executive attention, in particular, organizes and plans for action. Attention is also a filter, with a limited capacity to focus on and process internal and external processes. By linking attention to consciousness, the Buddhists are able to identify a cohering mechanism, which is phenomenological, and still doesn't contrive reason and affect as a dichotomy. Whereas Buddhists don't equate consciousness with self; they don't deny the importance of consciousness, and are very far away from the belief of an anthropomorphic creator God as well! There are several other facets of attentional processes that are central to Indian knowledge systems. These concepts can illuminate psychology and neuroscience. For example, the experience of attentional lock – Ekagrata. Ekagrata is usually translated as single pointed attention or concentration; it also means an effortless sustained conscious attention lock over sustained periods. Ekagrata may start as a voluntary practice of sustained conscious attention on a selected idea or thought or concept, however, a key phenomenological milestone is when there is sustained attention on the selected concept/thought or idea *effortlessly* and continues for long periods of time. This happens in case of musical phrases, for example, where one particular musical phrase continues effortlessly and for long periods of time.

Thus, we now have made the initial attempt towards the conceptual architecture of the Indian psychology of valid cognition. Attention, Attentional lock, Pramā-valid cognition, Viveka-valid cognitional reasoning and Vairāgya-valid cognitional-affective process. Next, we turn to concept formation.

Concept formation in contemporary psychology is part of schema and includes the steps of categorization, prototype, typicality and atypicality – which means that concepts are thought to be formed by first categorizing them, comparing them with typical examples of the concept and then looking at how far or close the stimulus is towards the typicality. A typical bird, for example, would be a sparrow, whereas an ostrich would be an 'atypical' bird. Because, this model of concept formation implies stereotyping error, another model – the exemplar model has been proposed. Perhaps, concept formation, esp. among humans, is aided by 'exemplars' that fall into a particular categorization without an assumption of typicality or a binary process of categorizing as typical and atypical. Note that since artificial systems need to be coded a priori, the flaws in human thinking of what human is about are then reflected in the codes for machines. Coding into machines first starts with categories and classes, humans learn the opposite way, through examples, categorizing and classifying dynamically/fluidly, according to their relational or task requirements, expectancies and information from the cultural carriers such as parents and grandparents, who might tell the child that an elephant is 'God' and an animal!!

The concept of Pramā as valid cognition is profound as it points to the observation that humans experience and conceptualize *at the same time* and not sequentially as in the current classroom learning or when machines are coded. Because humans learn integrating experience and conceptualization, they must use reasoning while experiencing, being affected, acting and forming concepts. *Pramā* means valid cognition and therefore, the implication is that whether one is cognizing correctly or not is dependent upon the application and use of the knowing in real time – feeling, thinking and action. In contemporary psychology, terms that are proposed are – embodied cognition and enactivism, etc. These words dialectically imply that cognition was disembodied and inactive. Pramā leads to Pramāna as explained by the Kasturirangan, Guha and Ramprasad; the cognitive routes to knowing are called as 'Pramāna', and different formal philosophical systems in IKT have permitted different cognitive routes-pramāna-s. Yoga allows for three pramāna-s – Prtyakśa (direct knowing), Anumāna (inferential knowing) and Āgama (knowing from trusted and credible sources).

It seems obvious that conventional mundane experience is centred on beliefs. A thought trap is to then take a recourse to 'all is subjective and, therefore, cannot be reasoned'. The question of truth – whether in belief or in reality, remains! There can be some experiences, which are subjectively real, inter-subjectively unshared and actually unreal, such as in creativity or imagination. Kasturirangan, Guha and Ramprasad, also identify that in Euro-American philosophy and psychology, there seems to be a profound yet subtle dichotomy between reason and experience; between the understanding of logical processes that underlie the assessment of the validity of cognition needs to be *necessarily impersonal and without emotion* in the Euro-American tradition. Indeed, in formal logic, one of the central pathways of making a cognition valid is to remove emotion and self-reference from it. Note the alternative route of Vairāgya taken in IKT and discussed in the earlier chapter on transformation of affective processes.

While discussing cognition and immersion, some students have asked – how is this different from obsession? The phenomenology of obsession in obsessive-compulsive disorder (OCD) comes very close to involuntary sustained attention – with a key and profound difference being that the object of attention is distressing and intrusive/non-self-selected in OCD.

This subtle overlap also creates the possibility of meditators falling off the track during their meditation practice and getting ensnared into sustained involuntary attention on a painful, anxiety producing thought/concept or ideas! If the person has not transformed/substituted painful contents of consciousness with neutral or peaceful contents of consciousness through practices of emotional transformation, as discussed in the earlier chapter, then this involuntary sustained attention can get locked in on intensely painful, anxiety provoking, unexpected and undesirable outcomes. Indeed, it would be a worthwhile project to study. Given that all of us would have experienced suffering and distress in our lives, this implies that if the person is able to sustain attention involuntarily *and* feel equanimity/śanta at the same time, as discussed in the earlier chapter, no matter what the object of attention/contents of consciousness then, alone, the person can experience what is popularly called as 'choice less awareness'.

To summarize, there seems to be a justified case for re-examining the case for Indian psychology of cognition. Three specific points to note – in the first place, psychologists need to explicate the processes through which phenomenologically 'voluntary' conscious sustained attention, becomes felt 'involuntary' conscious sustained attention and the consequences thereof. Next, it is obvious that only when involuntary conscious sustained attention which is non-threatening or co-occurs with a calm affect, that the person truly arrives at the possibility of well-being. Finally, If the body-mind-consciousness has to live, then, in parallel to the practice of involuntary conscious sustained attention, the process of affective transformation – of substituting or replacing or re-framing/structuring the painful or disturbing contents of consciousness with peaceful schema clusters must be emphasized. The self and self-intentionality as a cohering function is centrally involved here, in terms of being in equanimity and in allowing for the conscious sustained attention on internal contents without censoring. In advaita or what is popularly called as jnāna yoga, the applied implications of the idea of Brahman-an ownerless consciousness as the reality of the person-hood is profound precisely because, it effaces the phenomenology of fear and anxiety that comes with ownership/'I' consciousness. All content, whether positive or negative, cannot be self as consciousness or the true subject in Vedānta (Neti, Neti) given the phenomenal awareness of 'I', the socially constituted self is non-self.

Valid cognition: Symbols and play of consciousness

So, after looking at attention, valid cognition and methodologies to valid cognition, the next task is to replace the contents of consciousness from painful to peaceful. A complete erasure of the contents of consciousness is the last step of this process. Till now, the chapter has attempted to layer the cognitive concepts and discussed Pramā and Pramāna as valid cognition and cognitive routes, respectively. We have also briefly indicated the concept of Viveka, which is a lived experience of recognition of reality as it is. *Having recognized reality, even momentarily, or as abiding, doubtless experience – Viveka* engenders a profound shift in the lived experience. IKT then proceeds on a different approach from the conventional understanding. IKT, therefore, lays out a sophisticated framework for intentionally substituting, replacing and removing negative contents of the awareness with deeply positive concepts. Positive concepts are defined as those which bring peace. This can, of course, be trivialized into daily affirmations or brainwashing, but be that criticism as it may since the tradition of meditation implies a very deep healing, this section will attempt to layout the substitution and re-arrangement process. Note that in therapy, 'cognitive restructuring' is utilized; the power of this relatively ancient method is that it is self and relationally instantiated, without psychotherapists and other experts. This method is also less dependent on linear logic and reasoning. Neuroscience reveals to us that concepts are learnt by the brain through language and sensory symbols. Language itself is a set of auditory, visual symbols, thus, it is clear that the process of symbolization is the nub of the matter.

A general overview on current understanding of language and the brain: The brain structures directly associated with language are the temporal lobes, esp., left temporal lobe. The corpus callosum or the bridge between the two hemispheres plays a central role in language and cognition. Further, recent evidence suggests several other areas of the brain in language and cognition –including the motor and visual areas as well as the frontal lobe-which is implicated for attention and planning as well as abstract thought. In terms of measurability, Neuropsychological measurements can be done through electroencephalogram (EEG), positron emission tomography (PET) and functional magnetic resonance imaging (fMRI) and magnetic resonance imaging (MRI); through neuropsychological tests and batteries developed by psychologists and also through assessing neurotransmitter levels. Earlier research was limited to brains which had suffered insult or were damaged, etc. The recent advances give a great opportunity for research with healthy, non-traumatized brains. Language is enacted socially, and therefore, behavioural observations and measurements done by psychologists are also critical. It is easier to do research where an equivalence between brain functions and behaviour is straightforward, whereas abstractions such as understanding *the discourse* and complex behaviour such as humour/sarcasm/mockery/grace/gratitude, which are context and culture sensitive, are problematic for straightforward neuropsychological measurement of languages and imagery. Thus, for all complex and socially intelligent cognitive or linguistic activity, and even more so, contemplative transformation, neuro-psychological measurement and the scientific enterprise as of current status, will, unfortunately, fall short.

We briefly discussed Piaget (1896–1980) earlier (for basic understanding of Piaget's theory, see Goldstein, 2019). Cognitive development through symbols and language as a symbolic representation of the world is taken together in IKT but not always in contemporary psychology. Recent research has gone beyond the information processing approach and attempts to study metaphors, analogies and other such higher order transformations of basic symbols in linguistic and sensory coding. Note here that words – which are symbolic of objects and ideas, also carry the world-view of meaning and relations with other objects and processes with them. Vygotsky's socio-cultural theory (for details, again see Goldstein, 2019), is significant as it is known for its focus on the role of culture and symbols (through language) in the cognitive development of children; in comparison to Piaget, Vygotsky's formulation was truly culture sensitive, with focus on community scaffolding. As mentioned in IKT, language is central and through it, worlds are named and formed – **nāma-rūpa**. Infants and children are socialized into the world through language and culture right from naming concrete objects such as dogs and cats to naming abstract emotions – to be at peace! Language teaches us the relationship between doing (verbs) and being (nouns), the qualities and characteristics of the objects and actions (adverbs and adjectives), relationships, and thereafter, actions expected from the emotions associated with objects, relationships and processes. In this manner, we note that deeper meditative states and advanced practices are also named and cognized in a particular world-view. For example, the word – Prāna and the whole system and practice of Prānyāma was absent from Euro-American knowledge tradition till it was borrowed from IKT. Similar is the case of several cultural borrowings – words and the systematic practices of Tai-Chi, Qui-gong, Acupuncture, or in reverse-computers, technology, imaging, fMRI, camera, internet etc. The key point to note from above is the role of specific words/concepts, the knowledge they reveal and the world-view they manifest, which is learnt and enacted in socio-cultural ecologies. Thus, it follows that if we change the words or the word meanings, or if we consciously layer/substitute/replace word meanings with context specificity, the same words could be cognized and enacted differently in different contexts or at different levels of meditation practice. Note that this is not a trivial pursuit, like a daily affirmation of, say, Coca-Cola! The particular layering of the context specific word meanings is critical in understanding mantra and cognitive transformation. With this brief background, in the following section, the chapter will specifically look at the theory of language drawing from the non-dual tāntric Kashmiri Śaīva system and the role on maṇtra-s and saguna/nāma-rūpa (form and quality) meditation in cognitive and affective transformation (Brooks, 1992; Geoffery, 2008).

Maṇtra is an integral domain of Indian psychology, of Yoga, taṇtra and bhakti. As we discussed in the last chapter, bhakti discusses relational well-being and so centres on the sensorially processed world – nāma-rūpa, yet, this intentional cultivation of nāma-rūpa, with the affective transformation frees the bhakta – meditator, while engaged with nāma-rūpa (name and form consciousness). For more details, on nāma-rūpa, esp., from a philosophical view, the reader, may refer to the work of Heim (Heim & Ram-Prasad, 2018). Within taṇtra and maṇtra, the focus here is limited to cognitive and affective transformation therein both through linguistic codes and imagery.

The key point to trace here is the movement from Pramā to Viveka and Viveka to Mantra – in loop, bi-directionally. The systematic applied psychology of mantra and saguna dhyāna practices in Hindu spirituality, aim to radically transform the schema in the person and thereby prompt a chain of cognitive transformations in memory, thinking, reasoning and attention. Maṇtra works as a linguistic re/code and the saguna dhyāna as a visual re/code of all the conventional reality experienced till now, captured in the brain. Therefore, it is no surprise that mantra and visualization practice is frequently accompanied by 'altered experiences' and sometimes, so-called hallucinations/false beliefs, etc., both positive and sometimes negative. All such changes are resolved in the shared meaning making of the meditating practitioner cohorts, teacher and reality tested/rejected/confirmed in authentic living traditions. Mantra and Saguna dhyāna transformation is not just limited to an experience, but refers to a complete transformation in cognition, affect and behaviour in day-to-day life. Even as we know that maṇtra or deity meditation can enhance cognition as understood conventionally, through attention and working memory, for example, taṇtra and non-dual Kāshmiri Śaiva philosophy provides the explanation of radical cognitive healing.

Maṇtra, yaṇtra and saguna dhyāna; Re-coding and recognizing the world

Vedas celebrate language, listening and cognition. Concepts of Medhā, Prajnā, Vāni and Śruti are central in IKT. In some schools of IKT such as non-dual Kashmiri Śaiva thought, language is the core expression of consciousness as such-Brahman. Creation or the creative throb (spanda) is theorized to have happened through the vocalizations of consciousness herein addressed as Parama Śiva. Each of the vowels and consonants of the Saṃskrit varnamālā (garland of colours/alphabets) represents a specific principle of creation, existence and creative dissolution. Therefore, the varnamālā are called –mātṛkā (mothers). They act both as an avidyā māyā and obfuscate the true reality for the uninitiated as well as act as vidyā māyā to show the pathway of the reality for the initiate (for details of this study, please read Dyczkowski, 1987; Shāstrī, 1918; Somānandanātha & Shastriṇ, 1934; Vasugupta, 2012).

The Kashmiri Śaiva thought gives us an elegant theory of bījākshara and mantra-sādhanā, which is applied in Tāntric practices, esp. of the Samayā tradition. Among the three taṇtra pathways, Samayā is completely psychological in its approach in contrast to the Kaulā and Miśra traditions which use concrete objects *to symbolize* psychological principles and processes. It follows that if creation, maintenance and dissolution all arise from language, then not only is the world inherently sacred, and also, if language is enacted correctly (in meditation or otherwise), then the world can be re-transformed or re-created. Note that, this 'world' which is transformed is the subjective and the inter-subjective world as located in the life experience of the person. Most significantly, also note that, changing the subjective/inter-subjective world means changing the schema and the script, the belief structures and the cluster of concepts and therefore, the transformed person, is hypothesized to frame, cognize, perceive and enact (in) reality differently. Thus, changing the schema reflects in motor action and behaviour. Transformation in motor action and behaviour is called 'mudrā'. Intentional cultivation of mudrā is thought to bring about a change in the cognitive process. A detailed discussion on mudrā is beyond the scope of this book, but texts on Saivagama-s can be referred to.

Continuing the thread, the tāntric practices, whether Hindu or Buddhist, have three key components – Maṇtra, Yaṇtra and Taṇtra, which are rendered as linguistic code, visual code and the behavioural processes including the perceptual-motor code (mudrā). There is always a deity (visual/anthropomorphic code) associated with each of the maṇtṛā-s (linguistic code). These three components create a world-view. Yaṇtra is also a visual code, however, it is relevant specifically for advanced practitioners as each of the tāṇtric geometrical elements in the yaṇtra is consciously represented through an abstract principle. Some yaṇtra practices are done in groups as well, however, most are specifically 'given' to practitioners. The kālacakra initiation, as given by His Holiness the Dalai Lama over the years, is an example of a group tāṇtric practice, which is equally rigorous in its preparation and initiation. It could be tempting to empirically study the group practices such as kālacakra, however, the key statistically significant effects, given the floor and ceiling, can only be observed in advanced meditators, who have a semblance of regulation and control over their cognitive processes such as attention, response time and ability to fence off cognitive interference, mind wandering, etc.

The key psychological principle underlined here is that, if Attention, Pramā, Viveka and Mantra are bi-directionally related, then, through mantra and attention, the awareness can recognize that which is prior to linguistic and sensory symbolization. What would that state be and how would that be visible in the human brain? Texts such as Jīvanmukti Viveka call this 'Manonaśa' where mantra as linguistic codes lead to non-linguistic insight; sensory imagery leads to non-object awareness as such. Several students, at this point, discuss the glib idea of 'oceanic' experience! It would be educative to note that Paranjpe, has recently written a masterful book (Paranjpe, 2022). comparing the idea of regression in psychoanalysis with the framework of 'prati-prasava' in the PYS. As he discusses in the book, PYS and its commentaries also mention a sequential effacement of thought forms and senses as the person moves in Samādhi. Suffice it to say, the two ideas of 'regression' and 'prati prasava' look similar only on surface; nevertheless, these are quite entrenched in the popular imagination.

In terms of philosophy, the grand achievement of Kāshmiri Śaīva thought is that, it is able to articulate simultaneously – the non-dual trans-chronous, trans-local and trans-cultural, ownerless consciousness – Brahman along with the transformative nature of the world – Śakti, called as Māyā in Vedānta and Prakṛti in Yoga Sāmkhya. In this manner, the Maya as illusion/mithyā becomes a play – līlā of the consciousness as such. Readers may refer to religious texts and their interpretations by Indological, Sanskrit language and philosophy scholars. The psychological framework to note here is – language is experienced as sacred and potent for creating and re-creating the subjective and inter-subjective worlds of the seeker and his/her communities through *the re-symbolization* of the world and world-views inherent in the language codes.

With this interim solution, the central assumption remains the primacy to self-realization. In Advaīta Vedānta, the object of meditation is to fully cognize the ownerless conscious as essential nature of individualized consciousness (Jīva-Brahma-Aīkya). Some contemporary psychologists have termed it as a 'change in the understanding on the nature of self' see Rao et al. (2008). In non-dual taṇtra, esp., in Kashmiri Śaīva and Srī-Vidyā (Samayā) practices, the step is taken further, where the practitioner is established in non-dual self-realization and thereafter utilizes the power of language to radically reframe, recognize and re-schematize the subjective and inter-subjective worlds. As is consistently outlined in this book, unless non-dual realization doesn't occur, substitution and re-substitution of one schema with another will not bring liberation from the tyranny of thought itself. Mantra is defined as 'Mananaat Tryate iti' or 'that which liberates through thought'. However, manana is not mindless thinking, automatic thinking, deliberate conventional cognitive processing or over-thinking, words often used in current times. Mantra, though practised daily, is not a trivial pursuit. Mantra is that thought which liberates us from distress and tyranny of thought; note that our thoughts engage with the manifest world. Mantra-s are not conventionally constituted meanings and are used not only in Tāntric mantras but also in Hatha Yoga practices and music as well, where body parts and musical notes are layered to symbolize states of consciousness and specific auditory and visual imagery (Nyāsa). The process of consciously/intentionally 'placing' abstract principles and cognitive states on concrete objects and processes is called 'Nyāsa'.

Thus, starting from attention and stepping into valid cognition, we have now laid a profound framework, centred on reality, self as consciousness and the symbolizing process as the creative spark of that consciousness. All this appears now, that the gestalt: Attention, valid cognition, cognizing process, Viveka, Vairāgya, the symbolizing process, language and imagery – the lived world is created and recreated anew! (Ramachandra Rao, 1985). A caveat is in order – the classical texts acknowledge this path of working with re-symbolization as tricky and radical. Theoretically, all the alternate realities may be within the realm of possibility but not socio-legally valid! Suffice to note – the danger to fall into a completely unconventional re-schematizing of the world is clear and present on this pathway and has been recognized by texts. We had raised the question earlier – given that tantric practices have such a high risk of a completely non-conventional schematization, which is, in fact, acknowledged and emphasized in taṇtric literature, why even discuss it seriously? If these practices are to be taken up seriously, then what are the safeguards against dysfunctional schematizations? One of the first safeguards on this path is a very diligent practice of Yoga so that Vairāgya and Viveka is strengthened. Vairāgya is discussed in an earlier chapter as well. Second, in traditional sources, the Guru corrects the meditative practices of the disciple, so a mechanism of feedback with the Guru is maintained. Finally, texts discourage and dismiss the lure of easy accomplishments. Certainly, despite these safeguards, the temptations do lure incomplete practitioners. This is a high risk-high transformation path.

Till about a decade ago, in the scientific world, this would have qualified for a completely non-rational esoteric philosophy at best and mumbo-jumbo at worst. Today, however, with the advances in imaging and neuro-cognitive instrumentation, it should be possible to test some of these claims, systematically on a cohort of advanced maṇtra, yaṇtra and taṇtra practitioners. Recently, a study (Kozhevnikov et al., 2009) has shown that deity meditation from the Buddhist framework improves imagery tasks significantly and affects visuo-spatial memory and other cognitive functions. The authors note the paucity of research on cognitive effects of 'deity meditation', which requires extensive training in visual imagery. They also note that they travelled to Nepal and conducted the studies with highly advanced Buddhist practitioners (who consented) and then continued their data collection with other cohorts from Buddhist monasteries in the USA. It is entirely possible that research results on these tāntric and māntric practices will still get trivialized or reduced to 'cognitive enhancements' rather than their true radical implications. However, that issue can be discussed separately.

Before we jump down the rabbit hole of an 'Alice in Wonderland' kind, philosophers and Indologists should note here that, as Indian cognitive psychology, the section cannot scope a discussion on the content or philosophical differences between Buddhist or Hindu Tāṇtric practices. At this juncture, we are at the basic objective of tracing an Indian Psychology of cognition. We are interested in establishing the cognitive processes that lead to a transformation of meaning in a neutral manner and propose that the conceptual architecture of attention, Ekagrata, Vairāgya, Pramā, Viveka and mantra-tantra are independently arrived at and perhaps a better theory than schema and scripts!

Since all meditators practice within their body and brain, the assumption is that it must reflect in the brain function and neuro-transmitter levels and thereafter in behaviours, and therefore, research with neuroscience can reveal a global psychology of relevance. In the immediate term, at least in the advanced practitioners, it should be possible to do several studies with mantric practitioners. Hypotheses can be framed for affective transformations due to mantras, in carefully designed studies with various groups of cohorts. Longitudinally, long-term mantra practitioners can be hypothesized to show differences in terms of how they frame the situation, objects that they foreground or background in their perception (gestalt) and how they reason as well as solve problems. Similarly, affective changes can be assessed not only subjectively but empirically, removing placebo effects, by systematically observing their responses to stimuli and situations. It is important to note in good faith that all these hypotheses will still significantly run the risk of physicalists' or computationalists' interpretation, reduction or critique.

In terms of Hatha Yoga, the Sūrya namaskāra cycle is traditionally taught with associated bījākśaras; this can also be empirically tested (Rama et al., 1976). Similarly, the practice of Nyāsa in Yoga-nidra meditation (Satyananda, 2012) or in all meditations which involve Nyāsa, where the linguistic code and visualization of a deity is layered on a body part can also be specifically tested neuro-cognitively. It can be hypothesized that different pathways associated with body/cognition and affect will 'light up'. The caveat again is that – this must be conducted on intermediate and advanced practitioners and preferably not novices since novices will not be able to hold any ideas to sustained attention.

Similarly, in Indian music, certain sound phrases are theorized as co-creating and altering mood states, esp., songs by the great Vaggeyakāra–Muthuswami Dikshitar, in whose compositions, bījākśaras, notes and visualization through the sāhitya is seamlessly orchestrated. Advanced music students and teachers can be empirically tested in a series of studies on both linguistic as well as visual imagery correlates. The persistent issue of getting consent from an advanced meditator sample, esp., can be navigated through working with advanced students of classical music, who would be more likely to be available and easier to get consent from as compared to pure māntric practitioners.

In summary, we have traversed a vast and an unfamiliar landscape. Every other person, including students of psychology are aware of the hundreds of studies conducted on Yoga practices, etc. A current lot of studies prove that Yoga practices impact well-being and also have neuroplasticity effects. But, these studies are not fundamentally transformative as they fall within the physicalist, positivistic assumptions of both philosophy of mind and philosophy of science. The true consciousness centred psychology from India, would propose afresh, novel ways of conceptualizing cognition and cognitive transformation.

In terms of implications, firstly, from the practitioner perspective, maṇtra meditation involves a complete breakthrough – a changed world-view, a change in framing, in perceptual re-processes, in remembering and reframing memory and in reasoning and problem-solving. This implication alone, if proven empirically can have an impact on all aspects of psychology applications. Note here that visualization and visual imagery is increasing in focus in educational as well as clinical and counselling contexts. Research is ongoing for exploring augmented reality and virtual reality (AR and VR) for therapy, just as metaverse is the next frontier for new technology consumer experience. Visualization exercises are used in clinical and counselling psychology even now as well. Most importantly, it is a consciousness-based Indian psychology alone, that provides a theoretical explanation *and* a way forward for a complete well-being. It is a consciousness-based Indian psychology alone, that fences off getting enslaved to gadgets, which also use these principles but are driven by mindless commercialization and profit mongering.

Manonaśa: From mindfulness to 'no-mind'

Mindfulness arising from the Buddhist practice of Sati/Smrti has taken the world by storm! The key objective of Indian Psychology is to be free of suffering. Mindfulness, certainly provides one pathway to remain alive to the world – moment by moment. If we are able to perceive that we do see reality as it is, then, what could be the ways to live while being free of the conventionally constituted self-body-mind? In the next chapter, we will make an attempt to explore the terms we frequently read in primary texts – Manonaśa, Unmana-Manonmana. These allude to the possibility of a no-mind living!

References

Belzen, J. A. (2010). *Towards cultural psychology of religion: Principles, approaches, applications.* Springer.

Brooks, D. R. (1992). *Auspicious wisdom: The texts and traditions of the Sri-Vidya Shakta Tantrism in South India.* Albany, NY: State University of New York Press.

Buttle, H. (2011). Attention and working memory in mindfulness–meditation practices. *The Journal of Mind and Behavior, 32*(2), 123–134. http://www.jstor.org/stable/43854297

Dyczkowski, M. S. (1987). *The doctrine of vibration: An analysis of the doctrines and practices of Kashmir Shaivism.* Albany, NY: State University of New York Press.

Dy-Liacco, G. S., Piedmont, R. L., Murray-Swank, N. A., Rodgerson, T. E., & Sherman, M. F. (2009). Spirituality and religiosity as cross-cultural aspects of human experience. *Psychology of Religion and Spirituality, 1*(1), 35.

Evans, C. S., & Manis, R. Z. (2010). *Philosophy of religion: Thinking about faith.* InterVarsity Press.

Falk, M. (2006). *Nama-Rupa and Dharma-Rupa: Origins and aspects of an ancient Indian conception.* Jain Publishing Company.

Fields, C., Hoffman, D., Prakash, C., & Singh, M. (2018). Conscious agent networks: Formal analysis and application to cognition. *Cognitive Systems Research*, *47*, 186–213.
Fort, A. O. (1998). *Jīvanmukti in transformation: Embodied liberation in Advaita and neo-Vedānta*. State University of New York Press.
Fort, A. O., & Mumme, P. Y. (1996). *Living liberation in Hindu thought*. Suny Press.
Ganeri, J. (2017). *Attention, not self*. Oxford University Press.
Geoffery, S. (2008). *The origins of Yoga and Tantra: Indic religions to the thirteenth century*. London: Cambridge University Press.
Goldstein, E. B. (2019). *Cognitive psychology: Connecting mind, research and everyday experience*. Cengage.
Grossmann, I. (2017). Wisdom in context. *Perspectives on Psychological Science*, *12*, 233–257.
Harré, R. (2006). Resolving the emergence-reduction debate. *Synthese*, *151*(3), 499–509. Retrieved September 23, 2020, from http://www.jstor.org/stable/20118823
Hasenkamp, W., Wilson-Mendenhall, C. D., Duncan, E., & Barsalou, L. W. (2012). Mind wandering and attention during focused meditation: A fine-grained temporal analysis of fluctuating cognitive states. *Neuroimage*, *59*(1), 750–760.
Heim, M., & Ram-Prasad, C. (2018). In a double way. *Philosophy East and West*, *68*(4), 1085–1115.
Hoffman, D. D., Singh, M., & Prakash, C. (2015). The interface theory of perception. *Psychonomic Bulletin & Review*, *22*(6), 1480–1506.
Inbadas, H. (2016). History, culture and traditions: The silent spaces in the study of spirituality at the end of life. *Religions*, *7*(5), 53.
Inbadas, H. (2017). The philosophical and cultural situatedness of spirituality at the end of life in India. *Indian Journal of Palliative Care*, *23*(3), 338–340. https://doi.org/10.4103/IJPC.IJPC_61_17
Inbadas, H. (2018). Indian philosophical foundations of spirituality at the end of life. *Mortality*, *23*(4), 320–333.
Johnston, L. (2006). The 'nature' of Buddhism: A survey of relevant literature and themes. *Worldviews: Global Religions, Culture, and Ecology*, *10*(1), 69–99.
Kamath, M. S., & Ramanasramam, S. (Tiruvannāmalai India). (2003). *Sri Maharshi: A short life-sketch: Profusely illustrated* (9th ed.). https://www.sriramanamaharshi.org/ramana-maharshi/.
Kaplan, S. (2009). Grasping at ontological straws: Overcoming reductionism in the Advaita Vedānta – Neuroscience dialogue. *Journal of the American Academy of Religion*, *77*(2), 238–274. http://www.jstor.org/stable/20630117
Kasturirangan, R., Guha, N., & Ram-Prasad, C. (2011). Indian cognitivism and the phenomenology of conceptualization. *Phenomenology and the Cognitive Sciences*, *10*(2), 277–296.
Khisty, C. J. (2006). Meditations on systems thinking, spiritual systems, and deep ecology. *Systemic Practice and Action Research*, *19*(4), 295–307.
Kozhevnikov, M., Louchakova, O., Josipovic, Z., & Motes, M. (2009). The enhancement of visuospatial processing efficiency through Buddhist deity meditation. *Psychological Science*, *20*(5), 645–653. Retrieved September 20, 2020, from http://www.jstor.org
Mickey, S. (2015). *Whole earth thinking and planetary coexistence: Ecological wisdom at the intersection of religion, ecology, and philosophy*. Routledge.

Nathawat, S. S., & Menon, G. (2018). Mehendipur Balaji revisited: A descriptive phenomenological inquiry. *European Journal of Physical Education and Sport Science*, *4*(3), 61–65.

Oman, D. (2013). Defining religion and spirituality. *Handbook of the Psychology of Religion and Spirituality*, 2, 23–47.

Pakaslahti, A. (1998). Family-centered treatment of mental health problems at the Balaji Temple in Rajasthan. *Studia Orientalia Electronica*, *84*, 129–166.

Pandit, S. A. (2020). Viveka and Vairāgya: Empirical possibilities for cognitive concepts in Indian psychology. *Journal of Psychosocial Research*, *15*(2), 497–507.

Pandit, S. A. (2021). Advaita: Oneness as a lived reality – examining aspects of a profound and a radical psychology. *Psychology and Developing Societies*. https://doi.org/10.1177/09713336211038814

Paranjpe, A. C. (2022). *Yoga and psychoanalysis perspectives on the psychology of regression* (1st ed.). Routledge India.

Posner, M. I., & Rothbart, M. K. (2007). Research on attention networks as a model for the integration of psychological science. *Annual Review of Psychology*, 58, 1–23.

Pratt, J., Taylor, J. E. T., & Gozli, D. G. (2015). Action and attention. In J. Fawcett, E. Risko & A. Kingstone (Eds.), *The Handbook of Attention* (pp. 325–348). The MIT Press.

Rama, S., Ballentine, R., & Ajeya, S. (1976). *Yoga and psychotherapy: The evolution of consciousness*. Himalayan Institute Press.

Ramachandra Rao, S. (1985). *Sri Chakra – its Yantra, Mantra and Tantra*. Delhi: Sri Satguru Publications.

Ranganathan, S. (2018). Indigenous healing practices in India: Shamanism, spirit possession, and healing shrines. In G. Misra (Ed.), *Psychosocial interventions for health and well-being* (pp. 109–122). Springer.

Rao, K., Paranjpe, A., & Dalal, A. (2008). *Handbook of Indian psychology*. New Delhi: Foundation Books. https://doi.org/10.1017/UPO9788175968448.

Rothbart, M. K., Sheese, B. E., Rueda, M. R., & Posner, M. I. (2011). Developing mechanisms of self-regulation in early life. *Emotion Review*, *3*(2), 207–213.

Rukmini, T. S. (1981). Patañjali's Yogaūstras – a synthesis of many yogic traditions. *Annals of the Bhandarkar Oriental Research Institute*, *62*(1/4), 213–218.

Satija, D. C., Nathawat, S. S., Singh, D., & Sharma, A. (1982). A study of patients attending Mehandipur Balaji temple: Psychiatric and psychodynamic aspects. *Indian Journal of Psychiatry*, *24*(4), 375–379.

Satyananda, S. (2012). *Kundalini Tantra*. Munger Bihar: Bihar School of Yoga Press.

Sax, W., & Weinhold, J. (2012). Rituals of possession. In U. Husken & C. Brosius (Eds.) *Ritual matters: Dynamic dimensions in practice* (pp. 248–264). Routledge India.

Shāstrī, M. R. (1918). *The Tantrāloka of Abhinava Gupta*. Vol. 1. Commentary by Rājānaka Jayaratha. Allahabad: Indian Press.

Singh, R. P. B. (2017). Sacred ecology and transformative consciousness in Hinduism. *IJTC, International Journal for the Transformation of Consciousness*, *3*(1) 209–233.

Smith, F. M. (2010). Possession, embodiment, and ritual in mental health care in India. *Journal of Ritual Studies*, *24*(2), 21–35. http://www.jstor.org/stable/44368826

Somānandanātha, U., & Shastriṇ, M. (1934). *The Śivadriṣṭi (Śivadṛṣṭi) of Sri-Somānandanātha with the vritti by Utpaladeva*. Śrinagara: Government of Jammu and Kashmir.

Sood, A. (2016). The global mental health movement and its impact on traditional healing in India: A case study of the Balaji Temple in Rajasthan. *Transcultural Psychiatry*, *53*(6), 766–782.

Timalsina, S. (2012). Body, self, and healing in Tantric ritual paradigm. *The Journal of Hindu Studies*, *5*(1), 30–52.

Vasugupta. (2012). *The Aphorisms of Siva: The Siva Sutra with Bhaskara's commentary, the Varttika*. New York: SUNY Press.

Yang, X., Cheng, P.-Y., Lin, L., Huang, Y. M., & Ren, Y. (2019). Can an integrated system of electroencephalography and virtual reality further the understanding of relationships between attention, meditation, flow state, and creativity? *Journal of Educational Computing Research*, *57*(4), 846–876.

6 Unmana-Manonmana

Psychology and the 'no mind'

Mind as an appearance: Introduction

According to the tradition of Kevaladvaita in the Advaita Vedānta tradition, 'mind', which works through a subject-object duality, is the only unreality there is! All the rest is a mere manifestation of this mythical 'mind'. An excellent discussion on the nature of the mind from an Indian tradition can be seen in the scholarly book by Professors Paranjpe and Rao titled, 'Psychology in Indian Tradition' (Rao & Paranjpe, 2016). For all of us living with the idea of a mind as ultimately real and confusing it with consciousness, this is strange! The academic discipline of psychology and its practice is premised on the assumption that subject-object duality is real and consciousness emergent in its formal scope of study. So, the exploration in this chapter is to flip that assumption for consciousness-based psychology – what are the frameworks to look at mindlessness, mind, mindfulness, and no-mind in transcendence? The Indian knowledge tradition (IKT) do grant 'provisional reality' to the mind, and therefore, we are asking – are there frameworks of IP *that leverage the mind to transcend the mind*? Does consciousness-based Indian psychology provide the vocabulary and grammar for this transcendence?

The deity at the famous Meenakshi Sunderśwarār Temple, in the ancient town of Madurai, where Madurai Meenakshi is the queen of the town and the universe, Sundareshwar Siva is accompanied by his consort – Manonmani. The word-Manonmani is translated as mind-no-mind! An outsider to the Indian tradition may wonder – How can there be such a contradiction-a mind-no-mind? How can a God-Deity be accompanied by a 'mind-no-mind'? If we were to look at this as 'symbolism' since Śiva Sundareshwar is a yogi, then the question arises – can there be a state of 'mind-no-mind'? Can a 'no-mind' be conceptualized as the outcome of the practice of 'mind', which is the subject matter of psychology? Similar to the idea of transcendence as not a binary between 'this-world and other-world' as discussed in earlier chapters, in this chapter, we will discuss the Indic idea of 'mind-no-mind' in the lived experience. By implication, this conceptual framework of mind, non-mind, and 'mind-no-mind' indicates an

DOI: 10.4324/9781003336204-6

interwoven realization of consciousness as self, where mind emerges and dissolves, not just during advanced meditative states, but through everyday moment by moment lived experiences in this body and through these relationships in 'this world'.

In this chapter, we will discuss four key ideas. Firstly, for the present, we do acknowledge the presence of mind (mind as subject-object duality) in our conventional reality; define it as a 'representation of external world' and discuss the Indian practice ideas of Laya (dissolution) – a systematic immersion of losing mental representations and the accompanying self-consciousness, even if momentarily. Next, we will discuss 'Nirodha', which is different from the momentary loss of consciousness in flow states and is an important milestone in Yoga practice. Nirodha Pariṇāma in Yoga practice, as understood in Rāja Yoga or Patanjali's Yoga sutra-s (PYS), is indicated as losing phenomenal awareness progressively for longer periods of objective time to be stabilized as Samādhi in Aṣtānga and Rāja Yoga texts as a broader Yoga psychology (for details, see Bharati, 2001a, 2001b). Thirdly, we will briefly examine the Yogācāra framework on levels of consciousness to understand 'Ālaya Vijnāna' – an 'overmind' or a collective mind, beyond the individual mind that is assumed to be locked in the body.

Citta and Ālaya Vijnāna are currently proposed to model consciousness overflowing the individual locked in the body-mind (Chadha, 2013). Here we will briefly discuss the debates on Euro-American philosophy, esp. pan-psychism, and the physicalist argument in contemporary philosophy of psychology which reject pan-psychism and the overflow argument (Block, 2007b). Finally, we introduce the Indian idea of manonmana – 'mind-no-mind' – a delightful contradiction in terms. Manonmana is the fitting epitome to capture a realized life of freedom; a life that is able to transit from music to silence and then recognize that music and silence are interwoven with each other. Manonmana, mentioned in the foundation Hatha Yoga text – the Hatha Yoga Pradipika of Sri Svātmarāma and interpreted in contemporary times by Swami Satyananda (Muktibodhananda, 2012; Saraswati & Saraswati, 1998), is equivalently mapped with Samādhi, but is a fluid mastery of emergence and merging representational reflexivity to non-representational awareness. There is a most sophisticated tradition of oneness and a non-dual lived experience arising from Vedānta, Advaita specifically including the Indian perspectives on Jīvanmukti, and articulated in non-dual trika śaiva thought and the integration of hatha, tantra with Vedānta. First indicated by Sri Śankaracharya (Bhate, 2015; Chattopadhyay, 2012, 2016; Fort, 1998; Kachroo, 2005; Tagare, 2002) this is discussed in the text – Yogatārāvali, which is attributed to Sri Śankaracharya by insiders but questioned by other scholars as a later text. Be that as it may, the hathyoga tradition reached its fruition in the 11th and 12th century Hatha Yoga, Nātha Sampradaya and several traditions of bhakti.

The sheer possibility of mind-no-mind or manonmana revises the present scope of psychology; It should be seen as a reflective point for contemporary psychology and philosophies of mind in the European context that confuses consciousness and mind.

Mind and no mind in machine and human cognition

The predominant theory of mind is a representationalist view and this illuminates several initial facets of our understanding. Mind is accordingly defined as 'a representation of the external world' (Farmer & Matlin, 2019). This representation of the world is derived by our sense perception, our attentional processes, and later, our memory and linguistic processes. Creativity, problem-solving and decision-making are conceptualized as higher order cognitive functions. Cognitive psychologists have said that these representations can be in sensory analogues as well as symbolic/schematic/conceptual frames. Taking this definition further to its logical step, a computer can then develop a mind if the sensory processes are able to accurately capture and represent the world; if there is a system of schematic, symbolic and sensory analogue representations, and if we have the 'modules' of memory, working memory and language/expressive communication. These modules could then take decisions based on the moment-by-moment sensory inputs and the internal codes/rules or algorithms. In fact, the most updated intersections of AI and brain involve bionic chips that will stimulate the brain and make the mind work! For example, the microchip in the washing machine, which ordinarily has 'no mind' of its own, can also develop a mind. It can, through its sensors, identify you as the person who sets the machine to work every day; you could code the machine to do a warm wash during winter season through seasonal temperature sensors and the machine could be programmed to talk to you, in a language of your choice. Would this mean that the machine has a mind that has now generated a *consciousness of its own*? The identification of the modularities of mental functions represents an achievement of contemporary thinking.

The idea of the 'Internet of things' or IoT is premised on a representational theory of mind. One would say, possibly, that these are still machines, as they don't seem to 'learn' and need codes to function. Well, one can update one's knowledge now, as most of these complex systems will be self-learning. It is quite certain that machines in the near future, will be self-learning and, therefore, perhaps unpredictable as human beings. These machines will have such powerful computing systems that they will have gigantic memory records and will be increasingly precise in anticipating human behaviour. The machines will be able to communicate with each other as well, although their language of communication will be the mathematical and sensory analogue code transfers. If the systems will be self-learning, then, can they feel? We can argue that machines can be taught *to display* appropriate emotional expressions and, therefore, communicate with other humans and/or machines. These emotional expression codes can be made context, situation and culture sensitive, so does it matter, whether the machines will 'actually' feel or not? Possibly, the machines may learn to develop a dual system of an internal assessment and an outward expression, much like humans and keep a record of both. Will the machines misunderstand or become hysterical or dramatic? We can argue that such 'made to order' personalities, even spiritual guru personalities, can be coded in the machines. If so, then what is the difference between humans and machines? Cognitive scientists and philosophers have argued on this very complex and subtle question in terms of sentience and/or sapience (Duncan, 2006; Friston et al., 2020; Segundo-Ortin & Calvo, 2022). In what might sound strange to the Indian context, the scholars are arguing 'anew' for sentience in plants and animals.

At the next level, knowing (mirroring and reflecting) the non-self-other and being known by others could be seen as a characteristic of 'social' human and non-human beings such as animals and plants (plants communicate through fungi). Contextualized and translated into our earlier example, we can see that the washing machine can definitely come to 'know' you if you have been consistent in your lifestyle and set it up exactly at 8:00 am in the morning, say. Possibly abstract emotions such as 'a knowing' that comes from affection and love or even intense hate might be difficult for these machines, one might wager. Recently, some sci-fi movies have shown the possibility of machines and humans falling in love with each other; is that possible? Can a machine experience such delicate and complex emotions and the theory of mind that is implicit in these intimate interpersonal relations? Well, we have reached the point closest to self, as we need to ask the question – **in such non-self-worlds,** *why, for the life of us, is love experienced*? Hatred can be explained from a survival perspective, so can lust and sex.

We can now, at this stage, possibly look at the Vedāntic idea that consciousness as such, which is only understood through and as Self! Some of the most intriguing aspects of human experience may be difficult to code, at least currently. In the specific context of the example of the washing machine, the following conclusions can be drawn: Firstly, one of the key relatable points that we derive is that simple and complex organisms do conventionally have a representation of the external world that they then negotiate with, internally and externally. This can be understood as mind in a broad sense. In the IKT, the mind is not real, precisely because it is conceptualized as an interface between consciousness and the world (which is also consciousness, but appears as different). Secondly, we can surmise that, to the extent that this representation is aligned with our fitness to survive (Hoffman et al., 2015), we will call this as a conventional adapted mind. Thirdly, different organisms will have different representations according to their perceptual sophistication and living requirements and, therefore, would certainly have different minds with different structural and functional complexity; note that even if a bat experiences the same objective world differently than us, because it represents the world auditorily, it still *does represent* the world and connects to the organismic survival, even if we don't know, whether it may or may not have phenomenal awareness of an 'I' consciousness. Fourthly, there can be several structural aspects of representational complexity that can then be 'automated' or become automatic with the least or minimally conscious processes for creatures. Thus, the ability to act may or may not necessarily require a phenomenal 'I' awareness.

Fifthly, by this line of logic, then we can possibly create and construct artificial cognitions, driven by this modularity that can conduct almost human-like psychological processes in cognition, affect and behaviour and interact with humans and the non-human cohort. Note, in this trisection, affect is the weakest pillar, and therefore, we addressed it even before cognition in IP.

Delimited and therefore problematic in this view, is firstly, ethics and morality, where all the philosophical and cognitive science discussion is currently directed, esp. if there is a seeking to explore the possibility of consciousness without self (Ganeri, 2017). If we agree to this view then, developing a mind, is the first sign of a complex organism and Euro-American thought assumes the mind overlapping with 'consciousness', even while distinguishing conscious and unconscious aspects of the mind. Having agreed to this, we immediately run into serious issues – one, of course, is the question of emotions and affect, esp. complex poignant positive and negative emotions. Second, is the question of optimum functioning, flow, everyday creativity and excellence? Third, is the question of phenomenal awareness of well-being, which includes 'letting go of this mind'. In advanced meditation, why is there an experience of well-being, happiness and joy while letting go of the mind; why would this occur? In this chapter, the philosophical arguments for sentience, sapience and the question of qualia will not be discussed in detail. Suffice it to say, the chapter recognizes the real possibility of minded machines but, in line with the assumptions of Vedānta, distinguishes between mind and consciousness and, therefore, focuses on the very human journey of precise 'mis-identifying' the mind as self to 'detaching' from this false identity. The detachment that we discussed as Pramā, Viveka and Vairāgya, develops insight and progressively dissolves the identification. This finality leads to recognizing consciousness as self, which can constitute minds and social selves at will. In IKT, this is compared to the waxing and waning of the moon rather than an either or process of 'mind as self' vs 'consciousness as self'. As mentioned, consciousness as self is the immersed self of Sat-Cid-Ānanda and not the socially constituted self.

Emerging research on non-dual awareness: Creativity, flow, immersion and laya

As we have mentioned in the first chapter, in the last 30 years, there have been distinctive advances towards a decolonized, multicultural psychology, which has co-occurred with parallel movements towards an increasing acceptability of scientific research on consciousness, called as the consciousness boom by some scholars (Chadha, 2015; Damasio, 1998; Damasio & Meyer, 2009; Dreyfus, 1993; Thompson & Varela, 2001; Varela et al., 2017). Conceptually, most of the current neuroscience paradigms still mix up with the philosophies of mind and philosophy of consciousness since consciousness is understood as an 'emergent phenomena'. Some exceptions are pan-psychist, who is controversial and uber – non-mainstream. Block (1995, 2007a), for example, has consistently critiqued the reductions in physicalist, computationalist and functionalist arguments. He presents a view that consciousness overflows the mind! Of course, most representationalist/physicalist and functionalist philosophers of mind have rejected the idea of the 'overflow' of consciousness (Cohen & Dennett, 2011; Dennett, 1993).

Consciousness research has been based on advances in neurosciences. However, methods in neurosciences are always educated with first-person experience triangulation from advanced meditators. These meditators have been mostly from the Buddhist and yogic traditions. The neurophenomenological method is preferred over pure phenomenology or pure neuroscience. Meditators are preferred as they are trained in observation, reflexivity and self-regulation/intention, which is difficult for untrained lay persons. Recently, 'non-dual awareness' has been an interesting area of research on consciousness, which was earlier seen as the domain of 'idealist' Vedānta schools (Josipovic, 2010, 2019; Josipovic & Miskovic, 2020). Josipovic has argued that a 'minimal conscious experience' and an implied non-representational awareness might indicate 'non-dual' awareness. Therefore, at the very least, we can see that, there is an attempt to now explore that consciousness perhaps, 'overflows' a representational philosophy of mind, if nothing more; here mind is defined as the representation of the world and allows the possibility of a limited representation and or more radically a non-representational reflexivity/awareness.

Rather than framing it as an either/or speculative question, an Indian practice perspective which this book takes is of 'a topography and ecology of consciousness' – a consciousness as such, that reflects in specific states of mind-body-senses and the social world nexus, which causes representational reflexivity in specific instances, of the objective and the lived experienced world as processed by sensory perception and cognition. Connected to this idea is the implication that the phenomenal awareness is not static in its sensitivity; it continues to either get refined and more acute in awareness through practices or sadhana or 'denser' and rough in its acuity and sensitivity though an automatic living. Block's recent idea of access and phenomenal consciousness has been quite controversial among scholars. Whatever be the contours of this controversy, Block's idea of an a and p consciousness is fixed and static. In contrast, in the Indian philosophical systems and the applied psychology that it entails, both a and p consciousness can be transformed to either become more or less aligned and sensitive. Some easy to remember examples from the Indian knowledge systems of such topographical models are the Panchakosha in Taittriya Upaniṣad, the vyāhriti-s mentioned in the Vedas and the levels of consciousness in the Hatha Yoga tradition, most famously as Kundalini and the chakra-s. The Chakra-s are the states of mind-body-senses-social world nexus, while the Kundalini is the phenomenal awareness that gets stuck/identified with certain worlds or 'detached' and moves upwards – gets progressively refined, to finally transcend representations to reach an ownerless consciousness. In contemporary times, this point has been made by Shri T. K. V. Desikachar from Krishnamacharya Yoga tradition in their interpretation of the text – Yoga Tārāvali and the teachings of Sri Krishnamacharya – A contemporary Siddha Guru.

On a practical and even an academic psychology level, a topography of consciousness would mean that consciousness as such would be a vast multi-dimensional landscape, where under certain conditions, states of consciousness, with their particular states of mind-sense/s-body-social would emerge, including non-human minds! In this way, we have flipped the arguments of the contemporary philosophies of mind, where mind emerges from consciousness rather than the other way round!

A topography of consciousness would mean that at the substratum, interweave and transcendence would be an ownerless, non-representational awareness or an is-ness, from where representational reflexivity would arise and merge back. The substratum, interweave and transcendence is consciousness and not a philosophical category of a substance or an entity. In IKT, an applied psychology practice based on the principle of moving from a cluttered representational reflexivity to bare awareness is called Laya. Laya, in Saṃskṛit, means dissolution and is used in multiple nuanced contexts. Laya Yoga practice would mean to dissolve mentation *as it arises.* In popular psychology and self-help, there is a fashionable slogan of living in the present! Being in the present, moment by moment, would mean that all the accumulation of mentation till now has somehow been resolved – reflected upon and rendered insightful through a peaceful witness – metacognitive consciousness.

In the last two years, psychology research has started reporting on the idea of immersion and meta-cognition (see Lynch & Troy, 2021). Lynch and Tory explicitly explore the connection between non-duality in flow and meta-cognitive states. One of the characteristics of 'flow' has been an alteration in the awareness of self and time. In the Indian knowledge traditions, Rasa theory has been well researched (Higgins, 2007; Lynch, 1990; Nair, 2013; Sundararajan, 2010) which we discussed in Chapter 4, talks about the transformation of duality into a shared and thereafter, non-dual awareness through the exploration, experience and expression of emotions by the performer on the stage. The performer on stage starts with the dialogue to finally arrive at a shared consciousness of the emotional experience in performativity and receptivity both. The rasa theorists, gave the concept of sādhāraṇikaraṇa (universal sharing) – which means that before becoming a transcendental, otherworldly idea of 'no mind', the personal mind becomes a shared mind with other minds. During a rasa experience, the audience loses their self-consciousness, that too for a time being **in receptivity**, implying that sensory reception is not passive meaning making. Thus, they ordinarily don't lose consciousness, or get into coma or leave their body or enter into meditative states. The audience and the performer/s do, however, experience an awareness that is not jarred with I-absorption and I-consciousness.

Note here: the discourse on flow is typically individualistic in the Euro-American context for all legacy reasons. The discourse on flow typically focuses on the creative person and his/her/their performativity, but what about the receptivity and shared cognition of the viewers/audience and team members in the performance? Say, in a small music concert gathering, the accompanists, the listeners and the performer are in concert, similar to the audience, team members and the main players in a cricket match. Since this intense shared awareness is not personal and is shared with others, who experience the same or similar intensity at the same time, Ācārya Abhinavagupta, uses the term ekghana, which means 'massified as one'. Thus, non-dual awareness at this first level of a lived experience means an intense shared awareness, which has minimal personal/separate representation during that experience. Now, such processes are fairly common and possible in all intense experiences which are shared. An obvious example is the sexual intercourse and the actions, thoughts and emotional process leading to the sexual intercourse between two partners. Assuming both the partners are equally intensely involved in the shared experience, they do lose the jarring sense of a narcissistic self-absorption and I-consciousness for at least moments of time. Such an understanding of 'non-mind' would mean, losing a representational cognition and embodying and enacting in shared intense awareness alone. This fact has been noticed with technical terms such as 'Samyoga/Viyoga' as well as 'Sambhoga' referring to the intensity of the shared experience and awareness. In psychology, shared attention has been discussed, but mostly in the context of challenges in communication disorders, etc. It would be a moot point that, intense shared attention must be a feature of all activities of collective well-being and efficacy without being limited to a psychoanalytic focus on sex. We do observe intense shared attention in non-human actions pointing to the evolution of a primitive theory of mind and in the study of languages and empathy (Seyfarth & Cheney, 2013; Thompson, 2001; Zahavi & Rochat, 2015). The contemporary psychology discourse has not, however, looked at the shared attention and theory of mind in states of well-being through social aesthetics or relationality that runs parallel to life itself. In the experience of rasa – whether shared in sexual intercourse or in creative immersion or in food sharing, we are taking shared attention as a given psychological variable and are more interested in the quality of the attentional processes that then, at some point, merge into a shared, rasa.

In divergence to the popular obsession with the sexual intercourse, intense shared awareness is not limited to sexual intercourse alone, although it appears as the most 'relatable' example because awareness of duality and separation is keen and easier to acknowledge/reflect upon, before and after consummation through sexual intercourse. According to the traditions in tantra as well as in Yoga, consistently recognising non-dual awareness is the basis of all creativity and creative processes. Bhawuk, discussed this point in his work on creative processes and spirituality in the Indian tradition (Bhawuk, 2003, 2018). Prof Bhawuk has argued convincingly in his papers how experientially and through lived experiences of great spiritual masters, creativity in the Indian knowledge systems and Indian culture has been aligned with consciousness as such, similar to Pramā rather than as a cognitive activity alone.

Thus, a 'no mind' would imply a transcendence of a particular kind; a first glimpse, where a representational view of the world is erased and perception is direct, enactive and situationally embedded, at least for some moments. Gibson (Gibson, 2002), very famously in 1970s, discussed direct perception and affordances in goal directed actions that make perception and action coupled. Here again the role of losing self-consciousness and mentation towards shared consciousness has not been discussed in contemporary psychology.

In contemporary Euro-American psychology, when cognition is studied, usually it is simplified in terms of bottom-up processing, which is evidence-based, sense driven and data-driven processing; top-down processing, which is experience guided, schema-based processing and direct perception and processing, which is based on affordance in the environment and the goals of the organism. Gibson, as mentioned earlier, did not agree with a constructive nature of perception as proposed by the Gestalt school and instead proposed 'direct perception'. Direct perception is not a trivial, casual matter in the IKT; in Buddhism, for example, *Samjnā* is for sense drive perception and is distinguished from *Panna,* which is insight. The key insight that IKT gives us is that only under certain conditions of preparation, the representational nature of awareness is dissolved towards a direct perception. For all other conditions, the perception is not direct, esp. if it is driven by senses or cognition and remains representational. In the absence of a bare familiarity with Saṃskrit and Indian logic, it is easy to jump to the conclusion that 'direct perception' as described by Gibson is *pratyakśa*, which is casually rendered as direct experience. Some people mistakenly also look at it as sense-based empirical perception. Indeed the Indian knowledge systems have been quite sophisticated, where three kinds of Pratyakśa are acknowledged – Īndrīya Pratyakśa (sense based), mānasa Pratyakśa (cognition/representation based) and tatva Pratyakśa (direct experience of truth). In basic Buddhist understanding as well, we notice a distinction between sense-based perception called Samjnā and direct perception called Prajnā. The point of the matter is that Pratyakśa cannot be simplistically understood as sense-based direct perception precisely because the Indian knowledge traditions identify the limitations of sense-based perception. The concept proposed by Gibson of direct perception also is complicated by two factors-one the invariant structural features of the environment that the organism is aware of and called affordances. Second, the goal directedness in context and situated behaviour of the organism as it responds to the environment. Thus, Pratyakśa means 'no mind' transitionally.

This interaction between the environment and the goal-directed behaviour is observed in the case of creativity, flow and immersion states during which the person is an active and situationally embedded but directly perceives the context and the structure to act-as Pratyakśa. This is a limited moment by moment transcendence for a conventionally representational mind. In this momentary transcendence, one also tends to lose the jarring fragile ego, associated with a self-absorbed self-consciousness. However, the person doesn't lose the sense of self or the phenomenal awareness for an established extended period of objective time, enough to conclude (for themselves) that it is the non-dual awareness that is the basis, interweave and the summum bonum of all or any experience.

This brings us to the next step of transcendence, where using systematic induction processes in meditation frameworks, a seeker or the meditator systematically 'loses' cognitive elements in the consciousness to finally enter what have been called as 'altered states' for extended periods of objective time. Tart uses the evocative English word – 'induction process' (Tart, 1972, 2008). In summary, traditional texts claim three important points; first, texts claim that cognitive processes such as attention are to be leveraged internally to process internal contents of consciousness through two basic cognitive acts: (a) slowing down the speed or the stream of consciousness and/or (b) holding and sustaining attention on a single chosen object in consciousness. Second, the texts and the applied psychology practised by meditators assert that through a series of systematic processes, elements of the psyche related to either the selected object/element or the slowed stream of consciousness, a cohering process occurs and elements in memory and thinking are re-processed to progressively be 'given away'. This processing, also progressively deepens the quality of attentional processes, which is to say that instead of triggering a fear response, the attentional processes sustain and are sustained by a deep relaxation response. The final point is that the applied psychology of Yoga and meditation implies that seekers and meditators extend this process for longer periods of objective time such that in the final culminating process, the minimum phenomenal awareness, with the 'I' and the mineness of experience is also lost for extended periods of time. Before we continue, we need to note that these three steps are indicated as the three Pariṇāma (milestones) in the PYS-s and taught to students in a traditional teaching learning context. Also, it is important to note here that the measurability of neuroscience may be extremely limited in this framework. First, we don't know, for example, what happens in the brain, when the attentional cohering process starts, or the quality of attention 'deepens' or what would show on the MRI or fMRI the loss of phenomenal awareness. As mentioned earlier, Metzinger (Gamma & Metzinger, 2021; Metzinger, 2020) has proposed minimal phenomenal states' as associated with Ascending Reticular Activating System (ARAS) associated with being awake. But we don't know anything (neuroscientifically) as yet, since states of losing phenomenal awareness or entering into Samādhi States are very rare; these cannot be created or conjured up at will. Gamma and Metzinger have proposed a questionnaire, based on their review of literature to assess these minimally phenomenal experiences (MPE). It is sufficient to just note that such an effort is wonderfully ambitious.

Transcendence in Yoga is a step-by-step process during meditation through yogic practice but is *progressively subtle phenomenally* to finally recognize non-dual awareness over longer periods of time. This is a very subtle process, according to PYS, and cannot be a predictable trajectory. Note also that the texts claim that while 'coming back' to embodied consciousness, the seeker or the meditator follows the same process in reverse to finally become aware of the conventional self-embodied consciousness. This process of losing elements and contents of consciousness and then re-gaining them back continues longitudinally if the practice of meditation is consistent. According to texts such as Jīvanmukti Viveka, which is a revered Hindu Vedāntic text (Harshadananda, 2009), consistent practice of Manonaśa and Vāsanākśaya (destruction of mind and withering of desires) is emphasized and leads to a deepening of Samādhi or losing phenomenal self-awareness over extended periods of objective time, to finally arrive at *abiding* in no mind-called as Jīvanmukti and Turiya. With this brief interlink between creativity and flow states and what IP means by 'non-dual awareness', the next section deals with a particular term/concept used in Yoga Sutra called nirodha.

Nirodha: Altered states of waking consciousness, meditation and samādhi

The word concept '*nirodha*' is introduced in PYS in the very definition of Yoga as the spontaneous ceasing of the movements in the reservoir of consciousness. The movements in the reservoir of consciousness are understood with the word concept – Vrtti. Vrtti has been discussed well enough technically by philosophers, and is a word used in Indian languages to this day. Vrtti broadly implies the processes in the contents of consciousness and can include all or any of the following since Indian traditions do not bisect or trisect psyche into cognition, affect and behaviour. Cognition, affect and internal action and external behaviours are disjunct in disturbed mind-bodies but increasingly in tandem in processes of well-being, as indicated earlier. The definition of Yoga says that when all the movements in contents of consciousness cease, then one does arrive at the first step of transcendence, where one recognizes true 'self-nature'. Note that the self-nature is not a personal self (my self/your self) but the nature of self as such. Nirodha is that effacing of the contents of consciousness in conscious awareness at that particular point of time, necessarily based on resolution of the contents of consciousness that constitute the conventional self. Note that all automatic processes, as understood in contemporary psychology, are understood as 'karma-Samskāra-vāsanā' in Yoga psychology. These are all classified as belonging to citta – the repository of all the experiences, without or with conscious attention, recorded by and in body-mind. As mentioned, the citta organizes and re-organizes the contents of consciousness as past experiences of intention and action (Karma), past experiences of desires, thoughts, feelings and affect (Samskāra) and residual desires, thoughts and experiences of past events (vāsanā). Over a period of time and consistent practice, more and more automatic movements of karma, Samskāra and vāsanā emerge to conscious attention as 'reservoirs of consciousness' and are witnessed without engaging in them so as to not re-consolidating them. Alternatively, depending on the student's preference, a carefully selected attentional object or element is given so that all automatic processes as they arise are cohered around this attentional object. Thus, all contents of consciousness are re-versioned and linked to the attention of a chosen attentional object. Yoga Sutra-s, posit that over a period of time, depending on the quality of attention of the meditator/seeker and the ability of the seeker to either remain disengaged from the material that arises into conscious of awareness or merge and cohere into the carefully chosen attentional object, the person will reach states of without any contents –awareness as such.

Nirodha, according to several other later Hatha Yoga such as Yoga Tārāvali, is connected to 'Laya' and, at first, occurs in moments or very brief periods of time to then increasingly longer periods of time. As mentioned, the text Yoga Tārāvali, has recently been translated and interpreted into English, by Master T. K. V. Desikachar from Krishnamacharya's tradition (Desikachar & Desikachar, 2004). Yoga texts have timed these in terms of the number of breaths –spans called a 'matra' or breath measure. Note that breathing and patterns of breathing are seen in the Yoga texts as phenomenal markers of time similar to some other markers such as the opening and closing of eyelids and the beats of the heart. These phenomenal markers of time in terms of breathing are then systematically elongated by extending the in-breath and the out-breath and also inserting a pause between the breathing rhythms mindfully and consciously. This is generally well-known, at least to the students of pranayama across the world and in recent years, the pause in the breath, called as kumbhaka has now been fashionably called 'intermittent hypoxia'. Research shows that Kumbhaka improves oxygenation and induces Neuroplasticity (Malshe, 2011; Serebrovskaya & Xi, 2016). Yoga texts then posit that after consistent practice, not only does the out-breath becomes longer than the in-breath by the ratio of four to one, but the pause inserted between the rhythm of in- and out-breath becomes longer than both in- and out-breath; thus, kumbhaka or the pause 'overflows' the in- and the out-breath. Practically it would mean that the breathing not only becomes slower but also ceases/minimally aware for longer and longer periods of time. Yoga texts directly map the rate of breathing to the movements of thoughts in mind. In fact, the non-conscious desire to breathe arises as a thought in itself. Therefore, when breathing becomes minimally slow, then the thoughts, even of the desire to breathe (in or out) also become minimal. Finally, a person is able to observe a 'natural gap' between two movements arising out of mind similar to the gap between the in- and out-breath. This gap becomes longer and longer.

The PYS describes three Pariṇāma-s or outcomes in its aphorisms. They are Nirodha, Samādhi and Ekagrata Pariṇāma. The Nirodha 'ripens' into longer and longer periods of objective time when phenomenal self-awareness is progressively coherent and lost. Samādhi is one of the word concepts that indicates the complete, undoubted recognition of self-consciousness beyond thought. As has been mentioned often in this book, the source text for understanding Nirodha and Samādhi is PYS and the three authoritative commentaries on PYS in Sanskrit. As mentioned elsewhere (Pandit, 2020), Swami Veda Bharati, a master of Yoga Vedānta and Tantra, has given an authoritative commentary on the first two chapters of PYS in English, where he has also consolidated all the earlier interpretations and weeded out in-authentic commentaries. PYS and its commentaries identify levels of samādhi and the concomitant transformations in cognition, affect and behaviour/action of the committed meditators/seekers. Since the IKT does not dichotomize or trisect the psyche into cognition, affect and behaviour, the source texts, as well as their interpretations, initiate the discussions from an integrated step-by-step progression and transformation of the psyche from the states of fragmentation to an immersive no-mind via different topographies in the ecology of consciousness.

As we discussed in the first chapter, in current context, European and American psychology is deeply influenced by Buddhism, especially the influence of His Holiness the Dalai Lama. Most basic research studies have utilized what has been pioneered by Varela, Thompson and Rosch as a 'Neuro-phenomenological' approach. The phenomenological aspect of neuro-phenomenology has been derived from the phenomenology of a Buddhist applied psychology – both Abhidhamma/Theravada Pāli Buddhism as well as Mahayana Tibetan Buddhism (Chadha, 2015a; Johnston, 2006; Siderits et al., 2011). Even as these advances are in the right direction and co-create interdisciplinary learning and research spaces, several key gaps remain.

Firstly, basic research on consciousness and self, esp. as conceptualized and framed in several and diverse Indian philosophical traditions are not sufficiently studied by psychologists, esp. by psychologists in India. Indian knowledge traditions claim that the defining and central recognition is content and intent-less awareness. This central content and intent-less awareness is also trans-cultural. A phenomenological study of known advanced meditators who embody this recognition longitudinally has not yet been done. It is also the most challenging endeavour, because meditators are likely to remain silent about this most intimate and precious recognition of their existence. Such a phenomenological enquiry could, however, enlighten the path of neuroscience!

Secondly, Indian philosophical systems have a rich tradition of flourishing debates in formal philosophy as well as applied psychological practice. There is a striking diversity of viewpoints and a depth of textual material available. In recent years, 'comparative' philosophical projects have been attempted towards greater insight (Chadha, 2015a; Ganeri, 2003; Ram-Prasad, 2013). While this is indeed remarkable, very few broad collaborative researches have worked with the traditional counters to Buddhism in the Indian philosophical context, which is primarily non-dual advaita and Kashmiri Trika philosophers but could also include movements such as Baul and Kabir. This is important, in principle, because there has been a serious 2000 years history of debate and ideas. Therefore, collaborative projects that organize the phenomenology of non-dual perspectives, such as advaita and Kashmiri Trika practice, need a serious enquiry as well.

Thirdly, one of the most interesting aspects of the stages of Samādhi is the consistent experience of well-being. Well-being or subjective well-being has been well-studied in recent times. Psychologists such as Diener and Lyubomirsky have conceptualized subjective well-being and happiness. One of the features of this conceptualization is the focus on the interaction of the person embedded in the social and cultural worlds. While it is indeed true that persons need to interact with the environment, situational and contextual factors towards well-being, the key insight about psychological transformation in the Indian wisdom traditions is that they are not flat in time. In contrast, in the Indian conceptualization of well-being, there is lesser and lesser dependence on environmental, situational and contextual factors as the immersion becomes deeper and established. Indeed, the person becomes intrinsically coherent and lives frugally, with reverence and due honour-ing of the external world. Several life histories of yogis and meditators have documented that this intrinsic coherence continues, despite adversities and hardships, with lesser and lesser hedonistic cravings. Notwithstanding the nuances in the discussion, the role of well-being and affective process in advanced meditation and possibly no-mind states is a frontier area of enquiry, which is yet beyond the scope of most contemporary psychology research and knowledge endeavours. If taken for enquiry, we may learn from the cross-fertilization of ideas from Indic philosophies and applied psychologies.

In particular, Narayanan Srinivasan has recently written about the notion of 'ānanda' translated as well-being as particularly amenable to neuroscience investigation (Srinivasan, 2020). If there is no self and only attention, as Ganeri, in his supremely logical book, argues (Ganeri, 2017), then how is 'ānanda' (however defined) seen and experienced and lived through life? As mentioned, in the neuroscience traditions, there is a discussion on 'minimal phenomenal states', 'consciousness without content' (see Metzinger, 2013, 2020) and 'non-dual awareness' (please see Josipovic & Miskovic, 2020), where the role of ARAS system in the brain is proposed to be in nexus with these minimal phenomenal experiences. If it is so, then meditators must be able to direct the ARAS at will and also fire areas of positive affect at the same time! Is it possible that monks and advanced meditators can direct ARAS at will and how does that reflect in terms of well-being? These are some of the questions for neuroscientists and psychologists to cross-fertilize their existing conceptualization.

Finally, the fascinating idea of minimal phenomenal states as experienced and recorded by humans, and most recently taken seriously by Euro-American philosophers, emphasizes that we need to yet know a lot more than our current state of knowledge about mind sciences, including the question of whether it is possible to observe neural correlates of not just 'non-dual awareness' but of all systematic induction processes to enter into altered states of wakeful consciousness.

Citta, Ālaya Vijnāna and consciousness – Transcending the personal idea of mind

Ālaya Vijnāna and its mirror idea of Citta can be recognized as the first and original notion of an unconscious collective mind, about 2500 years before the Freudian and later Jungian concept of an unconscious. Indian knowledge systems are not fixed and frozen, as even in the texts demonstrate a continuous consolidation of dialogues and arguments. Ālaya Vijnāna represents the creative Buddhist interaction to the consistent dialogue and debate on the continuity of experience as such. The early Buddhists differentiated between momentary surface level consciousness and a deeper consciousness that seemed continuous. Thus, the intellectual challenge for the Buddhist schools was to conceptualize continuity of consciousness, without self, accounting for the moment by moment awareness and thereafter account for ethics and moral accountability, as they arise from a continuous 'owned' self! Similar effort is seen in current times, and indeed, Chadha, in one of her papers, proposed that the Yogācāra framework of 'Ālaya Vijnāna' could be utilized to understand the continuity of experience with an ethical framework without the necessity of self. Although Waldron (Waldron, 2008) compares Ālaya Vijnāna to the Freudian unconscious, this book disagrees with him. It is tempting to think of Ālaya Vijnāna as the unconscious, similar to Freud's notions. However, these surface level similarities of the word – 'unconscious' do not justify comparisons at all. The Buddhist framework is more logical, nuanced and delimited from sex and aggression compared to Freudian ideas. Table 6.1 shows the basic differences.

Abhidhamma texts could not conceptualize the deeper non-conscious continuous mind. The Yogācāra school responded with the 'third turning of the dhamma' and, in an adversarial dialogue and debate with the Yoga schools, presented a sophisticated theory of mind and consciousness. This conceptual framework looked at the *enminding process* in layers. At the first layer was sense awareness or Sannā (Samjnā). This gave rise to Sannā Vijnāna or sense consciousness. The Sannā of the form, visual cognition arises, dependent upon the eye and form and so on for all senses. Thus, there are five sense consciousness. Next layer was called as Vinnana (Vijnāna) – this technical term is understood differently than the similar term used in other Vedānta and Sāṃkhya frameworks. Vinnana in Yogācāra was understood as mental awareness that arises dependent on *karmic formations or Samskāra.*

Table 6.1 Comparison between the Buddhist Yogācāra Model and the Classical and Neo-Freudian Model of Unconscious

Buddhist Yogācāra models	*Classical and neo-Freudian models*
Sarvabija – All cognitive events constitute and sprout from the Ālaya	Classically, only sexual and aggressive are pushed into unconscious. What about other cognitions? Post-Freudians don't have specific views
Non-conscious is a home conscious and constantly interacts with conscious. There is no need for defence mechanisms	Unconscious is suppressed actively by conscious. Conscious life is a defence mechanism both for coping and for self-deception
Non-conscious is all events as they occur; 'I' consciousness is the root cause of craving and attachment; I consciousness is a false consciousness	Self is not explained; ego is conscious and a small part of structure; there is no freedom; just a Klienian 'depressive position'
Samskāra and vāsanās are contents of the mind; Ālaya Vijnāna (collective mind), pravritti vijnāna (individualized mind) and Sannā-vijnāna (sensory mind) are the structure of the mind	
Sila and Ethics are the positive basis of this interaction in Vijnāna	Super-ego is imposed upon the psyche by the society. It is necessarily negative and proscriptive

Source: Author.

The Buddhist theorists were very clear that this vinnana was conventional/worldly in its process and was called as sāmsāric vinnana. According to the Buddhist theory, awareness is two-fold and is recognized as a depersonalized event. The third layer beneath the five senses Sannā and manovinannā was called as 'kliśta manas' – a conventionally constituted but 'empty' sense of self that craves and is a cause of suffering. Finally, at the deepest level was a continuous stream of consciousness, which served as reservoir, and a home consciousness (Ālaya Vijnāna). Ālaya Vijnāna was again not personalized in its very definition and was seen as the eighth layer of consciousness. From this continuous stream of consciousness, all actions arose and merged in its repository, where they were in-record. Thus, Ālaya Vijnāna was base consciousness, persisting even after all conscious processes stopped. When they rise again, that is called 'Pravritti Vijnāna' or the beginning of creation. Ālaya Vijnāna was also called as the 'sarvabijaka citta' or mind with all the seeds. Kliśta manas in the ālaya is mostly filled with 'I' consciousness and 'pravritti vinnana' in Ālaya is filled with six functioning consciousnesses. Ālaya Vijnāna theory held that perception itself is 'constructed' on the basis of Samskāra. Samskāra thus was the content that regurgitated and ālaya was the structure.

No self, continuous mind: Ālaya Vijnāna and contemporary psychology

In current times, consciousness and its typologies such as extended consciousness (Damasio, 1998) have been broadly accepted by cognitive scientists. Panpsychism, as referred earlier, broadly implies that consciousness and sentience are available and possible for non-human beings. This argument in European tradition is examined against the idea of physicalism and the emergence of consciousness as a function of the complexity of the systems. The panpsychist argument is also seen through the meta-theoretical assumptions of Euro-American philosophy of science. Chadha (Chadha, 2015b) has proposed that Ālaya Vijnāna is an apt theoretical solution in debates and discussions on consciousness. The elegant framework of Ālaya Vijnāna turns the normative assumptions and arguments of the Vedānta upside down by proposing that while consciousness remains a correlated feature of minds, if not emergent to complexity, there could be a network of minds, instead. Abhidharmic texts question the 'social' convention of calling 'I'/'He'/'She' as the confirmation that the 'self' actually exists. *According to Abhidharmma texts, the cause of suffering is the assent to this cognitive error that there is an independent self just because there is a convention of calling it as 'I'.* The five skandhas or the 'aggregates of body and mind' cannot be called as the self. The appearance of self is false and the whole intention of meditation is to recognize the 'self-less' ness of (pudgala) persons, termed as *Pudgala-nairātmya*. In this, the Buddhist theoreticians were directly attacking the notion of *consciousness as self.*

A 'Pudgala' or a person refers to 'a conception of an object' – which by convention is referred as 'i' and by convention is said to possess the skandhas or the mind-body nexus. These aggregates are the cause on which the conception of 'I' is dependent. These causal continuums of aggregates exist in the past, present and future. In a cognitive error, humans conceptualize 'self' as the whole of the parts. Thus, 'I' or self is a mental construction that gets perpetuated by our agreement of it. Early Abhidhamma theoreticians or Pudgalavadin's argue that, there exists an entity that supports the five skandha-s of personality – similar to Nyāya –Vaiśeṣika, but that there is no permanent, causally independent self as an entity/substance. They also noted that rūpa skandha or the aggregate of sensory consciousness leads to Sannā and Vinannā as sensory-mental or mind-body perceptions called as mano-vijnāna. Mano-Vijnāna arises only in reference to itself – in the past and in the future in contrast to the five-sense consciousness or Sannā and clearly, the act of cognition is a simultaneity of Sannā and Vinannā. Who, then, is the agent of action? And therefore, suffering is experienced from actions arising out of this error filled, what was called as *kliśta manas*.

What would be the actual implications of this framework? The first one, would be the ethical and moral repercussions of a 'no-self, all mind, multiple minds framework', which can lead to a 'free for all' or more dangerous, 'power trumps all' notions of moral, ethical actions in a secular framework. The second implication is that the central question of the emergence of minds themselves still remains; un-illuminated as we seem to have just substituted consciousness with minds and removed self from the equation, probably because it fits our assumptions. When the Buddhists proposed their philosophy, they were radical pioneers as they were able to address the gaps in Indian Darśana on what was the nature of self. When the contemporary researchers appropriate the Buddhist ideas, it force fits into a confirmation bias, doesn't inform anything further, as the Buddhist arguments were later forced into retreat and critiqued, for example, Ālaya Vijnāna and the idea of 'Tathāgatagarbha' was critiqued for close parallels to the Sāmkhya-n Citta and Vedāntic Ātman. Finally, is this not a truly Indian Psychology that Indians need to engage in?

Minds as a play of consciousness: Multiple minds, cosmic consciousness

Innovation is not in convenient appropriation but arises as a response to a contextual imperative. It is in the context of the IKT and the dialogue between Buddhist and Vedāntic schools that we see this innovation. Vedantins had lost to Buddhist reasoning, and Ādi Śankara grappled with the Buddhist dialectic and reasoning, before he was able to find a profound reformulation or a minute gap that he used to re-frame the discussions. He agreed that the socially constituted, conventional self is indeed empty, yet the only pathway to understand and grasp consciousness is through the self-processes. This is subtle and, therefore, a radical reformulation; it implies that consciousness is all pervasive, but self – phenomenal awareness is an emergent phenomenon of the complexity of the ecology of consciousness. Just because self and phenomenal awareness arises out of the complexity of the systems, it does not limit the pervasiveness of consciousness but becomes the only window for recognition of the consciousness. Self-recognition is not of a conventionally constituted self, which is clearly empty but is the recognition that consciousness which pre-exists with or without phenomenal awareness, while self is the only pathway to recognize it. Second, it is the mind that constitutes and is co-constituted by the body and society. The nexus between mind-body and society is downstream.

As we have been discussing throughout this book, in the Indian civilizational context, the idea that consciousness animates at least those who are alive is not just found in the Hindu systems but also in the Buddhist and Jain systems. Thus, some scholars have now 'argued' that consciousness is indeed possible in a fly and what could be conscious awareness for the fly would be a non-conscious element among human experiences (Lamme, 2018; Roelofs & Buchanan, 2019). This idea of consciousness as deliberate awareness alone and everything else as non-consciousness is different from the Indian idea of consciousness as such. A few philosophers, who have studied Indian philosophy, have argued and re-emphasized (Albahari, 2019; Ram-Prasad, 2001) the idea that consciousness is all pervasive and is not limited by the physicalist personal body-mind–society complex. The most interesting and radical feature of the Indian knowledge systems was that not only did they philosophically argue the idea of consciousness as all pervasive or the Ālaya Vijnāna as continuous, but they also practiced these world-views without market-based pressures (mostly). Further, as a whole, these practices seem to work and result in well-being for those who practice. Thus, these frameworks were not pure speculative philosophy.

Indeed, the later developments of social psychology of the bhakti movement, as well as philosophical and applied psychological frameworks of Viśiṣtādvaita and dvaita, also arise from the idea that consciousness is pervasive and transpersonal; not limited by the human mind-body complex alone, but *is free to be human as well as non-human.* By this logic, are robots also artificially intelligent and pervaded with consciousness? A Vedantin would answer that – yes, consciousness pervades robots, just has it pervades stones and rocks, but the robot prakriti would not have enough 'Sattva' to reflect the luminosity of phenomenal self-awareness.

An important concept that underlines the continuity of consciousness, including the continuity of experiences recorded in consciousness, is the concept of Jivātman. Jivātman is an animated individualized consciousness that holds a particular personalized record and repository of experiences, which are required to get exhausted or brought to conscious awareness during the process of self-enquiry. According to Yoga Sutra, as the quality of attention matures and disturbances and distractions arising from the non-conscious awareness, memories, emotions, desires and past records of intentions and actions committed are effectively brought to conscious awareness and effaced through a variety of techniques which we discussed earlier. In this process of the maturity of attentional processes, the IKT traditions show that all the experiences which are held in the repository of the jivātman get effaced, eventually, so that the jivātman merges into the non-personalized consciousness as such. According to the practice and the maturity of attentional processes, the contents of mind, which itself is the construction *in* consciousness are cleansed, thus transcending the jarring narcissistic sense of conventionally constituted, 'I' absorbed 'I'-consciousness; the socially constituted self, which the Buddhists called as 'mano-Vijnāna' and kliśta manas is lost. Thus, Yoga processes and practice pave the way for a stronger or more long-term process of 'abiding' in 'no mind'. This clearly is longitudinal and lifespan transformation than just flow or laya or the easily measured bodily effects of relaxation.

As I have argued elsewhere (Pandit, 2020, 2021), Abhyāsa, Vairāgya and Viveka are a set of processes which would be not only amenable to neurological investigation but also would be hypothesized to show that regardless of situation, mastery over internal and external stimuli and consistent practice thereof allows for a minimally phenomenal state at will – the quietness of neural systems. Yoga practices also claim that this Dhyāna or deepening of meditative states results in less requirement of energy, a deeper relaxation response and the experience of well-being, finally we arrive at a point where all the contents of consciousness have been exhausted and effaced. Vedānta then prescribes a set of practices such that new impressions are effaced as they occur and later, none are recorded. Thus, it is possible to experience awareness which is nothing to own and is therefore recognized as 'ownerless'! (Siderits et al., 2011).

Manonmana (mind-no-mind): The frontier of mind as well as no-mind

In the later developments of Yoga-Sāmkhya, Vedānta and Trika Śaiva frameworks, including its cross-fertilization with the later Natha, and Hatha Yoga traditions, we arrive at the concept of Unmana and Manonmana. These conceptualization frameworks and their practice represent a gigantic historical process of integration and layering up of Yoga-Sāmkhya, advaita, trika, tantra and bhakti through Natha, Hatha Yoga and Srividya traditions (Swahananda, 2012). Although Hatha Yoga texts can be found at least till the 1st century CE, the consolidation and integration is most visible in the 11th century CE (for details, please see Mallinson, 2014). The practices of laya and the experiential aspects of Unmana and Manonmana are too far away, 'out there' and beyond the frontiers for the contemporary psychology and mind sciences.

Is it possible to explore that in an Indian framework, the deliberate and automatic cognitive processing framework is flipped such that advanced meditation means that well-being becomes 'automatic' or 'established' and the world-wise processes become odd and alien? This flipped idea of 'automatic' allows for the no-mind (Unmana), with deliberate episodes of time as 'mind'. If detailed seriously, by locating such rare cases, this flipped framework, can inform the scope psychology itself; Contemporary psychology, especially the theories of deliberate and automatic processing, are limited to the state of waking, where states of well-being seem constant and consistent in dreaming and dreamless sleep states. Is there an automatic and deliberate dreaming and dreamless sleep when the conscious mind is sleeping?

Do meditators who exhaust their personalized consciousness die and how soon? This question was debated and observed among those with a lived experience of Samādhi states. The detailing of the idea of Jīvanmukti and modelled by Swami Vidyaranya muni, in his Sanskrit text – Jīvanmukti Viveka captures several points about this radical idea of mind-no-mind. Swami Vidyaranya was an 11th–12th-century master, a monk, who is as revered as the next Ādi Sankarācārya in the Hindu canon, precisely because he detailed the mind-no-mind as a stage model. In order to bring clarity, he used PYS extensively. Euro-American scholars being outsiders to the tradition and familiar with a compartmentalized nature of knowledge have called the master – 'confused', revealing their own biases perhaps (see Fort, 1999). The stage model of Jīvanmukti captures several points that are important to understand mind-no-mind and has an underlying process of consistent practice called 'Samādhi abhyāsa'. As the master writes, this model of knowing and the consequent losing of 'I' awareness is given in Yoga Vāśiṣtha, a much earlier text, according to the tradition Note also that, this discussion sounds 'esoteric', but in contemporary times, Jīvanmukta-s have been documented and researched such as Swami Vivekananda, Swami Yogananda, Yogi Sri Aurobindo, Swami Rama and Swami Veda Bharati (Fort, 1999; Pandit, 2021). Most Yoga and meditation teachers, called as 'jivanmukta-s', are validated as being free while living from their teachers and elders in the meditator community through an internal community-based assessment; recall that Swami Yogananda was given the title of 'Paramahamsa' by his teacher when he returned back from America. The staging model of seven grounds of knowing (Sapta jnāna Bhumi) moves beyond the very familiar either/or binary model of enlightenment/liberation/transcendence that populates other nebulae – 'myth' making ideas about Yoga, meditation, transformation and transcendence.

The seven stages and their characteristics, are understood as occurring in repeated spirals rather than flat universal stages are shown in Table 6.2.

Table 6.2 Grounds of knowing from Jīvan mukti Viveka (freedom while living)

Knowing – Name of the stage of knowing	*Defining characteristics of the mind-no-mind*
First ground of knowing – Śubhecchā	Seeking and enquiry about the real nature of knowing and I awareness; desire to remove suffering.
Second ground of knowing – Vicāraṇa	A systematic and focused practice with contemplation, reflection and action.
Third ground of knowing – Tanumānasa	A practice that now purifies intention, cognition, affect and action; makes 'karma, Samskāra, vāsanā'. – disturbances weak in manifestation (tanukarana) for healing and transformation. This stage is comparable to the PYS, second chapter, first and second sutra.
Fourth ground of knowing – Sattvāpatti	The first experience of no-mind or awareness without phenomenality; this can be momentary or in some time, depending on the practice of the meditator. This is comparable to the 'Nirodha Pariṇāma' in Yoga Sutra-s.
Fifth ground of knowing – Asamsakti (first stage of Jīvanmukti)	Muni Vidyanaya, does not consider Sattvapatti as **Jīvanmukti**, as the knowing is not continuous and established. No mind intersects with mind. However, Sattvapatti initiates the process of exhausting the karma-Samskāra-vāsanā well. The fifth ground of knowing is indicated as the first stage of Jīvanmukti. In this stage, the Jivanmukta, does intense practice on three aspects according to Muni Vidyanya. (1) Samādhi Abhyāsa – the intense practice of deepening meditation; (2) Mano-nasha – the final resolutions and, therefore, the final 'destruction' of mind; (3) Vāsanākhaya – the withering of residual desires. Muni Vidyaranya forcefully emphasizes that all the three practices have to be intensely conducted ***in tandem and simultaneity***. Choosing one over the other will not accomplish Jīvanmukti.
Sixth ground of knowing – Padārthābhāvini (second stage of Jīvanmukti)	In this advanced and established stage of Jīvanmukti, the master (now) has almost completely exhausted their personal contents of consciousness. The word Padārtha-abhavini refers to the fact that the person is unable to perceptually, cognitively and affectively distinguish between 'I' and 'not I' or 'you'. They do hold their bodies but are unconcerned about it – including hunger, evacuation, thirst and sleep. Most of them stop speaking. Some of the recent masters who reached this state were Sri Ramana, Sri Lahiri Mahasaya and Sri Nityananda of Ganeshpuri. Such masters are revered and addressed as 'Avadhoota' – which is translated as 'washed/cleansed out'.
Seventh ground of knowing – Turyagā (a complete knowing and immersion in the consciousness; irreversible loss of 'I' awareness and final dissolution	In this final stage of mind-no-mind, Muni Vidyaranya says that there is a complete, final and irreversible dissolution of the mind. The body also is dropped. The minimal mind or phenomenal awareness is also completely given up/lost.

Source: Author.

Why should Indian psychologists be interested in mind-no-mind?

In the above model, we see the mind-no-mind as a continuum and not as a binary. Why do psychologists and particularly psychologists in India need to study this? For one, it defines the scope of psychology itself on a sliding continuum from automatic minds to freedom through no-mind! We need to discuss being free while living simply because, what would be the point of being free, while being dead or waiting for another birth (depending on one's beliefs). Freedom makes sense only while being alive. As psychologists, there are several interesting facets that need further theorization – Firstly, apart from removing the binary of unenlightened and enlightened, we note that the Jīvanmukta continues to live in the body-mind, identifying with a particular name, status and at least in the first stage of jīvanmukti, continues to operate in the social context. This implies that we are looking at a radical social psychology.

In the second stage of Jīvanmukti, the text says the person stops recognizing the other and may become socially inappropriate – Avaliya-s, Avadhoot-s, who walk around naked or live in a particular position for months are Jīvanmukta-s, who experience no 'I' and therefore, no 'other'. It is only in the last ground that the individuality completely and finally/irreversibly merges/extinguishes in the Brahman or the fourth, indicated to in the second chapter in reference to Māndukyopaniśad. From a research point of view, most contemporary Jīvanmukta-s have recorded and documented experiences of two or more than two such events when they lost phenomenal awareness as well. As mentioned in the texts, they did come back to that same phenomenological awareness of the body-mind and accessed the same content of consciousness, this is very interesting as it provides us with a new landscape and new insights, that texts have staged and theorized. Consciousness as such is conceptualized as trans-local, trans-chronic and transpersonal, and yet, after samādhi, and repeated samādhi, meditators do get back to the same synchronic, body-mind consciousness with earlier contents access once again. Why does that happen? It opens up possibilities of new research, more grounded in well-being than in the tyranny and cosmetic updating of mind – that which we see otherwise, including in a belief-oriented religious practice, therapy, etc. The idea of 'no mind' disrupts everything we take for granted in psychology as real. As we stated in the chapter – Mind is the only myth there is! So, here is an invitation from the Indian psychological thought to re-imagine not just psychology but human life experience itself. This is only possible in consciousness-based psychology.

The fact that we do not see the reality as it is one of the fundamental statements of Advaita Vedānta. This doesn't mean that we see a representational reality which is a hallucination or that there is no objective reality at all as has been misrepresented by various outsiders. The point made here is quite profound – that conventional reality as accessed is useful for conventional purpose, no more, no less. If and when our conventional motivations are removed, we experience and access an unvarnished reality beyond our personal selves. Note that this reality, which is beyond personal selves, is inherently moral and equal to all; it is not dead but alive to each one, including the tress, plants, insects, birds and animals. It is a live consciousness and is, therefore, sacred.

If we were to use this idea of a distributed conjured up social consciousness, then we arrive at two possibilities – first possibility is that all of us are conjuring a consensual reality which doesn't reflect the reality as it is, but it is organized and collectively conjured so as to ensure the survival of our groups or as individual self is. From this perspective, the world is a shared hallucination. Scholars, such as Anil Seth, have sensationally discussed this and framed their point that hallucinations that are seen as dysfunctional appear as coping processes for the consciousness to make sense of the world. The idea that consciousness conjures up a reality that we all agree to be a reality is not new. It is just that in case of a hallucination or a delusion that particular conjure of reality is not shared by other members of that person's network. Note that, in case of cults and extreme groups such as satanic groups or groups that believe in aliens/alien abduction or the idea of an apocalypse, a set of group members perceive that reality as the same. The key point here is that the body-mind processes can access social approval or assent towards a conjured reality, so the idea of consciousness as a network of conscious agents, doesn't free us of these possibilities either. The only way, according to Yoga, is to completely see through all mental constructions and still discover the live awareness and ability to be either silent or play along the game as it were!

As we move next to the chapter on consciousness and social selves, we see that, as a stepping stone, a relational and collective self is 'ownerless' and indeed, ownership/Ahambhāva/Ahamkāra is the marker for a socially constituted, 'empty' self. It is strange that in *contemporary social psychology, there is a striking diversity of frameworks and conceptualizations of individual minds and collective minds, which are consciousness blind* and without any significant attempt to tie the different compartments.

In Indian psychology, esp. bhakti frameworks, socially, the individual minds are purposeful collectively networked social groups as *Satsanga* (the connection of the insight). Satsanga in Indian psychology goes beyond the social consciousness or social collective consciousness of minds or the distributed forms of mind that pan-psychism seems to imply. Satsanga, or a conscious cultivation of the 'insight collective', is thereafter used as a mechanism for relational and self-transformation. As Ādi Śankara, the great Advaita master says,

'Satsangatve Nissangatvā Nissangatve Nirmohatavā: Nirmohatve Niṣchalatatva, Niṣchalatatve Jīvanmukti'!

The verse seems to imply that there is a step-by-step transition as follows:

1 Satsanga, which starts by a purposeful association with people who have experiential insight.
2 From satsanga, arises a desire for disengagement with all that one ordinarily engages in – that is, the sensory-motor, mind-body-society nexus that continually creates and regurgitates contents of consciousness which are constantly being created and churned.
3 An experiential disengagement is called, Nissanga. From Nissanga, comes the clarity about cognitive beliefs (these are called as delusions in the verse) we hold about the conventional realities that we are embedded in.
4 Through questioning these belief structures, the verse says that we become free from these errors. According to the verse, instead of arriving at emptiness, the seeker/meditator recognizes the principle of consciousness that never moves or changes and is without content or intent but creates content and intent at will. At this point, the master philosopher says that once this clear sky of awareness is recognized than one lives in freedom while living, that is Jīvanmukti, as mentioned in the Vedānta.

This verse then leads us to the next chapter on consciousness and social selves.

References

Albahari, M. (2019). Beyond cosmopsychism and the great I am: How the world might be grounded in universal 'advaitic' consciousness. In *The Routledge handbook of panpsychism* (pp. 119–130). Routledge.

Bharati, S. V. (2001a). *Yoga Sutras of Patanjali* (Vol. 3). Motilal Banarsidass Publ.

Bharati, S. V. (2001b). *Yoga Sutras of Patanjali (with the exposition of Vyasa)* (Vol. II: Sadhana-Pada). Motilal Banarsidass Pub.

Bhate, N. H. (2015). Yoga in the works of Ādi Śaṅkarācārya. *Yoga Mimamsa*, *47*(1), 30–36.

Bhawuk, D. P. S. (2003). Culture's influence on creativity: The case of Indian spirituality. *International Journal of Intercultural Relations*, *27*(1), 1–22. https://doi.org/10.1016/s0147-1767(02)00059-7

Bhawuk, D. P. S. (2018). Toward a spirituality-based theory of creativity: Indigenous perspectives from India. In *Asian Indigenous psychologies in the global context* (pp. 139–168). Springer International Publishing. https://doi.org/10.1007/978-3-319-96232-0_7

Block, N. (1995). On a confusion about a function of consciousness. *Behavioral and Brain Sciences*, *18*(2), 227–247.

Block, N. (2007a). Consciousness, accessibility, and the mesh between psychology and neuroscience. *Behavioral and Brain Sciences*, *30*(5–6), 481–499. https://doi.org/10.1017/S0140525X07002786

Block, N. (2007b). *Consciousness, function, and representation : Collected papers* (p. 786). MIT.

Chadha, M. (2013). Meditation and Unity of Consciousness: A Perspective from Buddhist Epistemology. *Phenomenology and the Cognitive Sciences*, *14*(1).

Chadha, M. (2015a). Meditation and unity of consciousness: A perspective from Buddhist epistemology. *Phenomenology and the Cognitive Sciences*, *14*(1), 111–127.

Chadha, M. (2015b). Time-series of ephemeral impressions: The Abhidharma-Buddhist view of conscious experience. *Phenomenology and the Cognitive Sciences*, *14*(3), 543–560.

Chadha, M. (2015c). The Problem of the Unity of Consciousness: A Buddhist Solution. *Philosophy East and West*, *65*(3), 746–764.

Chattopadhyay, S. (2012). Review of Vijñāna Bhairava: The manual for self-realization. *Prabuddha Bharata or Awakened India*, *117*(8), 429–430.

Cohen, M. A., & Dennett, D. C. (2011). Consciousness cannot be separated from function. *Trends in Cognitive Sciences*, *15*(8), 358–364.

Damasio, A. (1998). Investigating the biology of consciousness. *Philosophical Transactions of the Royal Society of London. Series B: Biological Sciences*, *353*(1377), 1879–1882.

Damasio, A., & Meyer, K. (2009). Consciousness: An overview of the phenomenon and of its possible neural basis. In S. Laureys & G. Tononi (Eds.), *The neurology of consciousness: Cognitive neuroscience and neuropathology* (pp. 3–14). Elsevier.

Dennett, D. C. (1993). *Consciousness explained*. Penguin UK.

Desikachar, T. K. V., & Desikachar, K. (2004). *Adi Śankara's Yoga Taravali* (Edited by K. Desikachar & TKV; Desikachar). Krishnamacharya Yoga Mandiram.

Dreyfus, H. L. (1993). *The embodied mind, cognitive science and human experience*. JSTOR.

Duncan, I. J. H. (2006). The changing concept of animal sentience. *Applied Animal Behaviour Science*, *100*(1–2), 11–19.

Farmer, T. A., & Matlin, M. W. (2019). *Cognition*. John Wiley & Sons.

Fort, A. O. (1998). *Jīvanmukti in transformation: Embodied liberation in Advaita and neo-Vedānta*. State University of New York Press.

Fort, A. O. (1999). On destroying the mind: The 'Yogasūtras' in Vidyāraṇya's 'Jīvanmuktiviveka'. *Journal of Indian Philosophy*, *27*(4), 377–395.

Friston, K. J., Wiese, W., & Hobson, J. A. (2020). Sentience and the origins of consciousness: From Cartesian duality to Markovian monism. *Entropy*, *22*(5), 516.

Gamma, A., & Metzinger, T. (2021). The minimal phenomenal experience questionnaire (MPE-92M): Towards a phenomenological profile of 'pure awareness' experiences in meditators. *Plos One*, *16*(7), e0253694.

Ganeri, J. (2003). Ancient Indian logic as a theory of case-based reasoning. *Journal of Indian Philosophy*, 31(1/3), 33–45.

Ganeri, J. (2017). *Attention, not self*. Oxford University Press.

Gibson, J. J. (2002). A theory of direct visual perception. In A. Nöe & E. Thompson (Eds.), *Vision and mind: Selected readings in the philosophy of perception* (pp. 77–90).

Harshadananda, S. (2009). *Jīvanmukti Viveka of Vidyāraṇya* (Translated by Swami Harshananda & Dr H. Ramachandra Swamy). Sri Ramakrishna Math.

Higgins, K. M. (2007). An alchemy of emotion: Rasa and aesthetic breakthroughs. *The Journal of Aesthetics and Art Criticism*, *65*(1), 43–54.

Hoffman, D. D., Singh, M., & Prakash, C. (2015). The interface theory of perception. *Psychonomic Bulletin & Review*, *22*(6), 1480–1506.

Johnston, L. (2006). The 'nature' of Buddhism: A survey of relevant literature and themes. *Worldviews: Global Religions, Culture, and Ecology*, *10*(1), 69–99.

Josipovic, Z. (2010). Duality and nonduality in meditation research. *Consciousness and Cognition*, *19*(4), 1119–1121.

Josipovic, Z. (2019). Nondual awareness: Consciousness-as-such as non-representational reflexivity. *Progress in Brain Research*, *244*, 273–298.

Josipovic, Z., & Miskovic, V. (2020). Nondual awareness and minimal phenomenal experience. *Frontiers in Psychology*, *11*, 2087.

Kachroo, M. (2005). *The goddess and her powers: The Tantric identities of the Saundarya laharī* [Master's thesis]. Department of religious Studies, McGill University.

Lamme, V. A. F. (2018). Challenges for theories of consciousness: Seeing or knowing, the missing ingredient and how to deal with panpsychism. *Philosophical Transactions of the Royal Society B: Biological Sciences*, *373*(1755), 20170344.

Lynch, O. M. (1990). *Divine passions*. Oxford University Press.

Lynch, J. M., & Troy, A. S. (2021). The role of nonduality in the relationship between flow states and well-being. *Mindfulness*. https://doi.org/10.1007/s12671-021-01627-3

Mallinson, J. (2014). *Haṭhayoga*'s philosophy: A fortuitous union of non-dualities. *Journal of Indian Philosophy*, *42*, 225–247.

Malshe, P. C. (2011). Nisshesha rechaka pranayama offers benefits through brief intermittent hypoxia. *Ayu*, *32*(4), 451.

Metzinger, T. K. (2013). Why are dreams interesting for philosophers? The example of minimal phenomenal selfhood, plus an agenda for future research1. *Frontiers in Psychology*, *4*, 746.

Metzinger, T. (2020). Minimal phenomenal experience. *Philosophy and the Mind Sciences*, *1*(I), 1–44.

Muktibodhananda, S. (2012). *Hatha yoga pradipika*. Sri Satguru Publications.

Nair, S. (2013). Rasa theory and neural mechanism. *New Zealand Online Journal of Interdisciplinary Studies*, *1*(2), 1–27.

Pandit, S. (2020). Viveka and Vairāgya: Empirical Possibilities for Cognitive Concepts in Indian Psychology. *Journal of Psychosocial Research*, *15*(2), 497–507.

Pandit, S. A. (2021). Advaita: Oneness as a lived reality – examining aspects of profound and a radical psychology. *Psychology and Developing Societies*, *33*(2), 190–207.

Ram-Prasad, C. (2001). Saving the self? Classical Hindu theories of consciousness and contemporary physicalism. *Philosophy East and West*, *51*(3), 378–392. https://doi.org/10.1353/pew.2001.0046

Ram-Prasad, C. (2013). *Advaita epistemology and metaphysics*. Routledge Curzon. https://doi.org/10.4324/9781315029399

Rao, K. R., & Paranjpe, A. C. (2016). *Psychology in the Indian tradition*. Springer India. https://doi.org/10.1007/978-81-322-2440-2

Roelofs, L., & Buchanan, J. (2019). Panpsychism, intuitions, and the great chain of being. *Philosophical Studies*, *176*(11), 2991–3017.

Saraswati, S. M., & Saraswati, S. S. (1998). *Hatha Yoga Pradipika*. Yoga Publications Trust.

Segundo-Ortin, M., & Calvo, P. (2022). Consciousness and cognition in plants. *Wiley Interdisciplinary Reviews: Cognitive Science*, *13*(2), e1578.

Serebrovskaya, T. V., & Xi, L. (2016). Intermittent hypoxia training as non-pharmacologic therapy for cardiovascular diseases: Practical analysis on methods and equipment. *Experimental Biology and Medicine*, *241*(15), 1708–1723.

Seyfarth, R. M., & Cheney, D. L. (2013). Affiliation, empathy, and the origins of theory of mind. *Proceedings of the National Academy of Sciences*, *110*(Supplement 2), 10349–10356.

Siderits, M., Thompson, E., & Zahavi, D. (2011). *Self, no self?: Perspectives from analytical, phenomenological, and Indian traditions*. Oxford University Press.

Srinivasan, N. (2020). Consciousness without content: A look at evidence and prospects. *Frontiers in Psychology*, *11*, 1992.

Sundararajan, L. (2010). Two flavors of aesthetic tasting: Rasa and savoring a cross-cultural study with implications for psychology of emotion. *Review of General Psychology*, *14*(1), 22–30.

Swahananda, S. (2012). *Vedanta Sadhana and Shakti Puja* (p. 336). Advaita Ashram.

Tagare, G. V. (2002). *The Pratyabhijñā philosophy*. Motilal Banarsidass Publ.

Tart, C. (2008). Altered states of consciousness and the spiritual traditions: The proposal for the creation of state-specific sciences. In A. K. Dalal, A. Paranjpe, & K. R. Rao (Eds.), *Handbook of Indian psychology* (pp. 577–607). Foundation Books. https://doi.org/10.1017/UPO9788175968448.032

Thompson, E. (2001). Empathy and consciousness. *Journal of Consciousness Studies*, *8*(5–6), 1–32.

Thompson, E., & Varela, F. (2001). Radical embodiment: Neural dynamics and consciousness. *Trends in Cognitive Sciences*, *5*(10), 418–425.

Varela, F. J., Thompson, E., & Rosch, E. (2017). *The embodied mind, revised edition: Cognitive science and human experience*. MIT Press.

Waldron, W. (2008). A Buddhist theory of unconscious mind (Ālaya-Vijñāna). In A. K. Dalal, A. Paranjpe, & K. R. Rao (Eds.), *Handbook of Indian psychology* (pp. 105–128). Foundation Books. https://doi.org/10.1017/UPO9788175968448.007

Zahavi, D., & Rochat, P. (2015). Empathy≠ sharing: Perspectives from phenomenology and developmental psychology. *Consciousness and Cognition*, *36*, 543–553.

7 Bhakti

Consciousness, social self and the aesthetic of transformation

Introduction: Is consciousness an abstraction locked in body-mind

Is consciousness *locked into* the body so to say? We view the self as isolated and autonomous; an unexamined assumption where, the self as embodied, is conceptualized as fixed with *boundaries of the body*; are we thinking of consciousness also as isolated and *locked* into these boundaries? How does the rigid and fixed locked-in body-mind/consciousness – fare at the next level of analysis – the social ontology? Is self *only* social, individualistic, social-relational or trans-social, but grounded in consciousness? Is self-recognized under different conditions of awareness – both social and trans-social?

The assumption of a locked-in consciousness is one of the most damaging consequential assumptions of a physicalist model of consciousness. In this chapter, two objectives will guide the discussions. First, is the 'mundane' consciousness shared socially, yet is not 'otherworldly'. What is meant by the term 'social consciousness'? Consciousness *certainly* abstracts from and therefore transcends the physical body and body awareness in a social sense. This chapter will first discuss social selves and Indian psychology.

As we have looked at self and consciousness from the broad Indian perspective, an interesting stream of research has looked at self-awareness which was supposed to be an exclusive human capacity, not found among non-humans, including marine animals and social insects such as ants. Of course, ants have chemical processes for communication and plants, as new research shows, use molecules as well as collaboration with fungi to be social! Suffice it to note that we cannot look at transcendental consciousness without first considering that consciousness, communication and self are tied together beyond the physical body and can be observed in non-humans, say, fish and self-directed behaviours (Kohda et al., 2019), social insects such as ants (Friedman & Søvik, 2021) and most famously, Asian elephants (Irie & Hasegawa, 2009).

Next, the chapter will introduce the constitution and, thereafter, transaction of a social self on the basis of the assumption of a transcendental consciousness – 'a cosmopsychism and beyond' a phrase used by Miri Albahari while connecting with the advaitic realization (Albahari, 2019;

DOI: 10.4324/9781003336204-7

Medhananda, 2022; Nagasawa & Wager, 2017). The key point is that an advaitic realization in Indian psychology, leads to fellowship, love and moment by moment creativity in a socially transacted self and loosens the conventional dogma about a fixed, rigid social self-concept. This rigid social concept that we study is a dead end of nihilism in mainstream social psychology. As discussed till now, in Indian psychology, a conceptual architecture of detaching from the social self to recognizing consciousness as such and thereafter re-engaging the social is seen through the Bhakti movement in Indian psychology. This is not sufficiently understood or appreciated.

In this chapter, we will introduce the key elements of bhakti as a social, psychological and philosophical transformation of day-to-day, moment by moment ordinary life. Next, we will examine this bhakti world-view along with the current contemporary psychology discussions on social self, the discovery of mirror-neurons in neuroscience and its profound implications on a relational co-constituted self. Finally, we will indicate everyday practices of creativity, positive emotion and intrinsic motivation – all centred in bhakti, to arrive at a sacred lived sense of fellowship that was presumably implied in the consciousness as Sat-Cid-Ānanda, seen in the discussions of the Vedas and Vedānta. In this way, we make a modest attempt to tie up the ideas of embodied consciousness, social selves, everyday creativity, and freedom while living or the idea of Jīvanmukti in Vedānta.

Social ontology of Indian psychology: Bhakti as the aesthetic of self – social transformation

We discussed rasa theory in the earlier chapter on emotional transformation. The rasa theory is central in understanding the appreciation of music, dance and indeed the appreciation of all aesthetics including the aesthetic of self-transformation. The distinguishing feature of rasa theory is that, it explains the experience and the phenomenology of joy, as mediated through presentation, mirroring and transformation of emotion always in a dialogical social context. The critical conceptual question for Indians is that – if consciousness is oneness, that how can it be grounded in relationality; emotion, in any case, is located in duality, presupposing two for the exchange. Secondly, an important question in Indian knowledge traditions (IKT) is the experience of suffering and pain in transactional and relational life. To discern the mechanism of transformation is to re-process both positive and negative raw emotion into rasa – joy, well-being and satisfaction in relational and social life. Why is it that emotions presented on stage, in an aesthetic context give satisfaction and well-being, but cause tremendous suffering in day to day lived experience; the same emotions, when enacted and experienced in life make us feel 'bound' in the Sāmsāra? This question of 'distance' is important to understand whether emotions can ever be leveraged towards self-realization or will always remain an obstacle towards it. We discussed these in the earlier chapter (Bansat-Boudon, 2013; Bharata et al., 1981; Muni, n.d.). However, it is important to ask – is transformation of emotion just limited and time-bound to the stage performance? If so, then, how is this different from catharsis? Bhakti, as a rasa, explains the mechanism of this transformation from performing on stage and viewing emotion as an audience to a complete overhaul, a day-to-day, moment to moment self-recognition in plurality of social selves. Note that the most sophisticated Trika Śaiva school also gives a framework, which is cognitive in its tilt; a detailed discussion is not in the scope of the social self.

Bhakti: From aesthetic appreciation to self and other transformation

Emotions are defined as responses that consist of subjective phenomenological and cognitive states, physiological reactions and expressive behaviours. All psychologists agree on three factors central to emotions – a subjective phenomenology and cognitive appraisal, the physiological/bodily response and an expressive behavioural (relational/social) response. Different theorists have focussed on these to derive a cross-cultural understanding of the construction and expression of emotion. In the Indian context, given the centrality of consciousness as such, theories in the Indian tradition have viewed emotion from a dual lens – in contexts where detachment is emphasized; emotion is viewed as the obstacle in pursuit of self-realization/Jnāna. In this context, it is set in the framework of ari ṣad varga, that is, emotions which cause distress – kāma, krodha, lobha, etc. However, emotion is also viewed as a upāya (a solution) where emotion is leveraged towards higher states of consciousness and well-being. It is only when emotion is viewed as a upāya, then it brings well-being, otherwise, raw emotional experience, located in the awareness of duality and fragmentation, binds the beings in saṃsāra chākra. So, how do we use emotion as upāya? In the context of music and dance, we find an elaborate theory of rasa in the sixth chapter of Bharat Muni's Natyaśāstra (Natyashastra (Sanskrit), 1989). The sixth chapter in Natyaśāstra identifies the objective of a dramatic performance as communication of the essential message of the Vedas and identifies the rasa as that essential message. Paranjpe, in 2009, proposed to use rasa theory as the indigenous Indian theory of emotion and emotional transformation (Paranjpe, 2009). Pandit (2011, 2013) tried to understand the idea of emotional transformation by interviewing experts in dance and music performance. A set of probes was identified, inclusion and exclusion criteria were set for the selection of the participants. Experienced teachers of dance, music and meditation were interviewed and transcribed. A thematic analysis was done for the interviews to identify core themes. As is normative in qualitative research methods, a purposive snowball sampling design was used to identify advanced dance, music and meditation teachers as the study participants. Guidelines regarding ethics, as well as the quality of documentation, were followed. These interview themes were then analyzed in the light of the text and the theories proposed in the texts (Gnoli, 1968.; Shāstrī, 1918). Some of the key findings that these interviews revealed were as follows:

The traditional Mārga/Paddhati as the process of 'evoking' rasa among collective relational and shared contexts: The interviewees suggested that the traditional format of Mārga (pathway) in dance and in music was the pathway of evoking rasa among the audiences. The interviewees expressed that the rasa was for the audience/seers/listeners and the performers were facilitating the evocation of that rasa in the others. One dance guru, however, also said that when she is performing, she is also the first recipient of the rasa. The interviewees equivocally said that, they start the presentation of an emotion with a very simple and/or a familiar expression of that emotion during a dance performance; they continue their exploration of the emotion and its presentation for the audience in increasingly particular, subtler and personally relevant ways. This increasing exploration of the emotion and its presentation is done through repetitions of the particular phrase (carvana), which is being sung again and again during music, as well as an accompaniment for the dancer to emote. All this is done in a shared meaning-making context. Over a period of time, the dancer/musician increasingly explores unfamiliar interpretations of the emotion and presents it to the audience. According to the interviewees, through this pathway, the audience is able to see the various possibilities of the experience and expression of that emotion. Among music performers, the process is a little more subtle and it is the emotion which is expressed through the notes of the rāga is given more importance than the Sāhitya or the literary content of the song presented. Among discerning audiences, called Rasika, this particular process is either approved or critiqued! During the dance performance, the music and the vocal accompaniment, the various aspects of your dance called as Nritta and the emotional experience and expression, which is shown primarily through the face and the body movements of the dancer, are experienced in totality (as unified consciousness) by the receiver/seer/audience. So, in summary, the teachers of dance and music identified a step-by-step process of increasing attention and an immersion (all cognitive elements) into the emotional expression which is embodied by the dancer and mirrored experiences by the audience. Attention is the central cognitive modality to enter in reflexivity and self-awareness.

From the audience's point of view, the dance and the music teachers expressed the view that the audience reflects upon the emotional expression both consciously and non-consciously. By deploying and locking the attention on that emotion, other cognitive processes get involved. They are memories, creative ideas, visual imagery as well as visceral sensations in case of some excellent performances. For example, audiences cry, have goose bumps or feel joyous and happy, laugh and communicate with each other or the performer.

Rasa exploration is a dialogue enacted socially: The format of presentation of dance as well as music in the Indian cultural context usually happens in the form of a dialogue. The dance and music teachers used the concept of **Manodharma**. Manodharma – which means the nature and the harmony within the mind of the performer is then communicated/shared with the audience. Manodharma allows for personally relevant explorations both in dance in the expression of an emotion through the face in the body as well as in music through the expression of various phrases within the framework of the Rāga. During the process of presentation of dance as well as music, the particular manodharma of the performer is appreciated or disagreed with by the discerning audience in light of their expectation of what the original intent of that presentation item could be. This is a very critical point-that all kinds of explorations are not appreciated. The audience already has in their mind a background expectancy derived from cultural shared meaning making of *what could be the original intent* of the presentation whether in dance or in music. One of the great dance teachers explained it in these words – 'we were presenting a programme for a village somewhere in North India, the dance was related to an event during Rama's exile. After we presented the song/dance and the concert ended, all the villagers came to meet us in the tent, bowed down to me and cried, saying that I exactly behaved as Rāma would have! That, they met *Rama once again*! I thought at that point – how would they know what Rama would have done?!' This points to the final theme from the interviews, which is called as Sādharanikarana as explained by the great Kashmiri Śaiva master Acārya AbhinavGupta. The audience sees the performance on the stage and, at one point, experiences that *emotion as social oneness* – transcending their personal subjective experience. It is inferred that looking at the performance through the modality of the stage is able to give the audiences that *distance* enough to see the emotion being enacted. Further, through the enactment, the audience is able to accept its mirroring in one's own life experiences. Thus, the theory is able to explain rasa experience through the reflexivity possible due to the modality of the stage. This particular point is further elaborated in later Kashmir Saīva texts with radical statements such as – Nartaka Ātmā, Rango Antarātmā (dancer is the self and the inner self is the stage).

Rasa and Spiritual Transformation: When the interviewees were asked if the experience of rasa is the same as the spiritual experience of self-realization, they said no – there was a one step difference! After several interviews as well as reading through the texts, one can say that the experience of the rasa allows you to look at your own emotional self from a distance and brings empathy and acceptance to oneself. On spirituality, however, the interviewees identified that Yoga and meditation experiences *need not have emotional content at all.* Apart from indicating śānta rasa as a quietude of emotion, one teacher pointed out that self-recognition of consciousness may be devoid of any content, whereas rasa experience is filled with a single content of peace! One dance guru said that 'all dancers are yogī-s, but all yogī-s may not be able to perform dance'!

This idea of immersion was discussed by an American psychologist Czsiksentsmihalyi and termed as 'flow'. However, rasa as social immersion, to then be called 'universal'. Thus, psycho-social framework of rasa provides the following key insights:

1 The modality of the stage provides us with the distance to observe and see. Here the point made by several contemporary practicing dance and music gurus that 'rasa is for audience' is well taken. The audience uses this distance in the beginning, as a concrete stage-audience distance, while seeing the enactment of emotion in the dance performance as well as the exploration of emotion in a more subtle way through music, to arrive at an **internal mirror** or a reflexive consciousness. Thus, we see the paradox of detachment and immersion in the process of viewing a dance or music performance – a 'Camatkāra' (paradox). We can say that, the concrete and later internal stage and the distance-immersion dynamic can give rise to an internal reflection and peaceful viewing of emotion. To that extent, the present emotion is 'ownerless'.
2 The experience of rasa is through a step-by-step's process of moving from familiar expression and experience of emotion to unfamiliar experiences and expression of emotion. This is similar to meditation and samādhi stages, esp., leading from distracted mind to quiet mind to 'no-mind'. In the whole experience, the audience is *also not segregating* music, accompaniments, stage and the performer as different – it's a unified experience of absorption. In fact, if the audience experiences any one aspect of the performance differently, then it is supposed to cause rasa bhanga (a violent distraction).

The modality of the stage is also a limitation as the performance-based understanding of emotional experience, enactment and transformation. So how do we then transform the whole experience of living and go beyond the otherworldly atmosphere created by the stage? This particular issue was addressed later in the conceptualization of bhakti as a rasa.

Bhakti as rasa: A transformation of relation, social and community living

The idea of emotional transformation was radically re-conceptualized in the later developments in Indian thought. Somewhere in the 11th century onwards, bhakti was conceptualized as rasa (Sharma Sen & Pandit, 2013). Note that, bhakti as a concept and intervention for self – recognition practice is mentioned in Śwetaṣvatara Upaniṣad as well as in the Bhagavad Gita. *Bhakti as a rasa,* however, was first mentioned by a Marathi philosopher Vopadeva (Haberman, 2003). Later developments in Indian historical, philosophical thought increasingly started using and re-conceptualizing bhakti as a rasa. The Gaudiya Vaiṣnava philosophers, residing in Vrindavan, gave an elaborate theory of rasa through bhakti. One of the key concepts that we see in the Gaudiya Vaiṣnava philosophers was the idea of **intentional role and relationship taking** in relation to the divine (Paranjpe, 2009). The second key idea in this theory was the intensity and immersion in the intentional role taken. It is an integral part of the Vaiṣnava framework to intentionally take a role and a relationship in reference to the divine principle, which is now viewed as anthropomorphic. We see this intentional role and relationship taking in the ancient Dravidian bhakti practices as well. For example, in the Pillaittamil literature, the authors – all-male, take the role of a mother and weave poems of maternal love for the divine child! This intentional role play was followed and taken up throughout life as a relational commitment and the intensity of that intentional role and relationship *was experienced as bhakti rasa*. Thus, life itself was a stage on which the relational role between the human and the divine was played out! Rūpa Gosvamiṇ (Haberman, 2003), the grandmaster and teacher of the Gaudiya Vaiśnava philosophy and the disciple of Caītanya Mahāprabhu identified several such intentional roles in relationship with the divine. The highest among them was the intentional role of the divine as the lover/beloved. Just below that was the role where the divine was a child in which the human was the parent! Below that, in a hierarchy, not of social power, but of intensity was a relationship, where the divine was a friend. Below that, was the relationship with the divine as a master. Sānta, which we discussed in the earlier chapter on emotional transformation, was the highest rasa according to Acārya AbhinavGupta; in a delicious irony, Śānta was placed lowest in the ladder of intentional relationships taking that one could have with the divine.

Now, not only has the human intentionally taken a role in a relationship with the divine, converted the world and the experiences of the world as a stage and a performance but has also transformed each and every moment of the embodied breath, thought, feelings in that relational and social self; suffusing each and every moment with the awareness and reflexivity in the intensity of their emotion for the self-chosen name and form of consciousness! Later bhakti texts have identified the physiological embodied responses associated with that intense mood of bhakti, such as crying and laughing at the same time, yearning, and feeling sad! Thus, bhakti rasa represents the triumph of a complete self-recognition and transformation, even in the presence of duality and multiplicity. *Note also that this relationality implied an inversion into the social. If humans related to the divine as a child, then the child and indeed all human children (as a conceptual schema) were looked at as divine. In this manner, clusters of schema and scripts, associated with childhood as such, were re-framed. Thus, all human relationships in the social context had the living possibility of a sacred transaction!*

This radical re-conceptualization of worldly relationships of duality and multiplicity and recognizing and reaffirming the inherent grounded-ness of consciousness is the true moment of Indian modernity. As mentioned, it engendered a spiritual, social and literary revolution in the historical consciousness as well as the psyche-Indian mindset with several values that we tend to associate with 'modernity' such as equality, fellowship, dignity and inclusion. This truly Indian modernity came much before European modernity and with little less baggage. In the Indian Bhakti movement and the revolution that it engendered – the question of caste and indeed anthropocentrism was directly engaged with. All people – upper castes and lower castes, Hindus and Muslims, men, women, transgender, birds, trees, plants, insects and animals – each one was entitled to partake in that intense, lifelong relationship of immersive, insane love and live a life of fulfilment – where liberation was here and now in fellowship for all. Thus, the transpersonal consciousness implied in Advaita Vedānta was personalized in each and every creature (Paranjpe and Rao, 2008). Note that later Vedāntin masters – particularly the great master – Sri Rāmanujācārya had already indicated this in his analysis of consciousness-as-such (readers may please read Sri Bhāṣya for further understanding).

In summary, the key psychological touch points of cognition, affect and physiological responses in transforming raw emotion into joy and well-being are distilled. This re-processed social self had gigantic social and political implications, and thus bhakti is a complete theory of social and spiritual transformation. Thus, we start from music and appreciation of dance and music performance on stage, which we have discussed in the chapter on emotion and affective process, where the framework suggests that the cognitive constructs of attention, locking and immersion open up self-awareness and reflexivity. Next step level change is *a conscious and playful distortion of conventional reality* – when the human being intentionally takes up a role and relation to the consciousness, with name, form, intention and qualities; and sets this relationship up on the stage of life. *This is the radical reconstitution of the relational self!*

In this relationship, in the initial phases, the relationality is anthropomorphized and separate from the lived world of the human, perhaps, in the form of an idol or a picture or a name and form; later, however, there is a re-coding of the schema cluster to each and every being – person, animal and all creatures is re-cognized as a form of the sacred consciousness! Thus, the life of bhakta is completely transformed, intensely immersed, and a highly emotional play that then further transforms the lives of those who are in the relational network of this person. Bhakti is lived in a social and political context, the lives of the bhakta-s also engendered social and political transformation. Thus, we have travelled from aesthetics on stage to aesthetics as life; even though aesthetic starts from listening to a performance on stage, the true object of aesthetic appreciation through rasa is to transform the social self and the world!

With this brief background, the next section examines how social self is conceptualized in the mainstream Euro-American psychology and how and whether it is related to consciousness.

Social self in European and American psychology

What could be the basis of social relationships? It is amazing to note that most of the experimentation of basic psychological processes or experimental psychology is on single subjects and conducted in an 'a-social context' with 'a-social' research design. Till about 30 years back, social learning theory approaches were relegated to the background of the psychology textbooks because social learning was difficult to prove and empirically test through rigorous 'scientific' experiments, quite similar to how today some aspects of consciousness are mindfully blinded. Classical and operant conditioning experiments were the gold standard for predicting human nature. Behaviourism was at its peak in the 60s and 70s and one of the ways to show the scientific nature of psychology was to construct experiments where context was removed. Even within Western European and North American psychology scholarship, this has been critiqued. Euro-American psychology, and especially the North American variant of contemporary Euro-American psychology, has been critiqued as biased towards what has been called as 'methodological individualism'.

Suffice it to say that these robust critiques and advances in neurosciences (Dreyfus, 1993; Varela et al., 1974) have led to a proposal of a new paradigm to look at cognition-behaviour as the **embodied cognition approach**. The embodied cognition approach and its variants – 'enactivism' and 'situated cognition' imply that not only is cognition embodied, but cognition is also situated in the context, as the organism dynamically adapts to such changes in the context, such as in music training and performance (Arzy et al., 2006; van der Schyff, 2015). This proposal has been debated and no consensus emerges, but it has found support among several interdisciplinary fields such as developmental, cross-cultural, cultural psychology and the study of creativity (Csikszentmihalyi, 1988; Lynch & Troy, 2021; Mirvis, 1998). At the embodied level, perceptual motor coupling (awareness X action) such as during sports or dance where the 'presence of mind' is required. At the same time, humans also either mindfully or automatically create a gap in their thinking and action, say in the legal process, where an authentic representation of the situation is sought for decision. So, cognition is embodied, situated and enactive, just as it is also, stretched, representational, dissociated and non-active, depending on the objectives; the Euro-American requirement to look for singularity in cognitive process doesn't work. In both cases, cognition must be contextual and social. Amazingly, it was only in the discovery of the mirror neurons in the 1990s that scientists were able to identify a specific, embodied pattern in the brain that explains why and how humans and non-humans learn from watching others, through modelling or mimesis (Kohler et al., 2002; Rizzolatti, 2005; Rizzolatti et al., 2002).

In the late 1990s, Italian researchers were working with baby monkeys and found something unexpected. While it made sense to observe that whenever the baby monkeys themselves shelled peanuts, their motor neurons fired/lighted up, it was *surprising* to observe that the baby monkeys' motor neurons fired/lighted up when they observed the other monkeys or the researchers shelling peanuts or peeling a banana. These motor neurons (a subset of all) that lighted up even when watching somebody else's action were named as *motor mirror neurons*. In the initial phases, there was scepticism that perhaps such mirror neurons exist in the brains of the primates but not of human beings! Over the years, starting from the late 90s, enough evidence has been gathered now to show unequivocally that mirror neurons exist not only in primate brains and bird brains but also in human brains (Keysers & Gazzola, 2010; Rizzolatti, 2005; Rochat & Zahavi, 2011; Turella et al., 2009). Again earlier, it was thought that mirror neurons primarily populate the occipital or the visual cortex. Now we know that for all perceptual and sensory systems, there is a subset of motor mirror neurons. What it means is that for all perceptual and sensory systems, such as taste, smell, touch, audition and vision there is a possibility of an immediate or a deferred action that can happen through *the brain imitating* the action. These mirror neurons are now understood as the basis for what is called 'social neuroscience', that is, communication among all humans and non-humans, including birds. Every time a songbird mother sings a song, the baby songbird tries to imitate the mother. This motor imitation is coupled with the perception of that sound from the mother songbird. Similarly, among human infants, it's a very well noted observation that the human infant closely *follows* stimuli in the context, including visual, tactile, olfactory, gustatory and especially auditory stimuli. The human infant, even before birth has a reasonably developed auditory system. As the human foetus, listens to the heartbeats of the mother and after birth is able to listen to and respond to the sound of the mothers or the primary caretaker's voice.

With the discovery of mirror neurons, scientists have established the possible pathways of a communication between two embodied selves; notwithstanding, the attendant debates and controversies, we know that these mirror neurons mirror the perceptions of others' actions, and therefore, we also have established the pathway towards a social self and the possibility of cognition, which is largely social. Zahavi, a philosopher of social ontology, has been writing on whether self is social and now, we can clearly see the linkage between a sensory, embodied shared self, where the actions of the other are followed as the actions of the self. This brings the possibility of a network of embodied social selves!

Thus, cognition becomes a broader understanding, where self is seen as a largely social system. Among philosophers, cognitive scientists, theorists of law, the question of self is also central because it ties up to the questions of accountability, ethics, moral action, responsiveness and responsibility towards each other, not only among humans but as part of the ecosystem. Therefore, mirror neurons and the principle of perceptual motor coupling not only help us understand that we are not isolated embodied beings but connected embodied beings, where the nervous system comprehends the 'other' through these mirror neurons.

Why is it that the brains do not distinguish between actions of the self and actions of the other, whereas, socially, humans and non-humans can easily distinguish the two? It appears that human infants learn the boundaries and distinctions between the self and others during socialization. The most significant implication seems to be that our mirror neurons in the embodied self link to a truly social and cultural shared self; a self which is *constituted* along with others and therefore, questions the ideas of autonomous individualistic self with rigid locked in consciousness in the body. In its very constitution during the early years of brain development, the embodied consciousness as self is relational. Scholars have also related this to the questions of empathy as the core basis of consciousness, with some controversy as well. In recent years, Menon and her collaborators have attempted to look at similar questions in emotions, empathy, consciousness and self (Anand & Menon, 2017; Kuchibhotla & Menon, 2014; Menon, 2005, 2013, 2014; Menon et al., 2014). For IP, note that, as discussed in the earlier section, the Bhakti movement emphasized on empathy and love for all as the central lived experience of a social self.

The mainstream Euro-American social psychology, views self, as largely a 'social' self, where 'largely social' is understood in terms of the socialization process. Broadly, there are two perspectives – reflexive and reflective. One line of though holds that the self independently reflects and, therefore, knows itself independently of others, or at least is so, most times. This is called the self-awareness perspective. The second perspective holds that the person and all the organisms can know themselves in reflection to the others. Both these views lead to the question of how individualistic, in reality, is the 'individual' in the social self. Indian scholars typically fall into the either/or trap and take either the self-awareness perspective, and focus on improving oneself, at the discount of the others and the structure. Others scholars typically dismiss the reflexive self and agency and overwhelmingly focus on the relationships and structures. The history of psychology debates shows that this binarization is nothing new.

Chadha (2011) has argued that *reflexivity and reflection-ism* may not be seen as dichotomies or opposites. In the lifespan perspective, we see that the human infant grows with both reflexivity and reflection-ism in concert. The particular *orchestration* of reflexivity and reflection-ism seems to be determined by niche micro-cultural networks, such as family and community, larger cultural and motivational context. For example, in the spiritual context in IKT, reflexivity and self-knowing are emphasized, whereas, in social transactional contexts, reflection-ism is emphasized in the same IKT. We see that the role of mirror neurons, observation of stimuli, imitation, deferred imitation, learning of languages and indeed all social learning show reflexivity and reflection-ism in concert. Children learn from each other; however, they also have their own independent understanding and reflections. Therefore, this binary of reflexivity and reflection-ism does not exist; rather, it is useful to look at both as different but supportive in a vertical spiral sequence. Among humans broadly and in Indian cultures specifically, children's learning through mirroring, imitation, language and other shared social practices and behaviours in certain contexts to allow for a shared and relational self. In certain pedagogies, reflexivity is foregrounded, in other pedagogies, reflection is. This relational self does not mean that individualism is lost as in the binary thinking between individual and social. Rather it means that, there is an additional layer *of micro-context and motivation specific* meaning making that human beings in diverse cultures engage in while reacting, responding and engaging with the social stimuli. Not only is the self relational, but it is also collective in the sense that we develop working concepts about events, processes and issues in the world as we relate to the world. Say we develop a working concept of an animal or a fruit. In my student cohort from Kochi, Kerala, they find my question very strange! It is not because they have not seen a banana; indeed, the story is quite the opposite; children in Kerala develop a very detailed and nuanced concept of a banana. The Kerala ecosystem provides for about 70 subspecies of bananas. Some bananas are green, red and some are conventional yellow. Some bananas are eaten as raw vegetables, some are cooked in curries, some are to be steamed and then eaten, and some are eaten ripe, which is the typically non-Malayali context way to perceive bananas and act (eat, in this case). Thus, the context and the motivation specify the task (motor) requirements and cultures provide several 'a-typicalities' in our concept formation. We discussed this briefly in the chapter on cognition. **Kasturirangan, Guha and Ramprasad** (Kasturirangan et al., 2011), **in their brilliant and innovative paper, convincing argue for an Indian Cognitivism that not only bypasses the binaries of reason, affect and action but also the frozen-ness** that is assumed in human concept formation, including social and self-schema.

This frozen-ness of concepts, especially concepts of self, others and social, contrives a fixed and frozen social self and the fixed and frozen other, which is convenient for academic reasoning but quite limited in relevance otherwise. If we were to understand the implications of an 'Indian cognitivism', we could examine a self and 'other' concept formation that allows for reflexivity and reflection-ism as a dialectic. This point is important to note as we will see this may be a reason for the 'Indian mindset', which as psychologists have proposed in extremely context sensitive and 'appears' contradictory (Sinha et al., 2010).

Thus far, we have identified the mechanisms in the human brain that allow for an embodied, enactive, situated and social cognition; this tight linkage between the embodied, enactive, situated and social cognition is a very recent phenomenon and interrogates all the earlier colonial implant theories from anthropology, sociology and history, which 'othered', 'exoticized', 'esotericized', 'dumbified', 'backwardized' and appropriated knowledge, culture and practices, in addition to being *'epistemically violent'* on the cultures and societies of the colonized cultures, nations and civilizations(see, Tuhiwai-Smith in the context of New Zealand). This is true not only of New Zealand from where Tuhiwai Smith writes, but also for all the colonized world (Smith, 2021). In particular reference to this chapter, it follows that consciousness is social and embodied and not locked-in, in the brain and nervous system. Consciousness in IKT is understood and experienced as pervasive, and therefore, it necessarily exists in the social. The consciousness that IKT calls as all-pervasive means that it is personal-embodied-enminded, social-cultural-economic-historical, and trans-social, trans-cultural and transcendental; consciousness is throughout the spectrum and the continuum, just appearing different. The transcendental nature of consciousness and self –realization as consciousness is *grounded in and routed through* the body-mind as well as social and cultural contexts.

Body and consciousness as trans-cultural pivots: Culture and psyche as organizing cognition

Even within the social self, cultural differences in the constitution of the self, directly translate as changes in affect, cognition and social behaviour, a widely acknowledged idea among cultural and cross-cultural psychologists and anthropologists. In cultural and cross-cultural psychological research, a well-accepted fact is that social selves are co-constructed with culture and the body-brain processes, where brain is termed as a 'bio-social sponge' (Ambady & Bharucha, 2009).

If culture and psyche co-constitute each other, then in what way is this constitution different? Several research studies across specializations in psychology focus on cultural differences. Studies in lifespan developmental psychology identify the cultural differences in nutrition, health, lifestyles, social interactions and their impact on the person throughout the lifespan, right from conception to death, focusing on both epigenetics and neuroplasticity through the lifespan. The key point to note here is that in the consciousness-based IKT, especially in Advaita Vedānta, the essential core is experience of self-recognition as consciousness (Swahananda, 2012; Vedanta Sadhana and Shakti Puja (p. 336). Advaita Ashram); cultural and therefore trans-cultural; social and therefore, trans-social. Indeed, it is precisely due to the fact that consciousness is understood as trans-cultural and social that people from across the world have sought this wisdom; it binds and brings all human and non-human societies and cultures in fellowship. Going forward and further to that, IKT assets that the self-realized persons are able to 'see' that this consciousness pervades all animate creatures in Buddhism and Jainism and indeed all creation including inanimate objects in Yoga-Sāṃkhya and Advaita Vedānta. It is this trans-cultural aspect of consciousness which is of interest in spirituality as practised in day-to-day life and recognized in meditative states.

Seekers from across the world have travelled to India in search of this living framework; trans-cultural, trans-social and trans-religious conceptualization of spirituality, which does not require the social constraints and categorizations of race, class, caste, religion and gender. All the Indic values that then move downstream from this recognition flow into social values of oneness, love and fellowship; realization and not mere belief of the trans-cultural, trans-social and trans-religious nature of unity and oneness of consciousness (Pandit, 2021). The power of this conceptualization is that it arises from social and cultural to then transcend the very same cultural, social and religious frameworks. Note also that this is not about a God and theology, but multiple pathways to Gods and Goddesses and multiple theologies.

There are two trans-cultural pivots, so to say, in our understanding of consciousness. It appears to be the body, and the physiological systems are the trans-cultural pivot that mainstream Euro-American traditions and philosophy of science depend on for 'generalizability'. The IKT locate their core on the idea of a trans-cultural consciousness and lived experience of embodied-enminded-social and transcendental self, emanating thereof. Note, however, that, our bodies and physiological systems are deeply embedded in our cultural and social systems, micro-contexts and their situatedness; the body-cognition-affect-behaviours are transacted as interwoven through these contexts as well. Similarly, even though consciousness is conceptualized and experienced as trans-personal, trans-embodied, trans-social and trans-cultural, the later movements in Indian history of spirituality empirically establish that consciousness is interwoven in all transactions; embedded in the embodied, personal, social, cultural and contextual superimpositions of realities.

Meditation practice: A bidirectional engagement between social and non-social

Yogis and meditators practice and train their content of consciousness to access advanced meditative states and realizations, which are progressively parsed out of the social and reflexive of the body and psyche as it is. They also mostly revert back to the same social, cultural and contextual realities to enact bodily and social transactions *situated* in them. If so, then how does that reversion back from advanced meditative states change the constitution of the social selves or contents of consciousness? The texts in the IKT and the documentations of living masters seem to suggest that, now, the meditator is able to reconstruct not only their own consciousness but also moderate, if not transform, the contents of consciousness relationally and in shared attention. The profound difference between a self-realized meditator and a non-meditator would be that the meditator knows that these contents of consciousness which constitute the 'social self' are not conclusive and cast in stone towards their self-identity. The meditator looks at the contents of consciousness as conventional realities but not ultimately real. Thus, there are two pathways to relationships and relational self. One, driven by our automatic citta, through automatic karma, sāmskāra and vāsana and *the other pathway of a re-constituted* citta based on the self-recognition as consciousness alone.

The profound difference between a Buddhist view and the Advaita Vedāntin view, is this – what the Buddhist views as the emptiness of the conventional self is what the Vedāntin views as the fullness of the consciousness, precisely because of this signature of *(re)creativity,* while re-animating the contents of consciousness. The realization that consciousness can create and re-create one or many embodied contents of consciousness is the ultimate signature of agency, creativity, freedom and fullness of consciousness. This agency and intentionality of consciousness as such is deemed sacred and divine, which expresses in all of creation, maintenance and destruction.

A consciousness-based social psychology, would imply that the *purpose of social order is to enact and transcend the empty social self and relations, every day in small and big ways.* In current contemporary times, the mindless repetition of *dharma* as religion has been accepted by almost everyone without question! In its original sense, dharma and social order would mean the creation of ethical social practices that enable an easy transaction of social life and, thereafter, an easy transition as migration as it were to meditation and easy self-recognition. Thus, there would be no need for Gurus dependency, fake Gurus and Ashrams if each person and their relationship, homes and communities, would be evolved and established in dharma. The purpose of social self and its core constitution with social, cultural and contextual realities is to enable the access to the trans-cultural recognition in a continuous moment by moment, day by day, month by month, year on year bi-directional loop. Note that, dharma also implies that if one followed one's own dharma socially, then the social self that is constituted in cultural and social realities is easy(ier) to transcend-momentarily as well as episodically through a life-long practice of both the being effective socially as well as merge or yield to meditative states simultaneously. This can be accomplished in the same 24 hours of the waking, dreaming and sleeping states of consciousness, as mentioned in the first chapter we started with.

According to IKT, all beings, including insects, animals, trees, marine creatures and creatures of the sky-birds, are motivated to follow their dharma which is the first purpose of living. The dharma, here, is not understood as a formal religion with a prophet, a book and a rigid practice. The IKT definition of dharma, is naturalistic and non-anthropocentric; when a tiger goes to hunt/prey, the tiger is following the dharma of tiger-ness, when the spider weaves a web or a bacteria or virus attacks a human, they are following the dharma of their self-nature. This principle of dharma, then is taken forward towards human beings to identify the essential purpose of being human. Taking this forward, when humans forage for food, procreate or work or have any social interactions, to the extent that they are following the principles of humanness (which is pivoted in self-enquiry and reflexive consciousness), they are fulfilling their dharma – purpose of life. This profound principle is accepted by Buddhism and Jainism, along with the later world-views and religions that arose in the Indian subcontinent.

In the current contemporary social psychology, the framework separates self-nature of humans and slots and caps their identities as social categories. With colonization, further profound distortions have come from translating the word dharma into English as religion. The definition of dharma in Sanskrit, is a be-ing that one holds (Dhārayate iti Dharma) and that which reflects the is-ness of the being/creatures (sva-dharma). In the IKT social psychology, layers of that is-ness start from sva-dharma to manuśya-dharma in a nested system; where self as relational and collective to their purposes as relational and collective. Note that after dharma, the next two Puruṣārthas are again primarily social, that is artha and kama. The fourth Puruṣārtha is moksha or freedom, which includes all freedoms *while living*. The IKT locates all the social selves, including selves of the animals, insects, birds, trees and plants as motivated to free themselves of their existential condition.

The fourth Puruṣārtha is specifically understood as 'spirituality/mindfulness' and is obviously separately studied in the current contemporary psychology. Note that in the Indian scheme of the social selves, consciousness is interwoven in all the four motivations of life and living and that too not just for humans but for all animate creatures on this planet and therefore, 'spirituality' and contemplative practice are interwoven in a civilizational value of a non-anthropocentric view of the social self, whose purpose is to ease of going back home to self-recognition.

Social self, self and the non-self: Other animals and subjects

One of the biggest difficulties arising out of the Cartesian dualism or what contentiously has been discussed as Cartesian error (A. Damasio, 1998; A. R. Damasio, 2006) is the dichotomizing of the self and *other as object*. The capacity to objectify other exists in humans, but relational selves imply the capacity to 'subjectify others'. From a non-Euro-American perspective, it is disturbing and intriguing that most discussions in philosophy, as well as in mainstream Euro-American psychology, have remained limited to looking at the other, including animals as 'objects'. This view is most predominant in the psychoanalytic schools of object relations and self psychology. In Kohut's self psychology, the mother is conceptualized to take the role of a self object for the growing and individuating child. However, studies have shown that infants and toddlers quickly learn and recognize the difference between actual objects and other subjects! In social contexts, during the lifespan, humans and most likely higher mammals/primates understand and see self-other relations both in terms of self and other non-self objects as well as self and other non-self subjects. As is clear, there is a profound difference between the two modes of relating with non-self, even from a body awareness perspective. Human beings relate to non-animate objects differently than animate non-human others. Research on flow experiences in creativity shows that when humans are 'objectified', they can't access the flow state; Note, flow states are characterized by a loss of self-consciousness, which objectification solidifies. Objectification has increasingly being studied as a predictor for depression (Jones & Griffiths, 2015; Quinn et al., 2011). So, clearly, the idea of others as social objects or the self as an object is a grave and inadequately examined idea in social psychology as is taught and practiced today.

Humans also relate to non-human animate beings differently from both non-animate objects and humans. For example, across cultures in social contexts, largely, people have a sense of relatedness with animals, insects, birds and plants. It is amazing that people across the world have cared for non-humans, but that doesn't constitute 'social knowledge' – a kind of a peculiar alienation in contemporary social psychology, even though humans have related with pets, domestic animals, etc. We don't see this relatedness of humans with non-human others in mainstream Euro-American psychology and in mainstream Euro-American psychological texts.

Finally, humans relate with other humans and at long last, it is here that you see an intellectual investment in the conceptualization of the social self in psychology! Humans seem to be able to shift from treating other humans as objects or as subjects and that particular aspect alone is identified in 'other-ing'. Psychologists have theorized that a sense of self non-self boundaries is a fundamental aspect of growth and development starting from infancy and is a hallmark of all human relationships including intimate relationships of love; they have not conceptualized the opposite – a mindful dissolution of the boundaries! In this reference, a locked-in individualistic self, would mean a different way of relating than a co-constituted shared relational self, as some psychologists have noted (Markus & Kitayama, 1991, 2003).

In the Indic tradition, due to the unique conceptualization of a trans-cultural nature of consciousness, beyond cosmo-psychism has implications for the constitution of social self; In contrast to body, this orchestrates as a shared self, which is also 'spiritual' in its constitution. From a consciousness-based perspective, the most profound implication is that even the social identity is *partly ownerless* since it is shared. Recall that we discussed in earlier chapters that the consciousness as such is self-recognized as 'ownerless'. Of course, in the socio-economic context of today, this constitutes as the problem of the 'commons' when it comes to behaviour and action. Note that, Indian communities, including tribal communities, even now, do not perceive this as a problem; problem of the commons is negotiated differently. How is the problem of commons negotiated with a shared identity – that is a matter of research.

The most externalized transactional social-cultural aspect presents self and consciousness as social and identity categories. These are the frozen identities of caste, gender, community and formalized religious identities. These projected identities are not fluid since they are transactional and it is these particular emanations of frozen identifications that have been the biggest challenge for the transformation of social self, esp. as there is social privilege inherent in caste, gender, class or status.

In this chapter, the focus is on the 'ownerless' shared relational self while acknowledging these social relations. One of the most intriguing and under-researched characteristics of the Indian cultural and wisdom traditions is that the cultural practices are leveraged so as to orchestrate and encourage the practice of an ownerless social self on a lived day to day basis. It is important to note how the Bhakti movement implied day to day creativity. The idea of *Navavidhā or nine ways bhakti* specifies nine lifestyle activities that engineer an ownerless social self, every day.

Apart from Navavidha lifestyle practices, another aspect which is not studied in the highly cerebral academic disciplines such as psychology has been the diversity of expressions of art, craft and performativity and their close connect with lived day to day practice (Dissanayake, 2015). Essentially, arts and crafts were the day to day practices of the people and reflected their 'ownerless' relatedness to the objects, creatures and other human subjects in their ecosystem. In each of the regions across India, in each state and possibly in each district, we find specific performative, fine arts and crafts traditions, as well as social gatherings and collective actions including festivals.

Everyday creativity can be better viewed as a daily practice of re-making social selves day to day. While positive psychologists have accepted the interconnections between motivation, positive emotion and creativity to the idea of self, there is a conceptualization gap in concepts of 'collective efficacy' and 'collective hope' and 'resilient communities'; skewed traditionally as they are towards individual self-efficacy and hope.

These insights are central in the context of everyday creativity as seen and observed in diverse aesthetic contexts in India and the larger conversation on a shared social self and an ownerless consciousness not locked up in an individual body. Scholars such as Dissanayake, studying everyday creativity such as Rangoli or wall art, have also commented that, *this creative expression is ephemeral* and un-named – there is no desire for ownership and citation on the creative moment (Dissanayake, 2001). Rangoli is created and re-created every day/every morning by the same person, implying a kind of 'ownerless-ness'. This is contrasted with the idea of creativity and art itself in the European and North American context, where art is kept in the museums for perpetuity.

The everyday art and creativity of a person drawing rangoli is recreated every day, afresh; therefore, the role of this creativity is not on the final product but on the process and what it delivers to the person's lived experience. This is, obviously, accounting and being mindful for the fact that creative process does result in a beautiful product on several other occasions and that indeed is wonderful, but that is not the point we are trying to emphasize. Going further, it could be surmised that this everyday act of creativity and re-creation the next day, generates a small amount or mild positive emotion, such as surprise or a small pocket of joy/amusement in that person. A mild positive emotion generated every day, could possibly relate to 'intrinsic motivation' (Ryan and Deci, 2000) and a changed 'sense of self' (Kristeller and Rikhye, 20008), in the morning can then be tied to the 'broaden and build framework' of Fredrickson (Fredrickson, 2004). Layered on the top of it is that early research done by Ison and her colleagues on the impact of mild positive emotions on future behaviours shows that even mild positive emotion brings a significant impact on other day to day social behaviours such as being helpful to others, being flexible in thinking, being and accepting of failure and being better self regulated (Joormann & Stanton, 2016). Thus, a daily practice of everyday creativity, as enabled by the IP cultures, which is essentially ephemeral and ownerless, would generate a mild positive emotion that would, in turn, reset that day for this person, *socially*! Sadly, very few Indian psychologists have worked on this mechanism of a day to day feeling of contentment in the life of an ordinary Indian person following their cultural practices and connected this to theorizations of an ownerless consciousness. Across the world, people have used everyday creativity acts – taking care of others, cooking new recipes and going for a walk on a different route! In the Indian psychology of bhakti, the key distinction is that these generate positive emotion, be filled with small 'c' creativity but, most *importantly, be ownerless, moment by moment*! In IP of bhakti, the practice of surrender mindfully accomplishes this ownerless-ness.

In summary, then, we have kept everyday creativity in the centre of the social self. Psychologists such as Simonton (Simonton, 2002) have differentiated between big 'C' and small 'c' creativity, as we have frequently referred in this chapter. Big 'C' creativity is the glamorous part of creativity, where certain ideas disrupt paradigms, thought processes and civilizations. Big 'C' is mostly owned up creativity. According to Simonton, small 'c' creativity is the incremental creativity. Indeed, one might think, that small 'c' creativity is not so jazzy! However, from Indian consciousness-based psychology, it is the small 'c' creativity, that is of great interest for a social ontology of self and other. These moments of transformation create and re-create a positive self, a resilient relationship and a positive other, at no cost or incentive/reward.

Small 'c' creativity is that every day, moment by moment creativity, where social consciousness might overflow the social, into pure reflection and immersion, even if for moments! Every time, consciousness 'overflows' the socially constituted self, moment by moment, it brings surprise and joy! Note that this overflow is still not binarized in terms of this worldly and otherworldly consciousness but valenced within the very same socially and culturally constituted, a conventionally experienced and expressed self. Every time, small incremental positive emotion is experienced, the person is likely to be not only (a) pro-social/helpful, (b) flexible and (c) express better self-regulated, as Isen and her colleagues' research shows (Ashby & Isen, 1999; Isen, 1987; Isen et al., 1987). A 'here and now' transcendence, which is not even as immersive as 'flow' is experienced by the person that is enabling to meditative states whenever the person decides to meditate. It is probable, that such a person, may not disrupt a discipline like Einstein or cause a paradigm shift, but certainly, such a person experiences well-being on a moment to moment and day to day basis. Thus we can say that small 'c' creativity is linked with small 'w' well-being! And such a small 'w' well-being is likely to get accumulated to remake moment by moment 'karma and sāmskāra'; these dually make the person resilient to face adversities that they are likely to experience in their lives as well as be a step towards altered states of consciousness or advanced meditative states.

Simonton and several other contemporary creativity researchers also note that what in 'best case scenarios' is termed as flexibility and less self censoring also is correlated with 'cognitive disinhibition' that affects our ordinary adjustments in our social contexts. According to psychologists, cognitive disinhibition correlates with maladjustments and mental health concerns among creative individuals. This is important to note as we don't have any evidence to assess whether every day, small 'c' creativity causes the extent of cognitive disinhibition as seen in big 'C' creative process. It is possible to hypothesize that everyday creativity as a cultural practice might be correlated with 'just enough' positive emotion and overflow without cognitive disinhibition. It should be possible to explore the moment by moment awareness and aesthetic appreciation due to dialogical cultural practices, which reduce cognitive disinhibition as well. Creativity is notoriously difficult to model in predictive equations and computational modelling! This presents the nub of the question for a physicalist vs a non-physicalist idea of consciousness. Can creativity be modelled through mathematical equations?

In the IKT, one of the fundamental characteristics of consciousness is creativity, fertility and abundance. Unpredictability is also a characteristic of consciousness but is framed as 'playfulness' of consciousness. In the Vedas, the first experience of self-consciousness is described in feminine terms. It is stated that, when the self first became self aware, the first intention that arose in the 'self-aware' self was to become many. Scholars and traditional teachers have identified this moment as the moment of creativity, fertility and abundance. Later traditions of Tantra identify this as the primordial feminine energy that is contradictory, only if viewed from a limited human perspective and is ever free, ever playful.

Thus, while the Vedas conceptualize creativity as the central aspect of Cit or consciousness, different philosophical and wisdom traditions try to articulate and resolve the contradictions inherent in the idea that while consciousness is transpersonal, it is expressed and experienced through an embodied and a personal, relational and social self; while consciousness as such is without intention, knowing and action, it is expressed and experienced through animated intention, knowing and action and while consciousness as such cannot be limited to and is without form, qualities and name, it is expressed and experienced through infinite names, forms and qualities! This paradoxical nature of consciousness was articulated and aligned in the bhakti scholarship and practice. Thus, by the 15th and 16th centuries CE in India, we see a consolidation of theory and living practices that are lived, experiential, embodied and integrative of the paradoxes about consciousness commonly understood. In the next chapter, we will take this line of thought further.

Bhakti movement and Indian modernity: The second moment of Indian social self

The Bhakti movement that we briefly discussed in the chapter on emotional transformation was also a moment of Indian social modernity, in that it accomplished three profound innovations: first, it grounded the transcendental consciousness as such, in the day to day lived experiences of embodied humans and inferred in non-humans. Secondly, Bhakti movement, accomplished this through aesthetics and emotional transformation rather than intellectual regurgitation. It, thus, 'bound' people with the meaning, values and lived practices implied in the idea of consciousness. This bondage of love was a positive bondage, whereas the bondage of automatic cognition, unprocessed affect and an unhealthy body was a negative idea of bondage-a fetter. Third, Bhakti as movement achieved this moment of modernity, much before European modernity. The values that one associate with modernity – inclusion, justice and fellowship – were all emphasized and lived during the four centuries churn of the Bhakti movement in Indian history. Bhakti movement was an accomplishment of grounding the philosophical and conceptual frameworks of an all-pervasive consciousness as such, discussed in the Vedas and Vedānta, as Brahman, Paramātman and Dharma in day to day, ordinary life of people from all creeds, castes, genders and regions, which was accomplished through the lived life of its practitioners, whether famous or not, in their written texts, songs and dances and everyday life experience. The lived experiences of these wandering minstrels, were also documented in some cases as philosophical and scholarly treatises, as layers of meanings and interpretations on social events/festivals and everyday actions in their poems and songs. Thus, Bhakti movement was the true social ontology and applied social psychology of the Indian context, inherently pluralistic and inclusive of all, fighting discrimination of caste, creed, language and gender.

Possibilities of Indian social psychology: How does this link with the social psychologists of today

All this is good for the past, the critic might say, what does it mean for the social psychology of India today? Firstly, psychologists in India need have no right-left hesitation in reclaiming this aspect of past! Indeed, the bhakti tradition breaks the stereotype of an internal homogeneity of Indian psychology. Second, for academicians, esp. social psychologists, the question is whether we look at the social psychological landscape of India, from the Euro-American analytical categories and see the imposed etic or do we recognize this emergent universal longing for a collectively crafted well-being for humanity. After all, this is the eutopia that the so-called 'modern' liberal values promise; the same was lived, and therefore, there is a 1000-year lived experience of communities. Across the world, as distress and anguish are experienced, this is the 'future forming' social psychology. In the Indian context, Bhakti movements generated a radical mindset shift; and this is still practised in the households, relationships, communities and regions of the Indian subcontinent. Bhakti still flourishes in India, and rather than looking at it as sociologically, more research, not limited or reduced to surveys, needs to be done on psychological and existential processes and lived experiences of the persons embracing this life. The social psychology of bhakti, does not deny suffering or injustice; these exist, but it offers alternative theorizations of addressing these real existential and human concerns towards well-being – individually, interpersonally, socially and at the level of communities.

Of course, the yearning for love and friendship, compassion and altruism is universal; the practises of caring and fellowship also exist across the world; there is just no mainstreaming of this, which IP does. Indeed, positive psychology talks about the balanced conceptualization of what a 'psyche' or mental health is, but they struggle to understand community hope or collective efficacy, locked as they are in legacy of the binaries between individual, social, markets and the state. Clammer, for example (Clammer, 2013, 2014), takes this point that the social theorizing in Europe is itself interwoven with the predominant ideas of power and authority; obedience and governmentality. Such a social theorizing is unable to imagine alternate and creative theorizing, which in fact, Buddhism and Jainism do, even when they disagree with several other foundational ideas in IP. Indian social psychology presents the possibility of looking at the social with trust and fellowship. In any case, at the bare minimum, the academic texts of social psychology, esp. in India, can certainly go beyond Euro-American social psychology. With these brief concluding remarks, in the next chapter, we will look at the everyday creative processes in detail.

References

Albahari, M. (2019). Beyond cosmopsychism and the great I am: How the world might be grounded in universal 'advaitic' consciousness. In *The Routledge handbook of panpsychism* (pp. 119–130). Routledge.

Ambady, N., & Bharucha, J. (2009). Culture and the brain. *Current Directions in Psychological Science*, *18*(6), 342–345.

Anand, G., & Menon, S. (2017). Body, self and consciousness according to Tirumūlar's Tirumandiram: A comparative study with Kashmir Śaivism. *International Journal of Dharma Studies*, *5*(1), 1–13.

Arzy, S., Thut, G., Mohr, C., Michel, C. M., & Blanke, O. (2006). Neural basis of embodiment: Distinct contributions of temporoparietal junction and extrastriate body area. *The Journal of Neuroscience : The Official Journal of the Society for Neuroscience*, *26*(31), 8074–8081. https://doi.org/10.1523/JNEUROSCI.0745-06.2006

Ashby, F. G., & Isen, A. M. (1999). A neuropsychological theory of positive affect and its influence on cognition. *Psychological Review*, *106*(3), 529.

Bansat-Boudon, L. (2013). The World on Show, or Sensibility in Disguise. Philosophical and Aesthetic Issues in a Stanza by Abhinavagupta (Tantrāloka I 332, Locana and Dhvanyāloka I 13). *Around Abhinavagupta. Aspects of the Intellectual History of Kashmir from the Ninth to the Eleventh Century.*

Clammer, J. (2013). *Culture, development and social theory: Towards an integrated social development.* Zed Books Ltd.

Clammer, J. (2014). *Art, culture and international development: Humanizing social transformation.* Routledge.

Csikszentmihalyi, M. (1988). The flow experience and its significance for human psychology. In *Optimal experience* (pp. 15–35). Cambridge University Press. https://doi.org/10.1017/cbo9780511621956.002

Damasio, A. (1998). Investigating the biology of consciousness. *Philosophical Transactions of the Royal Society of London. Series B: Biological Sciences*, *353*(1377), 1879–1882.

Damasio, A. R. (2006). *Descartes' error.* Random House.

Dissanayake, E. (2001). *Homo aestheticus: Where art comes from and why.* University of Washington Press.

Dissanayake, E. (2015). *What is art for?* University of Washington Press.

Dreyfus, H. L. (1993). *The embodied mind, cognitive science and human experience.* JSTOR.

Friedman, D. A., & Søvik, E. (2021). The ant colony as a test for scientific theories of consciousness. *Synthese*, *198*(2), 1457–1480.

Fredrickson, B. L. (2004). The broaden–and–build theory of positive emotions. *Philosophical Transactions of the Royal Society of London. Series B: Biological Sciences*, *359*(1449), 1367–1377.

Gnoli, R. (1968.). *The aesthetic experience according to Abhinavagupta* (Vol LXII, 2nd ed.). Varanasi: The Chaukhamba Sanskrit Studies.

Haberman, D. l. (2003). *The Bhakti Rasamrta Sindhu of Rupa Gosvamin.* New Delhi: Indira Gandhi National Centre for the Arts in association with MLBD Publishers Pvt. Ltd.

Irie, N., & Hasegawa, T. (2009). Elephant psychology: What we know and what we would like to know. *Japanese Psychological Research*, *51*(3), 177–181.

Isen, A. M. (1987). Positive affect, cognitive processes, and social behavior. In L. Berkowitz (Ed.), *Advances in experimental social psychology* (Vol. 20, pp. 203–253). Elsevier.

Isen, A. M., Daubman, K. A., & Nowicki, G. P. (1987). Positive affect facilitates creative problem solving. *Journal of Personality and Social Psychology*, *52*(6), 1122.

Joormann, J., & Stanton, C. H. (2016). Examining emotion regulation in depression: A review and future directions. *Behaviour Research and Therapy*, *86*, 35–49.

Kasturirangan, R., Guha, N., & Ram-Prasad, C. (2011). Indian cognitivism and the phenomenology of conceptualization. *Phenomenology and the Cognitive Sciences*, *10*(2), 277–296.

Keysers, C., & Gazzola, V. (2010). Social neuroscience: Mirror neurons recorded in humans. *Current Biology*, *20*(8), R353–R354.

Kohda, M., Hotta, T., Takeyama, T., Awata, S., Tanaka, H., Asai, J. Y., & Jordan, A. L. (2019). If a fish can pass the mark test, what are the implications for consciousness and self-awareness testing in animals? *PLoS biology*, *17*(2), e3000021.

Kohler, E., Keysers, C., Umilta, M. A., Fogassi, L., Gallese, V., & Rizzolatti, G. (2002). Hearing sounds, understanding actions: Action representation in mirror neurons. *Science*, *297*(5582), 846–848.

Kristeller, J. L., & Rikhye, K. (2008). Meditative traditions and contemporary psychology. In K. Ramakrishna Rao, A. Paranjpe, Ajit K. Dalal (Eds.), *Handbook of Indian psychology* (pp. 506–539). New Delhi: Cambridge University Press.

Kuchibhotla, L., & Menon, S. (2014). Self and empathy. In S. Menon, A. Sinha & B. Sreekantan (Eds.), *Interdisciplinary perspectives on consciousness and the self* (pp. 177–192). Springer.

Lynch, J. M., & Troy, A. S. (2021). The role of nonduality in the relationship between flow States and well-being. *Mindfulness*. https://doi.org/10.1007/s12671-021-01627-3

Markus, H. R., & Kitayama, S. (1991). Culture and the self: Implications for cognition, emotion, and motivation. *Psychological Review*, *98*(2), 224–253. https://doi.org/10.1037/0033-295x.98.2.224

Markus, H. R., & Kitayama, S. (2003). Culture, self, and the reality of the social. *Psychological Inquiry*, *14*(3), 277–283. https://doi.org/10.1207/s15327965pli1403&4_17

Medhananda, S. (2022). The playful self-involution of divine consciousness: Sri Aurobindo's evolutionary cosmopsychism and his response to the individuation problem. *The Monist*, *105*(1), 92–109.

Menon, S. (2005). What is Indian psychology: Transcendence in and while thinking. *Journal of Transpersonal Psychology*, *37*(2), 83.

Menon, S. (2013). Consciousness, love and well-being: Indian Psychology and the Bhagavad Gita. In *PsycEXTRA dataset*. American Psychological Association (APA). https://doi.org/10.1037/e627722013-057

Menon, S. (2014). *Brain, self and consciousness*. Springer.

Menon, S., Sinha, A., & Sreekantan, B. V. (2014). *Interdisciplinary perspectives on consciousness and the self*. Springer.

Mirvis, P. H. (1991). Flow: The psychology of optimal experience. *Academy of Management Review*, *16*(3), 636–640. https://doi.org/10.5465/amr.1991.4279513

Muni, B. (n.d.). *Natyasastram with Abhinavabharati* (Edited by R. Kavi), 4 vols. Gaekwad's Oriental Series. Published under authority of Government of His Highness the Maharaja Gaekwad of Baroda.

Nagar, R. S. & Joshi, K. L. (1981). Nāṭyaśastra of Bharatamuni: With the commentary Abhinavabharati by Abhinavaguptācārya. Parimal.

Nagasawa, Y., & Wager, K. (2017). Panpsychism and priority cosmopsychism. In G. Brüntrup & L. Jaskolla (Eds.), Panpsychism: Contemporary Perspectives (pp. 113–129). Oxford University Press.

Natyashastra (Sanskrit). (1989). Sri Satguru Publication.

Pandit, S. A. (2011). The concept of rasa in Indian psychology: A preliminary qualitative study. *Journal of Psychosocial Research*, *6*(1), 135–144.

Pandit, S. A. (2021). Advaita: Oneness as a lived reality – examining aspects of a profound and a radical psychology. *Psychology and Developing Societies*. https://doi.org/10.1177/09713336211038814

Pandit, S. A., & Misra, G. (2013). Emotions in Indian psychology. In G. Misra (Ed.), *Psychology and psychanalysis* (pp. 663–691). Centre for Studies in Civilizations, Project of History of Indian Science, Philosophy and Culture, Indian Council for Social Science Research.
Paranjpe, A. (2009). In defence of an Indian approach to the psychology of emotion. *Psychological Studies*, *54*, 3–22.
Paranjpe, A., & Rao, K. (2008). Psychology in the Advaita Vedanta. In K. P. Rao (Ed.), *Handbook of Indian psychology*. New Delhi: Foundation Books.
Quinn, D. M., Chaudoir, S. R., & Kallen, R. W. (2011). Performance and flow: A review and integration of self-objectification research. In R. M. Calogero, S. Tantleff-Dunn, & J. K. Thompson (Eds.), Self-objectification in women: Causes, consequences, and counteractions (pp. 119–138). American Psychological Association. https://doi.org/10.1037/12304-006
Rizzolatti, G. (2005). The mirror neuron system and its function in humans. *Anatomy and Embryology*, *210*(5–6), 419–421.
Rizzolatti, G., Fadiga, L., Fogassi, L., & Gallese, V. (2002). 14 from mirror neurons to imitation: Facts and speculations. *The Imitative Mind: Development, Evolution, and Brain Bases*, *6*, 247–266.
Rochat, P., & Zahavi, D. (2011). The uncanny mirror: A re-framing of mirror self-experience. *Consciousness and Cognition*, *20*(2), 204–213.
Ryan, R. M., & Deci, E. L. (2000). Self-determination theory and the facilitation of intrinsic motivation, social development, and well-being. *American Psychologist*, *55*(1), 68–78. https://doi.org/10.1037/0003-066x.55.1.68
Sharma Sen, R., & Pandit, S. A. (2013). Exploring Vatsalyam: The emotion of love for the child. *Psychology and Developing Societies*, *25*(1), 165–193.
Sen, R. S., & Pandit, S. (2013). Exploring Vātsalyam: The Emotion of Love for the Child. *Psychology and Developing Societies*, *25*(1), 165–193.
Shāstrī, M. R. (1918). *The Tantrāloka of Abhinava Gupta* (Vol. 1). Commentary by Rājānaka Jayaratha. Allahabad: Indian Press.
Simonton, D. K. (2002). Creativity. In *Encyclopedia of psychological assessment*. SAGE Publications Ltd. https://doi.org/10.4135/9780857025753.n60
Sinha, J. B. P., Singh, S., Gupta, P., Srivastava, K. B. L., Sinha, R. B. N., Srivastava, S., Ghosh, A., Siddiqui, R. N., Tripathi, N., Gupta, M., Srivastava, S., Mulla, Z., Vijayalakshmi, C., & Pandey, A. (2010). An exploration of the Indian mindset. *Psychological Studies*, *55*(1), 3–17. https://doi.org/10.1007/s12646-010-0001-x
Smith, L. T. (2021). *Decolonizing methodologies: Research and indigenous peoples*. Zed Books Ltd.
Turella, L., Pierno, A. C., Tubaldi, F., & Castiello, U. (2009). Mirror neurons in humans: Consisting or confounding evidence? *Brain and Language*, *108*(1), 10–21.
van der Schyff, D. (2015). Music as a manifestation of life: Exploring enactivism and the 'eastern perspective' for music education. In *Frontiers in Psychology* (Vol. 6, p. 345). https://www.frontiersin.org/article/10.3389/fpsyg.2015.00345
Varela, F. G., Maturana, H. R., & Uribe, R. (1974). Autopoiesis: The organization of living systems, its characterization and a model. *Biosystems*, *5*(4), 187–196.

8 Purṇa

Creative living and transcendence here and now

Completion: Towards everyday creativity and joy

Adhika Dekhane Tari Niranjan Pahane; Yogiraj Vinavane manā āle vo māye

(to really see, is to see the transcendental ownerless; For that, one learns yoga and distinguishes the apparent and real)

Dehabaḷi Deoni Sādhili mya sādhanā; Tene samadhan mani jodale vo maye

(I let go of my body awareness and accomplished my practice; Letting go of my body awareness, allowed me contentment)

Anangapan fitale, mayachandā sāthavile; Sakal dekhile ātmaswaroop vo maye

(Letting for of attachment and self-centered desire, I collected all of them; O, mother, I saw all my self-centered desires as not mine and for the all/whole-ownerless)

Pure Pure āta prapanca pāhane; Nijānandi rāhane swaroopi vo maye

(Now, let us not get caught in seeing the apparent five; O, Mother, It is good to rest in the ownerless consciousness)

(Jnāneśwara, a 13th century Marathi Nātha yogi and poet, translation by the author)

Above is a short excerpt of the 'abhanga' written by the great Nath yogi master of 13th century Maharashtra which describes, in its gentle simplicity, the everyday self-recognition as a lived practice (Karhadkar,1976). The song also nudges the listeners to engage in everyday creative living. The Bhakti movement, in Indian history from all regions, not only reconciled the apparent dichotomy of the embodied and transcendental consciousness indicated in the Vedānta; the theoretical pathways laid by the commentaries on Brahma sutra by grand masters such as Ādi Śankarācārya, Rāmānujacārya and Madhvācārya led to the grounded living as Brahman.

DOI: 10.4324/9781003336204-8

Note that Ādi Śankarācārya even while writing about pure consciousness, celebrates love and devotion for embodied consciousness as Saguna (Brahman with name, form and quality) as the self-same expression of the sacred consciousness as such. Jnāneśwara exemplifies the scholarly, aesthetic and day-to-day lived experiences of the galaxy of self-recognized, embodied, situated lived life trajectories of teachers in the Indian consciousness-based psychology (Karhadkar, 1976). Several such teachers and masters from different parts of India, wrote extensively, in the languages of the common ordinary people, travelled across the land, danced, cried, and sang – communicating with the people, and with other teachers of the tradition to weave the fabric of the culmination of an integrated applied psychology over the period of next 200 years. The Indian psychology that reached its fruition in the 17th century, much before the advent of British colonizer and the idea of European modernity, integrated embodied consciousness through Hathyoga traditions, which as the texts show, integrated advaita, tantra and bhakti traditions together. Thus, many of the Bhakti saints, such as Jnāneśwara, were Nath Yogis and masters of Vedānta. In their scholarly and poetic writing, they converted the philosophical Vedāntic realizations into lived day-to-day experiences, writing poems and songs, dancing and teaching, breaking the barriers of caste, creed and region. These great masters lived a life of everyday creativity and joy without denying the challenges they faced. This chapter, therefore, closes with the performativity and receptivity of everyday joy and relational well-being. This chapter merely restates the positive earned and accomplished by the master teachers in 16th century India, which students currently in India at least have forgotten and tangentially study as 'positive' psychology.

In this chapter, we will look at everyday creativity and how psychologists have discussed this as the small 'c' creativity in contrast to the big 'C' creativity, which is supposed to be disruptive and paradigm changing. As briefly mentioned in the last chapter, Simonton distinguishes between big 'C' and small 'c' creativity (Simonton, 2013). This chapter holds that instead of a paradigm changing big 'C' creativity, it is the small 'c' everyday creativity, with its small connection with positive emotion, and a day-to-day life satisfaction that leads to well-being and contentment. Perhaps, it is contentment which is central to understanding the small 'w' – well-being as an everyday process rather than a transcendental idea of an end state self-realization or recognition of consciousness as such! Who is a liberated person – a Jīvanmukta, a person who looks at samādhi as an end state, much like a long-term promise or a person who lives in freedom every day – moment by moment?

Psychologists, esp. positive psychologists and earlier anthropologists, have studied what *we call as everyday creativity*. Everyday creativity is not monetized and is done and undone every day. An example of that everyday creativity would be the rangoli or alpanā or Koḷam; free hand or geometrical patterns drawn on the floor in front of the Indian homes, using rice flour every morning and especially during the special occasions such as festivals or marriages. Anthropologists such as Ellen Dissanayake, studied this everyday creativity and wondered what could be the adaptational outcome of a rangoli or, indeed, even a cave painting found in several cases by prehistoric human societies (Dissanayake, 2001, 2015). This book proposes the idea that it is these shared cultural and collective practices that link, everyday lived experience, positive affect, shared relational self and a social consciousness that easily steps into a transcendental consciousness. Let us look at everyday creativity and positive affect, which then relates to a day-to-day mindset of satisfaction and Śānta, leading to a transcendental self.

As self and relational expression, day-to-day creative acts are not intended to be monetized and their subsequent monetization reflects alienation; an other-ing and a reductive market-based framing. Colonization and later globalization, have possibly hijacked the original intention of this self-expression into a large-scale commodification of the performative and fine arts as well as the crafts traditions in the colonized cultures as means of 'survival' across the world. More specifically in the Indian cultural traditions, actual material poverty and deprivations in living conditions have forced the choices of people. Having lost this clear and concrete connection with self-expression and turning all craft, art performance and collective lived experiences into products, events, tourism and market trends, questions then arise about the authenticity of these 'products' as what we see are defined by market-based discourses, reified and alienated from the self. Thankfully, several everyday small 'c' creativity practices such as the Indian tradition of Rangoli/Alpanā/Koḷam has not yet been commodified, but might be getting lost, precisely because of the mainstream framing; there seems to be no monetary value. About 50 years back, it was normative to see either freehand or geometric patterns drawn using rice flour in front of Indian houses across India. Called as Rangoli, Rāngoli, Koḷam and Alpanā in different Indian languages, it is an everyday act of creativity; an un-sensational, day-to-day practice and an expression of self and self-experienced was not directly linked to adaptation and survival of species. Indeed, this was the first social act, every day.

Anthropologists have long noted that across societies, human collectives have often painted, drawn and expressed themselves through the arts; through aesthetics, collectives have found joy and well-being (Kargól, 2021; Lavie et al., 1993; Narayan, 2016; Richards, 2018). In the increasingly commodified times of today, most of these arts and crafts and, indeed, everyday living practices have been removed from their sacred roots, modified, monetized and are increasingly seen as business opportunities rather than as expressions of self and self-experience which they probably were originally intended to be. Anthropologists have also questioned why it is that human beings starting from early human collectives have expressed themselves in ways which were not utilitarian or at least had no direct connection to survival and adaptation. Psychologists have also studied creativity in their own bubbles – trying to theorize it a-contextually. In the last 30 years, as the Western European and North American academia, confronted multicultural societies and evidences, the understanding of creativity has broadened.

As we will examine this small 'c' creativity and its connection with positive emotion, day-to-day experience of emotion and day-to-day satisfaction that is a much specific construct than a broad 'life satisfaction'. As we will see, *it is contentment rather than happiness* which is central to understanding Indian Psychology practice as a process rather than a milestone. Similarly, it is a well-being as a lifelong process rather than a transcendental idea of an end state that is central to the Indian understanding of being free while living or Jīvanmukti.

The objectives of this particular chapter, therefore, are firstly, to review the evidence on everyday creative processes as expressed through arts and crafts of the collectives/societies, specific to the Indian context. Next, the chapter hopes to examine the evidence relating to creativity in contemporary Euro-American psychology. As mentioned above, the everyday lived experience of the teachers in the bhakti movement lived and reconciled all the dualisms and analytical contradictions in an academic understanding of consciousness. The chapter, then attempts to delve into the Indian knowledge traditions to identify the pathways to words moment by moment day-to-day well-being as expressed and experienced through day-to-day positive emotions and everyday creativity. Everyday creativity as everyday self-recognition is a fascinating element of Indian psychology, and on a strong conceptual ground of the consciousness as such.

The chapter will attempt to tie in the ideas of embodied consciousness, everyday creativity, positive emotions and freedom while living or the idea of Jīvanmukti in Vedānta. Finally, the chapter closes with the idea of *Sahaja* – which captures the idea of an innocent, spontaneous living as well-being. Sahaja, according to Indian traditions, is manifest in everyday creativity but more significantly arises from a quiet and uncomplicated mind, which coheres the elements of day-to-day living, simply and in harmony with the ecosystem. Thus, we hopefully restate the grand thought and theoretical achievement of the Indian psychologist masters – combining philosophy and philosophical schools of Yoga-Sāmkhya, Vedānta, bhakti, tantra and body; all with their lived practices in individual relational collectivity. Note how seamlessly, the legacy binaries and analytically categories of Euro-American thought come together. Indeed, knowledge was always organized in integrated form as the hidden structure of the disparate outer expression.

Creative and performing arts in the everyday Indian context

One of the fascinating and mind-boggling characteristics of the Indian cultural traditions has been the diversity of expressions of art, craft and everyday performativity. India, in its regions, has specific classical and folk traditions of performing, fine arts and craft traditions. If you look at the north of India, in each state and possibly in each district, we find specific performative, fine arts and crafts traditions. For example, you will find the most beautiful craft traditions starting from Leh Ladakh, traditions of performances and performativity and you will also find unique traditions of singing/dancing and social engagements in groups and collectives. *Each of them is linked with the sacred.* Similarly, you would find the same for the state of Himachal Pradesh, the union territories of Jammu in Kashmir and so on. The Crafts Council of India, in association with World Crafts council, has worked on a craft map of India, but that is just scratching the surface. Overall, the Ministry of Culture is tasked with documenting and sustaining the mind-boggling diversities of heritage – built, tangible and intangible heritage, the craft traditions in textiles, metalwork, mud work, pottery, ceramics, jewellery design and so on. Apart from these classical and folk traditions of performative and fine arts as well as the crafts, UNESCO has now started to identify the 'bio-cultural heritage' and living communities. Then there are discursive spaces called 'kshetra' – larger than a temple complex, holding the collective memories, schemas and scripts. Thus, the larger lived practices of the diversities of the Indian communities are not understood and studied by Indian psychologists. Indeed, the various folk and tribal traditions have withered as this study was outsourced to anthropologists.

These living practices are not studied by psychologists, esp. in India, perhaps, because they are un-sensational. Everyday creativity and lived practice is also not monetized and is *done and undone* every day. An example of that everyday creativity would be the rangoli or alpanā or Koḷam; free hand or geometrical patterns drawn on the floor in front of the Indian house homes, using rice flour every morning and especially during the special occasions such as festivals or marriages in India. As mentioned, Dissanayake, studied this everyday creativity in the Indian subcontinent and noted the 'ephemerality'. Dissanayake enquired about the adaptational outcomes of art and questioned the utilitarian meta-theoretical assumptions of art and aesthetics, indeed, what is the adaptational value of a cave painting found in several cases by prehistoric human societies; calling 'neuro-aesthetics' as *narrow aesthetics* (Brown & Dissanayake, 2009; Dissanayake, 2001, 2008, 2015). Indian societies have traditional looked at everyday creativity as expressions of self as consciousness, which typically show day-to-day experiences or cultural ecologies; signatures such as a parrot, a peacock, the form of a mango or a wish fulfilling tree! At the moment of that self-expression, these are not intended to be monetized either!

Across all societies, with the advent of colonization and the other-ing of the indigenous societies, *these acts of self-expression* which were materially looted, then traded but became esoteric and other-ed. Colonization and later globalization, have possibly hijacked the original intention of that self-expression into a large-scale commodification of the performative and fine arts as well as the crafts traditions across the world. More specifically in the Indian cultural traditions, these have removed the sacredness and everyday joy. Having lost this clear and concrete connection with self-expression, questions then arise about the authenticity of these 'products' as what we see are defined by market-based discourses, reified and alienated from the self.

Everyday activities make and remake the self – the embodied enminded self as consciousness; what does the contemporary psychology, esp. positive psychology reveal? In the next section, we will examine the interconnections between every day creativity, motivation, positive emotion and creativity as intricately tied to the idea of self itself. This, we will examine through the updated research from the field of psychology and neuroscience.

The field of creativity, as studied in psychology, has undergone a huge 'advance' in the last 50 years. The earliest researches in creativity were primarily done by Terman in the North American context. Terman wanted to study the life trajectories of gifted children and this wonderful research assessed these gifted children called as 'termites' longitudinally (Hastorf, 1997). He found that the so-called gifted children did not have very high IQs rather more likely to be just above-average in the IQ. These children were also likely to be more adaptive, hardy and experienced positive coping methods. Later research, revealed that the so-called 'gifted' children were also likely to experience less physical health problems, more socially adaptable and resilient, turning the popular stereotypical perception of a creative genius as maladjusted upside down.

The early models of creativity particularly focused on the paradoxical nature of the creative process as well. The creative process is quite paradoxical, where there are phases of focused attention followed by completely de-focused attention (also called incubation) followed by a sudden insight or a 'revelation'. Because of this paradoxical nature of creative insight and process, early European thought also viewed creativity from a theological perspective as the 'revelation'. Some of the classic case histories that we recall to understand the paradoxical nature of creative insight are the insight about the structure of benzene by Kekule, the 'aha' moment experience by Archimedes and the revelatory reporting of mathematical equations in the case of Ramanujam.

The significant departure from the earlier ideas of creativity and creative process came through the research of Mihalyi Czsiksentsmihalyi (Csikszentmihalyi, 1988; Ma et al., 2018). Czsiksentsmihalyi, foundationally contributed to Euro-American psychology in three ways: firstly, he used the process mapping of the emotional states of the creative person through moments. For this purpose, he worked with those who were identified as high functioning or creative persons. Second, he was a pioneer in using technology to map emotional states by moment, called 'experience sampling', through the use of gadgets such as pagers. Thirdly, he contributed to illuminating the paradoxical nature of the creative process and coined the key term 'flow'. Some of the key characteristics of the creative process, as identified by Czsiksentsmihalyi, are particularly instructive for our future discussion. The research found that the creative person uses less self-censoring and allows for multiple ideas; thus, even the 'wild', the 'lame' and the politically incorrect ones are attended to. This less self-censoring in attention as a cognitive variable can then be discussed along with Fredrickson's model of 'broaden and build' (Fredrickson, 2001). Fredrickson, in her famous model looks at how positive emotions broaden the momentary thought-action repertoire. It basically, means that momentary positive emotion, leads to flexibility of choices in decisions to act, which further lead to openness to experience. The research by Czsiksentsmihalyi also noted that the creative process needs to present the right amount of challenge – that which does not threaten the person to get overwhelmed with survival and fear and yet is not so easy that the person is pushed to boredom and lethargy. The third key insight of the creative process was that the creative person in the creative process does not look at failure as a conclusive judgement on the self; *rather failure is looked at as temporary setback*. This makes the creative person pursue ideas in different iterations/titrations is so to say, till the idea is not elaborated sufficiently. Thus perseverance in light of failures and negative judgements is key to understand creativity and indicates the role of self-systems, studied by creativity researchers (Mirvis, 1991). Later creativity researchers have also noted a distortion in self-time during the flow process. Now, how do we interpret and translate these insights into the context of everyday creativity as seen and observed in the Indian context of diverse performative and fine arts as well as crafts traditions? Let us take the example of rangoli, what would trigger a common ordinary person in the Indian context to draw a geometrical or a free hand pattern using rice flour in front of the house every day in the morning. Certainly, for one, the person would have a repository of traditionally used and practised geometrical patterns, possibly inherited from the mother/the mother-in-law/the other women in the family. However, women typically create **their own patterns** after drawing the basic matrix, on a moment by moment decision! Secondly, many women decide to draw freehand, again possibly choosing from a culturally inherited repository of figures and forms such as the form of a mango, a peacock or a wish fulfilling tree. Finally, certain patterns, in that moment, lead to changes in the freehand as well as in geometric rangoli. Circles and semicircles, then lead to triangles and half triangles; triangles lead to connections between the triangles and so on, *the form keeps expanding*. There is no fear of failure and forms are erased and redrawn. Traditionally, the rangoli is always started with a dot and thereafter expanded. It is interesting to note that In texts, starting from the 'dot' thereafter expanding from the 'dot' is also taught as the creative principle of this universe itself. Most rangoli patterns use colours, but the day-to-day rangoli is usually done with white rice flour. In some states, such as Kerala, rangoli is made with a variety of flowers, especially during the festivals, in collectivity. As mentioned, Dissanayake, studying everyday creativity from the context of Sri Lanka, has also commented that, this creative expression is *ephemeral* and recreated every morning by the same person. This is contrasted with the idea of creativity and art itself in the European and North American context, where art is not only monetized but also kept in museums *for perpetuity*. The everyday art and creativity of a person drawing rangoli are recreated every day, a-fresh. We just took a very ordinary, mundane example of rangoli, now, it could be possible to accept that this everyday act of creativity and re-creation next day, generates a mild positive emotion in that person. The mild positive emotion generated every day in the morning can then be discussed with the broaden and built framework of Fredrickson without any controversy. Early research (Ashby & Isen, 1999; Isen, 1987; Isen et al., 1987) on the impact of mild positive emotions on future behaviours shows, that even mild positive emotions show a large impact on behaviours such as being helpful to others, being flexible in thinking, being and accepting of failure is and being better self-regulated.

Thus, in reference to the lived Indian psychology, that reached its fruition in the 15th century CE and was led by masters of advaita, hatha and bhakti, we can agree that a daily practice of everyday creativity through the cultural processes such as drawing rangoli, painting on walls, community cooking and singing, etc. would generate a mild positive emotion, in togetherness/shared attention and memory that *would in turn reset that day* for this person – even an ordinary person; thus connecting to the sacred/the relationality of consciousness as God, that we discussed in the chapter on social selves.

It is so unfortunate that, none of the Indian psychologists have worked on this mechanism of a day-to-day *feeling of contentment* and mild positive emotion in togetherness in the life of an ordinary Indian person following their cultural practices. Neither have they connected this to positive psychology, which would generate a global and relevant theory and application nor have they viewed this as fresh theorizations of a continuing and lived Indian psychology.

This key element of contentment and flexibility of thought-action repertoire, as empirically demonstrated by Fredrickson, in her study context of positive emotions, has been identified as a living practice of sacred in the day-to-day life of the societies and communities since long. In addition, this everyday creativity, also made it possible for the advaita practitioners' masters *to live an embodied mind-no mind, such that, the social self and the psyche were constituted and dissolved moment by moment.*

Contemporary psychology evidence: Creativity, motivation, positive emotion

It is noteworthy that recent trends in contemporary psychology, especially in positive psychology, have not only acknowledged the role of culture in constituting and expressing emotion but also thrown light on gaps found earlier in the very conceptualization of emotion and emotion focussed processing. Researchers such as Stanton and her colleagues (Austenfeld et al., 2006; Austenfeld & Stanton, 2004; Stanton & Low, 2012) have noted that **the earlier questionnaires that sought to answer questions related to coping, seemed to frame question on emotion, with an unexamined bias – in a way that, intense emotions were insinuated with maladjustment and low self-efficacy.** Recent positive psychology research corrects these mistakes and advances our understanding of emotion focussed coping in terms of which emotions are processed and which are avoided while being in stress or pain. Similarly, this dynamic between emotion processing and avoidance is connected with the set of behaviours that are activated and/or inhibited. Thus, we see a 2×2 matrix of emotion processing and avoidance with behaviour activation and inhibition.

We should note that, across cultures, the combinations of processing and avoidance with behavioural activation and inhibition might be schematized differently, thus, giving a contextual specificity as well as an adaptational edge to emotion processing. Psychologists now accept that emotion focussed processing and coping is central to emotional intelligence and includes pathways through which we can direct thoughts and cognitive processes simply by a better understanding of our emotional landscapes. Emotional intelligence, itself was a contribution in recent years, which comes as a great sense of relief after at least three confused colonized generations in the Indian context (Salovey & Mayer, 1990).

Be that as it is, at this point of time, note that we have moved past the idea of positive and negative emotion as dichotomies. It appears now that not only are negative emotions capable of being used to direct thoughts and cognitions towards creative process but that the self is central in these negotiations. If the conventionally understood, socially constituted self is overwhelmed by the valence of emotion, then whatever that emotion be, it is difficult to process it, whereas, note that if the self feels adequate to

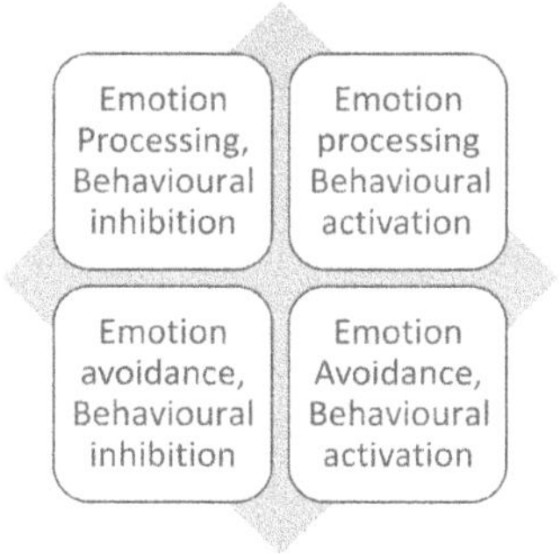

Figure 8.1 The interconnections between emotion and behaviour – processing, activation and inhibition.

Source: Lopez, Pedrotti, and Snyder. (2019).

process the emotion, then the self can be a resilient self – whether for negative or for positive emotion. The question then loops back to our earlier chapters – how is the self-constituted; both conventionally through Yoga and bhakti as well as its recognition as consciousness alone in advaita? The point to note here is – two strategies directly radiate out of affirmation of the social self and its negation. In affirmation, if the social self is constituted, then according to the Indian Psychology frameworks, it is likely to be more coherent, social relational and yet easy to dissolve, moment by moment – whether through Buddhism, or advaita or bhakti. While popular psychology discusses the interconnections between negative affect and arousal, again, we see that behavioural activation and inhibition are connected to the self-system. Thus, a theorization must include a self (even if it is socially constituted in a physicalist universe); second, the self needs to include a positive identity and a higher self-efficacy. The next step question would be – How does a higher self-efficacy accrue?

Positive identity and self-efficacy are central to understand the true import of the research on creativity, briefly summarized in the earlier section. It is positive identity and self-efficacy that allow the creative person to look persevere and look at failure as a temporary setback, to be flexible and less self-censoring so that new or unfamiliar ideas, thoughts and emotions are not appraised as 'threatening' to the self. This point directly relates to the Indian traditions of Yoga-meditation and advaita-non-dual recognition. If the idea of self is upstream beyond the socially constituted self; if the self is viewed as ever expanding, unbroken and ever-stable *witness*, then such a 'belief' (even if it remains a belief) itself, provides for a strong and positive identity and self-efficacy. Of course, it goes without saying, but it needs to be again emphasized that 'consciousness as self' in the Indian knowledge traditions is not based on beliefs but on self-recognition and, thereafter, the lived experience of the meditators in unbroken traditions of more than 4000 years.

This brings us to the final point on the nature of motivation itself; motivation is defined as the internal triggers that drive action. The nuanced understanding of motivation itself has undergone a gigantic shift in Euro-American psychology in the last 50 years. About a century earlier, psychologists viewed motivation in terms of the terms such as 'drives', 'instinct' and homeostasis. The deterministic idea that humans are 'driven' to specific actions related to survival alone reduced theoretical possibilities and incomplete 'knowledge' about human nature. Now, we know that even the so-called survival-related motives, such as hunger and sex, are significantly moderated by cultural and situational factors. While, it is true that human organisms are motivated to eat to survive at the basic either/or level, beyond that binary, hunger itself, at least in the contemporary societies, is moderated and regulated by (A) market-based triggers such as advertisements, portion sizes, food choices, cost, etc.; (B) cultural factors such as historical and culturally inherited food preferences, local produce and (C) situational factors such as availability and access, including deprivation, poverty and war. Similar points can be extrapolated about drives such as sex and sleep.

The key learning is that organisms have complex navigations of triggers to act and the simplistic models of motivation based on the organism (and not the self) might distort our understanding about human psychology itself! The humanistic and existential traditions in the Euro-American context did focus on self and motivation. Note that philosophers in the European tradition have always discussed terms such as will, connation and intention. Even while Maslow explicitly located his model of hierarchy of needs in self-actualization and transcendence, this model was critiqued for being theoretically nebulous and conceptually weak precisely because, Euro-American context, did not have the conceptual toolkit in the extant mainstream physicalist/computationalist and functionalist universe and philosophy of mind to explain 'peak experiences', self-actualization and transcendence. Indeed, philosophers and psychologists in European and American contexts have given theorizations of self but have been unable to ground them on theoretical frameworks of the sacred, simply due to the theological idea of an anthropomorphic authoritarian God and not consciousness as God or consciousness as self or consciousness as ānanda. Spirituality thus wanders around untethered to other aspects of psychology.

Ryan and Deci, in contemporary psychology (Deci, 1975; Ryan & Deci, 2000, 2001), through a series of studies, connected motivation with the self-systems and proposed that high functioning individuals show an intrinsic motivation pathway. What this means is that high functioning individuals are motivated to act by causes and triggers internal or intrinsic to them. Simply put, they act because they are intrigued, curious or immersed in a task, and the task is inherently satisfying them. On the contrary, extrinsic motivation implies that the person is triggered to act due to some factors such as rewards and punishments external to either the task or the self. Later research studies in cognitive psychology have shown that creativity and intrinsic motivation are strongly linked (Auger & Woodman, 2016). This seems logical and does not surprise; indeed, it is surprising that it took so long to prove. In the specific context of IKT, intrinsic motivation is culturally privileged but note also that extrinsic triggers are not demonized or reduced to reward and punishment. The social self in Bhakti experiences as well as processes humiliation, social ostracism, adversity and injustice not as a punishment or a reward but as duties to be completed through compassion and insight. This loops back to the chapters on emotional transformation and cognition.

The assumptions of rational analysis in European philosophical tradition, are different from plural logical systems such as Jain, Buddhist and Hindu Nyāya (Frazier, 2011; Ganeri, 1996, 2002, 2004; Koller, 2000). The tri-sectional fragmentation between philosophy, theology and science in European history, is stark as compared to the IKT, which examined the possibility of a non-anthropomorphic idea of consciousness without a legacy of this trifurcation. The Indian traditions entertained the frameworks of pluralistic logic and rationality and did not view science, theology and philosophy as speculative and/or separative from each other; divorced from human experience. It is obvious that such allowance to plurality, was a relief; emphasizing that, it is these systems of thinking and reasoning, that brought an underlying order to the diverse Indian context. These key points are well elaborated by contemporary philosophers such as Ganeri (Ganeri, 2002) and Ram-Prasad (Ram-Prasad, 2013) in reference to social theory and pluralism. Both have written about Jaina logic of Anekantavada as the basis of Indian cultural acceptance of diverse views as well as the basis of epistemology as the common ground to debates and discussions among Buddhists, Jaina and Āstikā scholars.

In summary, then, we have kept creativity and creative process in the centre and examined associated concepts and constructs, such as emotion and motivation, without reducing them to simplistic ideas. As we started this chapter, Simonton (Simonton, 2013) has differentiated between big 'C' and small 'c' creativity. Big 'C' creativity is the glamorous part of creativity, where certain ideas disrupt paradigms, thought processes and civilizations. According to Simonton, small 'c' creativity is the incremental creativity. One might think that small 'c' creativity is not so interesting; in fact, it is the small 'c' creativity, that is of great interest to this book, as small 'c' creativity is that every creativity, where consciousness overflows! Every time, consciousness 'overflows', moment by moment, it brings surprise and joy! Note that this overflow is embodied, day to day; not binarized in terms of this worldly and otherworldly consciousness, but valenced even within the socially and culturally constituted self. Every time, small incremental positive emotion is experienced, the person is likely to be not only (a) prosocial/helpful, (b) flexible and (c) express better self-regulated, as Isen and her colleagues' research would inform us; a here and now transcendence, which is not even as immersive as 'flow' is experienced by the person. It is probable, that such a person may not disrupt a discipline or cause a paradigm shift, but certainly, such a person experiences well-being on a moment to moment and day-to-day basis. Thus we can say that small 'c' creativity is linked with small 'w' well-being! And such a small 'w' well-being is likely to make the person resilient to face small and micro adversities that they are likely to experience in their lives.

Simonton and several other contemporary creativity researchers also note that what in best case scenarios in termed as flexibility and less self-censoring also is correlated with 'cognitive disinhibition' that affects our ordinary adjustments in our social contexts, correlating with maladjustments and mental health concerns among creative individuals. This is important to note as we don't have enough evidence to assess whether every day, small 'c' creativity causes the extent of cognitive disinhibition as seen in big 'C' creative process and therefore, everyday creativity as a cultural practice might be correlated with 'just enough' positive emotion and just enough overflow! It should be possible to explore the moment by moment awareness and aesthetic appreciation due to other dialogical cultural practices in the Indian cultural contexts by interdisciplinary researchers, observing performative and fine arts, crafts practices as well as culturally structured practices such as wandering or travelling without a specific intent and *an intentional frugality* in living, that then allows for small 'c' creativity throughout the lifespan.

Thus, we have discussed and summarized the key insights in our understanding of creativity, creative person and the possibilities of everyday creative living. In the next section, we will examine what the Indian knowledge traditions have to inform and illuminate about creativity, creative process and possibilities of creative living.

Computational creativity and Indian psychology

In a workshop on computational models of the human mind, a very interesting statement was made by the course instructor about the nature of creativity. It was said that, creativity is notoriously difficult to model in predictive equations! Indeed, this presents the nub of the question for a physicalist vs a non-physicalist idea of consciousness. Can creativity be modelled through mathematical equations or maybe can mathematical equations come alive and form and re-form themselves? There is no denying that, there is order in the universe, implying a certain kind of predictability, leading to statements by scientists that 'God' is a mathematician. At the same time, there are disjunctions and the possibility of a moment by moment unpredictability can never be denied in reference to not just human ecologies but also physicalist domains such as the arrival of the monsoons. Why is it that conditions are better specified/specifiable in all cause-and-effect relationships in the so called 'natural sciences'? At the centre of this question are the intersections of biological and life and the chemical sciences. Scientists are divided and controversies continue to erupt! Biologists such as Sheldrake (Sheldrake, 2011) have proposed ideas that can be considered as 'wild' from the current positivistic perspectives. Sheldrake and several others, such as Roy Bhaskar (2013, 2014), not only put their professional lives on line of fire but have also been shunned and 'ghosted' after being earlier feted, at least in the case of Bhaskar!

Indian knowledge traditions, specifically the advaita perspectives state that, consciousness alone explains and sustains creativity and all life as creative impulse (Bhawuk, 2003, 2018). The interesting and provocative (even if you disagree) points made by biologists such as Sheldrake are that they try to locate characteristics of consciousness away from the body into abstract ideas of 'information or memory fields'.

In general, we see that innovations in scientific thinking have only arrived after the reconciliation of the binaries and contradictions inherent in scientific thinking itself, for example, the case of dissipative structures

(Prigogine & Stengers, 1997). In their 1997 book, Perigigone and Stengers argued that determinism in thermodynamics is no longer a tenable scientific belief. This was called as paradigm shift and thermodynamics evolved thereafter. Similarly, the biologist Sheldrake proposes that a transpersonal, trans-chronous consciousness is the only possible explanation for this living universe, through his hypothesis of 'morphic resonance and memory fields'! This has been called as complete pseudoscience. Sheldrake has also proposed that, we are on the cusp of a Kuhnian paradigm shift in mind sciences. He might be proven wrong and might be effaced in the history of ideas. If Sheldrake is proved right in future, then, that would need a serious revision in the philosophies of science, esp. positivism and their assumptions.

In the Indian knowledge traditions, one of the fundamental characteristics of consciousness is creativity, fertility and abundance. Unpredictability is also a characteristic of consciousness but is framed as 'playfulness' and acknowledged in the later non-dual Trika Śaiva texts as the 'Svātantrya Śakti' (ever emergent power of freedom) inhering in consciousness. In the Vedas, the first experience of self-consciousness is described in feminine terms. It is stated that, when the self first became self-aware, the first intention that arose in the 'self-aware' self was to become many. Scholars and traditional teachers have identified this first moment as the moment of creativity, fertility and abundance – *Ekoham Bahusyām Prajāyai.* Later traditions of Tantra identify this as the primordial feminine energy that is playful and ever free, appearing contradictory only from a human thinking perspective.

Note that different world-views in IKT have addressed these questions with their own formulations. According to Sāṃkhya, non-self-aware impulse, intention as well as intuition comes from Prakrti (also called as Pradhāna), which is a primordial feminine energy; this conceptualization would look at prakriti as non-self-aware and conscious, whereas the principle of consciousness and awareness is Puruṣa. The advaita perspectives re-interpreted the Sāṃkhya – Yoga with the writings of Acārya Śankara. Śankara's advaita, also tried to address this contradiction in understanding consciousness and framed the principles of materiality, manifestation, ephemerality and intentionality as 'Maya' – the unreal, mesmerizing, charming manifest world. Advaita located the only reality in consciousness as such, untouched by intentionality, self-awareness and the unpredictable, ephemeral materiality of the manifest world. However, this sophisticated theorization of non-duality, was also co-taught with poly-theistic worship of an embodied understanding of consciousness. The sophisticated advaita world-view, which is non-dual and awareness alone, has been stated up by brilliant logic and argumentation, making it the crown jewel of Indian philosophical contribution; yet difficult to be understood empirically. Immediately, after Āchārya Śankara's monumental work, two great philosopher-teachers disagreed with Śankara's advaita. The great teacher – Sri Rāmānujacārya, argued that the materiality, ephemerality and the manifestation of this world are not unreal but are real expressions of the consciousness as such. Thus, Sri Rāmānuja, in fact, innovated philosophically and proposed a resolution of contradictions held together in the very characteristics of consciousness as such. As Sri Rāmānuja viewed that the world is not a playful charming illusion but a real expression of consciousness; Viṣiśtādvaita philosophy led to social reform and serious attention to human and non-human life and experience while accounting for the consciousness as such as the very self, channelled through forms, with qualities and names (Nāma-Rūpa-Guṇa). Later movements in Kashmir Śaiva non-dualistic thought as well as in Tantra, specifically reframe the connection between the seer and the seen as one and non-dual and, at the same time, attempted to reconcile the contradictions perceived in the characteristics of consciousness as such and consciousness as experienced in the manifest embodied world. In the later Tantric as well as the non-dual Kashmiri Śaiva thought, it is the consciousness alone which is self-aware and also becomes the world in a playful manner – it enjoys seeing, sensing and being itself!

Thus, while the Vedas conceptualize creativity as the central aspect of *Cit* or consciousness, different philosophical and wisdom tradition try to articulate and resolve the contradictions inherent in the idea that while consciousness is transpersonal, it is expressed and experienced through an embodied and personal self; while consciousness as such is without intention, knowing and action, it is expressed and experienced through animated intention, knowing and action and while consciousness as such cannot be limited to and is without form, qualities and name, it is expressed and experienced through infinite names, forms and qualities!

Whereas in the earlier non-dual Advaita systems, luminosity or self-reflexivity/knowing is emphasized, free and liberated intentionality unfettered by any compulsions is emphasized equally along with the self-luminosity of consciousness. Therefore, following the earlier Advaita tradition, the meditator reaches a realization of a self-luminous and completely unintentional awareness, whereas practising the Trika Śaiva non-dualistic tradition, the practitioner realizes a self-luminous and a fully intentional awareness in the embodied consciousness as a person. This profound acknowledgement explicated in the non-dual Trika Śaiva tradition allows for a living and becoming universe which is then worked through the collective agencies of those who have realized this truth. While it is true that, Acārya Śankara also focused on what has been called as the Satkāryavāda – or the doctrine/argument of creating in recreating the universe as is lived, both Sāmkhya and Advaita, were commonly misinterpreted with a passive consciousness and an active universe dialectic. The later Trika Śaiva non-dualistic tradition and the tantric tradition seem to explicitly mention what was implied by the Advaita and the Sāmkhya traditions. As I have argued elsewhere, the living traditions of Hindu thought may have had their significant differences as well as debates, but they all focused and guided their students through a set of processes and methods towards the final living realization of the trans-cultural, transpersonal and trans-chronus all-pervasive consciousness-the Brahman, which is also experienced as the glory of the infinite embodied consciousness forms, names and qualities! This reconciliation of contradictions and opposites, indeed is the hallmark of consciousness-based mind sciences.

Going further, one of the key features of all human and non-human systems that we currently count as conscious all exhibit a strong characteristic-of creativity, including but not limited to the ability to reproduce! Creativity and generativity go beyond a simple reproduction or mating systems, and dialectically, intelligent expression alone would count as 'creative'. This would mean that there would need to be a self-system that interacts with the world and has the capability of (a) a moment by moment enactive, intelligent response capacity, (b) a moment by moment as well as an enduring sense of awareness and (c) a moment by moment as well as an enduring positive and stable affective response, that allows for unpredictability or dynamism, change and transformation, without feeling threatened for survival. This precisely would be an elaboration of Sat-Cid and Ānanda. This is a shocking thought – that the world is alive, not in an isolated creature by creature sense, but alive to each other.

In the current discussions on artificial intelligence and artificial consciousness, several fundamental questions about the agency of self, boundedness of self-systems and affective response of the self-system are discussed. A fundamental question that can be asked as the difference between artificial consciousness and non-artificial consciousness is not in the sense of learning-because systems seem to learn by themselves; it's also not in the sense of memory because systems can have enormous repositories of memories which can be triggered using the right keywords; we can't even call something an object or an entity as animated with consciousness if that system is able to reason, or use logic or see patterns or gaps, because humans frequently fail to use reason or logic and organized knowledge, whereas non-human systems unfailingly use reason and logic. Systems can possibly **act** as agents and agency itself does not require or define consciousness. Note that both in Sāṃkhya and Advaita, consciousness – as such, is not intentional and also is not an agent, knower, experience and owner of any action.

We move a step closer if we were to examine emotionality and consciousness. In the questions of affect, again when it comes to survival related threat related questions, a system can be programmed to either destroy the objects that threaten or self-destruct, but can the systems feel? Emotion focus involves emotion processing and emotion display. Some scholars argue that it does not matter whether the system can feel something; what matters really is that the system can 'show/display' emotion appropriately. This display of appropriate emotion can be coded into the machines and can fool humans to think that the machine is 'feeling' and is able to respond. This idea is very problematic and, in fact, central to the objectification of 'others' – other humans, genders, cultures and races that we as human beings have subjected each other to. While the repertoire of appropriate display of behaviours, including emotional expressions, fits the transactional idea of intelligence and consciousness, it still accepts that somewhere the ability to feel, the ability to be affected by and the ability to respond to through emotions might be a step closer to understanding what consciousness is. The key insight to emphasize is that even closer than emotion in understanding consciousness is the paradoxical nature of creativity, the creative process and the embodied and transcendental consciousness that lives and expresses this creativity while paradoxically remaining unaffected.

A manifesto of a consciousness-based psychology

Thus, we have travelled a long distance and a wide landscape. Starting from the current excitement in consciousness studies, mind sciences and cross-cultural and cultural psychologies, that seek to decolonize the academic discipline of contemporary global psychology, the book has argued that the Indian consciousness-based psychology needs to be reclaimed and studied afresh. Colonization has created a huge rupture in indigenous knowledge systems and consciousness and the mindsets of the colonized countries and civilizations are still struggling to address their internalized prejudices and stereotypes, such that they look at their own cultural selves and their psychologies as backward, superstitious and the other. This has been recognized by several scholars across disciplines and specializations in humanities and social sciences with some key consolidations in recent times (for details, see Banavathy & Choudry, 2015; Chaudhary et al., 2022).

Till recently, contemporary psychology and science were either dismissing consciousness as an unscientific mystery, perhaps rubbish or studying consciousness with fragmented selves and unrefined subjectivities of both the researchers and the subjects. By unrefined, we mean untrained to observe and realize the fallacies of reasoning processes as such. One of the first documented difficulties of inter-disciplinarity between the rich history of very sophisticated models of consciousness and mind in the IKT is that the Euro-American history of ideas has continued its battle with binary thinking and dichotomies, arising from Greek Philosophy (Singh, 2010). This has profound implications on how research is conceptualized, conducted and interpreted. This point holds good for the research method in general across disciplines – be it ecology, sustainability as well as psychological science.

In the IKT, as is well-known, consciousness is a central concern. Even when Buddhists and Jaina, have disagreed with the identity of consciousness with self, even with their negation, consciousness has still been a central concern, along with the acceptance of certain central principles in the civilizational discourse. These key principles across Indian knowledge systems cohere and structure ideas, concepts, frameworks and models to then detail out theories and practices. The meta principles of Dharma, Karma, the cycle of birth, death and re-birth (sāmsāra cakra) and mukti/nirvāna all assume the centrality of consciousness and the lived worlds without denying either. Not only has each principle been theorized in detail, with several books written of aspects of these principles, but they have also been cohered and included in practices, which have been followed through centuries and are still practices. Thus, they are lived realities. The meta-coherence to these principles is provided by consciousness. Thus, it is emphasized that in the conceptual topography of the civilizational discourse, consciousness coheres to all psychological knowledge and practices. Due to this coherence, dualities, even if they exist downstream in the conceptual flow, are reconciled.

It is critical that the Indian consciousness-based psychology, is accessible and visible not as a compulsion or authority but certainly to those who seek it. For this, psychology, beyond the constraints of social identities, extends the invitation to a life of fulfilment and well-being. This fulfilment and well-being are seen in the lives of the practitioners and their everyday creativity. We end this book with a joyous song – again, by Jnāneśwara and translated by the author.

अरे अरे ज्ञाना झालासी पावन । तुझें तुज ध्यान कळों आले ॥१॥
Are! Are! Jnāna Jhālāse Pāvan; Tujhe tujh dhyāna Kaḷo āle
(Oh Jnāna, you have been purified!; you recognized your own self now)
तुझा तूंचि देव, तुझा तूंचि भाव । फिटला संदेह अदे न्यतत्त्वी ॥२॥
Tujhā tuchi Deva, tujhā tuchi bhāva; Phitla sandeha, anya tattve
(you are 'that'; and you are the feelings towards 'that'. There is nothing else, without doubt)
मुरडूनियां मन उपजलासी चित्तें । कोठें तुज रितें न दिसे रया ॥३॥
Muraduniya mana, upajalāsi citte; kothe tujh rite na dise raya
(you arose as mind from the vast stream of consciousness; there is no emptiness, everything in and out is effulgent)
दीपकीं दीपक मावळल्या ज्योती । घरभरी वाती शून्य झाल्या ॥४॥
Dipaki Dipak Māvalayā Jyoti; Gharbhari Vāti Shunya Jhālya
(light a lamp, with another, all apparent are empty)
वृत्तीचि निवृत्ति अपणांसकट । अवघेंची वैकुंठ चतुर्भूज ॥५॥
Vritti chi Nivrtti, apana sakat; avaghechi vaikuntha, chaturbhuja
(the vritti ceased spontaneously; all within and without is the abode of Vishnu)
निवृत्ति परमानुभव नेमा । शांतिपूर्णक्षमा ज्ञानदेवो ॥६॥
Nivrtti Parama Anubhava Nema; Śānti Purṇa Kśamā Jnāna Devo
(by the grace of guru (Nivrtti); all – peace, fulfilment and knowledge is experienced)

References

Ashby, F. G., & Isen, A. M. (1999). A neuropsychological theory of positive affect and its influence on cognition. *Psychological Review*, *106*(3), 529.

Auger, P., & Woodman, R. W. (2016). Creativity and intrinsic motivation: Exploring a complex relationship. *The Journal of Applied Behavioral Science*, *52*(3), 342–366.

Austenfeld, J. L., Paolo, A. M., & Stanton, A. L. (2006). Effects of writing about emotions versus goals on psychological and physical health among third-year medical students. *Journal of Personality*, *74*(1), 267–286.

Austenfeld, J. L., & Stanton, A. L. (2004). Coping through emotional approach: a new look at emotion, coping, and health-related outcomes. *Journal of Personality*, *72*(6), 1335–1364.

Banavathy, V. K., & Choudry, A. (2015). Indian psychology: Understanding the basics. *International Journal of Yoga-Philosophy, Psychology and Parapsychology*, *3*(1), 9.

Bhaskar, R. (2013). *A realist theory of science*. Routledge.

Bhaskar, R. (2014). *The possibility of naturalism: A philosophical critique of the contemporary human sciences*. Routledge.

Bhawuk, D. P. S. (2003). Culture's influence on creativity: The case of Indian spirituality. *International Journal of Intercultural Relations*, *27*(1), 1–22. https://doi.org/10.1016/s0147-1767(02)00059-7

Bhawuk, D. P. S. (2018). Toward a spirituality-based theory of creativity: Indigenous perspectives from India. In *Asian Indigenous psychologies in the global context* (pp. 139–168). Springer International Publishing. https://doi.org/10.1007/978-3-319-96232-0_7

Brown, S., & Dissanayake, E. (2009). The arts are more than aesthetics: Neuroaesthetics as narrow aesthetics. *Neuroaesthetics*, *43*(57), 43–56.

Chaudhary, N., Misra, G., Bansal, P., Valsiner, J., & Singh, T. (2022). Making sense of culture for the psychological sciences. *Review of General Psychology*, *26*(4), 399–415.

Csikszentmihalyi, M. (1988). The flow experience and its significance for human psychology. In *Optimal experience* (pp. 15–35). Cambridge University Press. https://doi.org/10.1017/cbo9780511621956.002

Deci, E. L. (1975). Conceptualizations of intrinsic motivation. In *Intrinsic motivation* (pp. 23–63). Springer US. https://doi.org/10.1007/978-1-4613-4446-9_2

Dissanayake, E. (2001). *Homo aestheticus: Where art comes from and why*. University of Washington Press.

Dissanayake, E. (2008). The arts after Darwin: Does art have an origin and adaptive function. In K. Zjilman & W. Van Demme (Eds.), World Art Studies: Exploring Concepts and Approaches (pp. 241–263). Valiz.

Dissanayake, E. (2015). *What is art for?* University of Washington Press.

Fredrickson, B. L. (2001). The role of positive emotions in positive psychology: The broaden-and-build theory of positive emotions. *American Psychologist*, *56*(3), 218.

Frazier, J. (2011). Reason and rationality in Hindu studies. *Journal of Hindu Studies*, *4*, 1–11. https://doi.org/doi:10.1093/jhs/hir014

Ganeri, J. (1996). The Hindu syllogism: Nineteenth-century perceptions of Indian logical thought. *Philosophy East and West*, *46*(1), 1–16.

Ganeri, J. (2002). Jaina logic and the philosophical basis of pluralism. *History and Philosophy of Logic*, *23*(4), 267–281.

Ganeri, J. (2004). Indian logic: *A reader*. Routledge

Hastorf, A. H. (1997). Lewis Terman's longitudinal study of the intellectually gifted: Early research, recent investigations and the future. *Gifted and Talented International*, *12*(1), 3–7.

Isen, A. M. (1987). Positive affect, cognitive processes, and social behavior. In L. Berkowitz (Ed.), *Advances in experimental social psychology* (Vol. 20, pp. 203–253). Elsevier.

Isen, A. M., Daubman, K. A., & Nowicki, G. P. (1987). Positive affect facilitates creative problem solving. *Journal of Personality and Social Psychology*, *52*(6), 1122.

Kargól, M. (2021). Knitting as a remedy: Women's everyday creativity in response to hopelessness and despair. *Cultural Studies*, *36*(5), 821–839. https://doi.org/10.1080/09502386.2021.2011933

Karhadkar, K. S. (1976). Dnyaneshwar and Marathi literature. *Indian Literature*, *19*(1), 90–95. http://www.jstor.org/stable/24157251

Koller, J. M. (2000). Syādvāda as the epistemological key to the Jaina middle way metaphysics of Anekāntavāda. *Philosophy East and West*, *50*(3), 400–407.

Lavie, S., Narayan, K., & Rosaldo, R. (1993). *Creativity/anthropology*. Cornell University Press.

Lopez, S. J., Pedrotti, J. T., & Snyder, C. R. (2019). *Positive psychology: The scientific and practical explorations of human strengths* (4th ed.). Sage.

Ma, D., Wang, A. C., Parikh, I., Green, S. J., Hoffman, J. D., Chlipala, G., Murphy, M. P., Sokola, B. S., Bauer, B., Hartz, A. M. S., & Lin, A.-L. (2018). Ketogenic diet enhances neurovascular function with altered gut microbiome in young healthy mice. *Scientific Reports*, *8*(1), 6670. https://doi.org/10.1038/s41598-018-25190-5

Mirvis, P. H. (1991). Flow: The psychology of optimal experience. *Academy of Management Review*, *16*(3), 636–640. https://doi.org/10.5465/amr.1991.4279513

Narayan, K. (2016). *Everyday creativity: Singing Goddess in the Himalayas*. University of Chicago Press.

Prigogine, I., & Stengers, I. (1997). *The end of certainty*. Simon and Schuster.

Ram-Prasad, C. (2013). Pluralism and liberalism: Reading the Indian Constitution as a philosophical document for constitutional patriotism. *Critical Review of International Social and Political Philosophy*, *16*(5), 676–697.

Richards, R. (2018). *Everyday creativity and the healthy mind: Dynamic new paths for self and society*. Springer.

Ryan, R. M., & Deci, E. L. (2000). Self-determination theory and the facilitation of intrinsic motivation, social development, and well-being. *American Psychologist*, *55*(1), 68–78. https://doi.org/10.1037/0003-066x.55.1.68

Ryan, R. M., & Deci, E. L. (2001). On happiness and human potentials: A review of research on hedonic and eudaimonic well-being. *Annual Review of Psychology*, *52*(1), 141–166. https://doi.org/10.1146/annurev.psych.52.1.141

Salovey, P., & Mayer, J. D. (1990). Emotional intelligence. *Imagination, Cognition and Personality*, *9*(3), 185–211. https://doi.org/10.2190/dugg-p24e-52wk-6cdg

Sheldrake, R. (2011). *The presence of the past: Morphic resonance and the habits of nature*. Icon Books Ltd.

Simonton, D. K. (2013). What is a creative idea? Little-c versus Big-C creativity. https://doi.org/10.4337/9780857939814.00015

Singh, K. (2010). Beyond mind: The future of psychology. In M. Cornelissen, G. Misra, & S. Varma (Eds.), Foundations of Indian Psychology Volume 1: Theories and Concepts (p. 86). Pearson India.

Stanton, A. L., & Low, C. A. (2012). Expressing emotions in stressful contexts: Benefits, moderators, and mechanisms. *Current Directions in Psychological Science*, *21*(2), 124–128.

Index